The
Moston Story

Fr Brian Seale

Published by Father Brian Seale, St John Vianney's Presbytery, Poynter Street, Moston, Manchester M40 0DH, UK. Telephone: 0161 681 6844.

Printed and bound by Deanprint, Stockport Road, Cheadle Heath, Stockport, Cheshire. Telephone: 0161 428 2236.

LAUDETUR JESUS CHRISTUS

The knight he rode east, t'wards the uprising sun,
But the broad heaths of Moston lay silent and dun.
The Wild Rider of Lancashire
Samuel Bamford

The first thought that strikes the mind when contemplating the past fortunes of Moston is the degree of favour in which that township was held by our forefathers. Possessing, as it might seem, but few advantages in point of situation, the very names of its subdivisions - White Moss, Nuthurst Waste, Theile Moor, and Chadderton Waste - suggesting much of dreariness and discomfort, Moston enjoyed a reputation unequalled by all the other suburbs of Manchester, as the residence of families of distinction.
A History of the Ancient Chapel of Blackley
Revd John Booker

The smell of the hawthorn in spring, and of the grass and the hay in summer, and of the fading leaves in autumn, and the scent of burnt wood or peat in winter was more delightful to me than all the sweets of Araby: and the wind-swept fields of Moston carried quite as much vitality in them as any place I have since visited.
Moston Characters at Work
John Ward

CONTENTS

PREFACE TO
SECOND EDITION

It is twenty three years since the first edition of *The Moston Story* was published, and it has long since been out of print. I have had many enquiries about a second edition. But frankly, I could not be bothered. In recent years, several people asked if they could produce a reprint to satisfy a demand. I gave them my permission; but nothing transpired. Then Peter Emerson Jones, the chairman of the Emerson group of companies and a former classmate from Mount Carmel, Blackley, not only offered to reprint it but also to pay the cost. I began to think: is it that good? While I could not accept Peter's most generous offer, it did prompt me to compile an index (something sadly missing from the first edition) and I started to think of ways to improve it.

I had come into possession of a rare photograph of Lightbowne Hall, which would fit in nicely at the end of chapter 6. There were slight emendations needed to the text, which has otherwise remained intact. I decided against replacing the photograph of St John Vianney's church hall on page 92 with one of our new ultra modern church. After all, *The Moston Story* is a kind of time capsule, which has become part of local folklore. It encapsulates all the information I could garner, and which I was able to preserve for future generations. Many of my contributors have passed away. May they rest in peace. This edition is a memorial to them. With rising costs the price is the cheapest I could manage.

The primary dedication remains **Laudetur Jesus Christus**, Praised be Jesus Christ. But if I may be allowed a secondary dedication it is as follows: To Sheila Kelly, my devoted housekeeper and wise counsellor for twenty seven years (who thinks I am mad to invest my savings in this venture at my age); to my wonderful G.P. Dr John Fallon; to the dedicated staffs of North Manchester General Hospital (especially I.C.U.), and Manchester Royal Infirmary; and to the congregation of St John Vianney's and my many Catholic and non-Catholic friends, who by their love and prayers have helped me through hard times. I still need the prayers of all the good people out there. Oh, and by the way, a final plea: Please buy this book and prove my housekeeper wrong!

BRIAN SEALE, Moston, January 2006

ACKNOWLEDGMENTS

I am greatly indebted to the staffs of Manchester Central Reference Library (Local History Department); Manchester Polytechnic Local Studies Department; Abraham Moss Centre; Simpson Memorial Library; Oldham Local Interest Centre.

I wish to acknowledge the assistance of the City of Manchester Civil Engineer's Department, Cultural Services Department, Planning Department; Courtauld Ltd; Ferranti Ltd; National Coal Board; Geographia; Ordnance Survey; The Manchester Evening News; The East Manchester Reporter; The Blackley Guardian; The Oldham Chronicle.

I thank S.R. Publishers (East Ardsley, Wakefield) for permission to quote from 'Roman Lancashire' by W. Thompson Watkin; and Ian Allan (Shepperton) for permission to quote from 'The Lancashire & Yorkshire Railway' by O.S. Nock.

The photographs of old Moston and old New Moston, charts, maps, plans and sections, are reproduced by kind permission of Donald Anderson, Manchester Central Reference Library, Manchester Polytechnic Local Studies Department, National Coal Board, Ray Dunning, Chris Makepeace.

The photographs of present-day Moston and New Moston were taken specially for this book by Ian Barlow of New Moston.

Special thanks are offered to John Moorhouse and Barry Moran for helping me to illustrate the book.

Moira Rowe, aided by Monica Downes, typed the text; a mammoth task, for which I owe them my deepest gratitude.

I appreciate the generous assistance of Tom Parkinson, Julian Hunt, David McRae, and especially Keith Warrender.

My great gratitude to Rob Howard of Robaccord Publications, Stockport; and Mike Broome of Deanprint, Cheadle Heath, Stockport.

CONTRIBUTORS

Many more people have contributed to this book than are listed below. To those whose names I have forgotten I tender my heartfelt apologies. Some contributors wished to remain anonymous. My thanks to all who have helped me in this enterprise.

Sister Patricia Abbott
Sister Clare Adams
Donald Anderson
Peter Berry
Molly Betney
Alec Booth
Des Booth
Vin Booth
Edna Boulton
Alex Brown
Cath Browne
Sheila Butterwick
Edith Buxton
Bob Campbell
Frank Campbell
Bill Carter
Mary Carter
Lawrence Cassidy
Very Revd James Christie
Leslie Clough
Amy Cocker
Revd Arthur Collin
John Corcoran
Donald Cornthwaite
Hilda Coulthurst
Jim Croarkin
Revd John Low
Kevin Madden
Ian Marland
Ted Maurice
Fr Bernard McGarry
Joe McMurray
Fr Gerard Meath, O.P.
Paddy Meehan
Barry Moran
Frank Murphy
James Murphy
Tommy Murphy
Revd Harry Ogden
Pat O'Neill
Ron O'Neill
John Robinson
Moira Rowe
Revd Gordon Roxby
Philip Ryan
Jim Schofield

Bill Davies
Jim Davy
John Donnelly
Ernest Doughty
Betty Dunning
Ray Dunning
Sister Monica Dwyer
Brother Gerald Fitzgerald
Agnes Franklin
Cecilia Gerard
Fr Martin Gosling, O. Praem
Ken Goulding
Barry Greenwood
Joan Griffiths
Mike Harker
Dermot Healy
Margaret Higham
Jack Holt
Walter Hopkins
Jennie Jennings
Julie Jones
Joe Joy
Sheila Kelly
John Kulikowski
Reg Latham
Leslie Scholes
Doreen Scott
Gina Shakespeare
Sister John Shaw
Ken Stell
Tony Sweeney
Rita Tavernor
David Taylor
Joe Taylor
Maureen Toms
Elsie Toner
Steven Turner
Ralph Wagstaff
Michael Walsh
Barney Ward
Ann Watson
Isabel Webb
Lucy Wheelton

BIBLIOGRAPHY

A DICTIONARY OF MODERN HISTORY by A.W. Palmer (Penguin Books)

A HISTORY OF NEWTON CHAPELRY by H.T. Crofton

AN UNFINISHED HISTORY OF THE WORLD by Hugh Thomas (Pan Books)

GUIDE TO MANCHESTER 1936 (Manchester City News)

JOHN WESLEY by C.E. Vulliamy (Epworth Press)

MAMECESTRE by J. Harland

MANCHESTER AS IT WAS by C. Makepeace (Hendon Publishing Co. Ltd)

MEDIEVAL BRITAIN by D. Richards & A.D. Ellis (Longman)

MINES AND MINERS OF SOUTH LANCASHIRE by J. Lane & D. Anderson

MOSTON CHARACTERS AT PLAY by John Ward (Charles H. Barber)

MOSTON CHARACTERS AT WORK by John Ward (Charles H. Barber)

ROMAN LANCASHIRE by W. Thompson Watkin (S.R. Publishers)

ROMAN ROADS IN BRITAIN by Ivan D. Margary (John Baker)

RURAL ENGLAND 1066-1348 by H.E. Hallam (Fontana)

SECTIONS OF STRATA OF THE COAL MEASURES OF LANCASHIRE by G. Hickling

TAMERS OF DEATH by C.J. Kauffman (Seabury, New York)

THE ANCIENT CHAPEL OF BLACKLEY IN MANCHESTER PARISH by J. Booker

THE COURT LEET RECORDS OF THE MANOR OF MANCHESTER

THE GEOLOGY OF MANCHESTER & THE SOUTH EAST LANCASHIRE COALFIELD by L.H. Tonks

THE HISTORY AND ANNALS OF BLACKLEY AND NEIGHBOURHOOD by P. Wentworth

THE LANCASHIRE CHARTULARY ed. by W. Farrer

THE LANCASHIRE AND YORKSHIRE RAILWAY by O.S. Nock (Ian Allan)

THE MINISTRY OF HEALING by C.J. Kauffman (Seabury, New York)

THE MANCHESTER HISTORICAL RECORDER (Hayward)

THE MANCHESTER MUNICIPAL CODE 1897

THE PELICAN HISTORY OF THE WORLD by J.M. Roberts (Penguin Books)

THE PENGUIN DICTIONARY OF SAINTS by D. Attwater (Penguin Books)

THE RESPLENDENT SIGN by L.W. O'Neill

THE STORY OF THE OLD FAITH IN MANCHESTER by J. O'Dea

THE TEXTILE MILL ENGINE by G. Watkins (David & Charles Library of Textile History)

THE VICTORIA HISTORY OF THE COUNTY OF LANCASTER (vol. 4), W. Farrer, J. Brownbill

TRANSACTIONS OF THE LANCASHIRE & CHESHIRE ANTIQUARIAN SOCIETY

A NOTE ON SOURCES

In his preface to 'A History of the Ancient Chapel of Blackley in Manchester Parish,' published in 1854, the Revd John Booker lamented: 'From causes which need not here be adverted to, all opportunity has been denied for tracing the descent of lands in Moston township, a neighbourhood most fruitful in records of the past. This is greatly to be regretted, since much that is interesting might have been expected from such a source.' More than fifty years later H.T. Crofton laboured under the same disadvantage. In his essay 'Moston and White Moss' (1907) he wrote: 'For a full statement of the "personal history" of Moston we must wait for the publication of the Salford Hundred volume of the Victoria History of Lancashire.' Eventually, in 1911, the long awaited information came to hand with the appearance of volume four of 'The Victoria History of the County of Lancaster,' edited by William Farrer and J. Brownbill. The copious footnotes between pages 264 and 270 would have gladdened the heart of John Booker, had he lived to see them. Surprisingly, to this day no effort has been made to sift this material. In the early chapters of the present work I have attempted to make good this deficiency. The chapter on Theyle Moor owes everything to H.T. Crofton's investigation into the mass of documents bearing on the century long litigation.

During the early years of this century John Ward produced two works of considerable interest, 'Moston Characters at Play' (1905) and 'Moston Characters at Work' (1911). In the absence of any other published account of Moston since 1911, Ward's books have become the staple diet of local readers. Unfortunately, while the author has preserved a large amount of valuable information, he eschews chronology; it is extremely difficult to date his episodes. Nevertheless, it has been possible to construct a historical framework, and to locate much of Ward's material within it. By dint of importunity I was given access to private papers, unpublished monographs, company records, legal documents, log books, etc. Many wonderful people have given me the benefit of their expertise. I regret that it is not possible to include the names of all who have helped me in this compilation. The book is the most comprehensive treatment I could manage. Many professional people did not bother to answer my letters, requesting information. Consequently, some areas have not been as well explored as others. I think I know just how poor John Booker felt!

BRIAN SEALE, Moston, October 1983

PLAN OF THE TOWNSHIP OF MOSTON

— TRACED FROM 6 INCH ORDNANCE MAP —

PUBLISHED, 31ˢᵗ MARCH 1848.

— Area of the Township of Moston, 1297. 0. 33. —

The ▬▬ Line indicates the boundary of the Township of Moston.

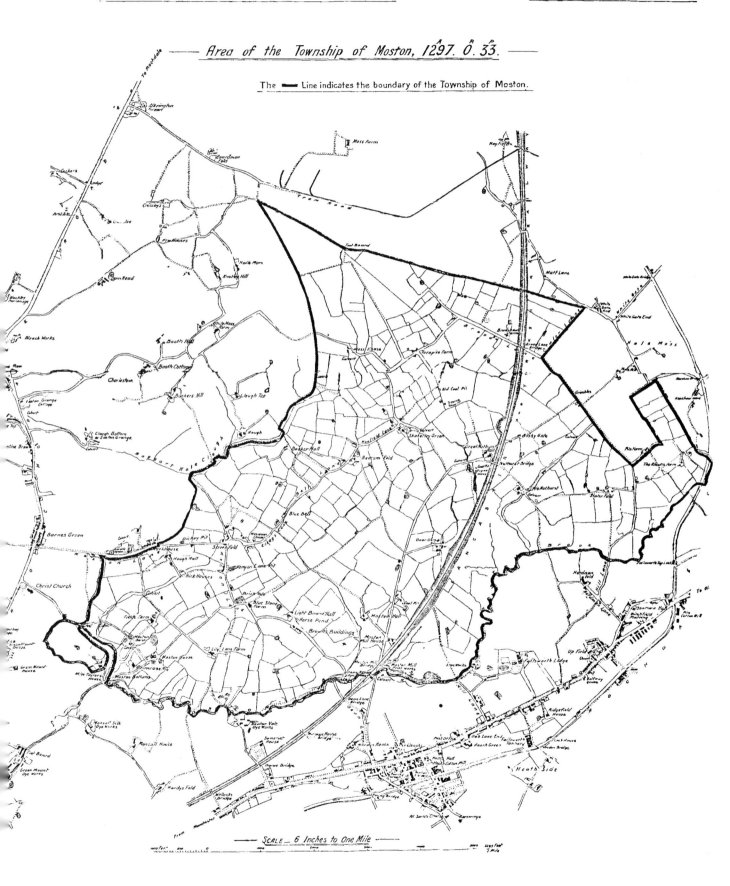

— SCALE — 6 Inches to One Mile —

1

The Origins of Moston and Nuthurst

The Romans were the greatest road-builders of the ancient world. Starting from Rome itself, highways fanned out through an empire that stretched from the Black Sea to Hadrian's Wall in the north and from the Atlantic coast of Africa to the Red Sea in the south. About the time of the empire's greatest extension, A.D. 117, soldiers of the 28th Legion, based on the newly erected fortress camp at Castlefield (in the heart of downtown Manchester), were employed in constructing several roads out of the busy staging post. Their task was a difficult one. Primeval forest and swamps covered the region. But, nothing deterred the Roman legionaries - in this instance probably Frisian mercenaries, hard men from Germany's north sea coast.

On the northeast side of Manchester two roads have been traced by archaeologists - one certainly, the other supposedly, emanating from the town. The first road came from the area of Central Station, by Mill Street, Cemetery Road and Briscoe Lane, straight through the site of All Saints church, Newton Heath, and on by Roman Road in Failsworth. It then made its way through Oldham and on into Yorkshire, passing to the north of the Roman fort at Slack near Halifax. The second road, surrounded by mystery, crosses Blackstone Edge on a more-or-less straight line between Littleborough and Halifax. It has been described as the most remarkable construction of any Roman road in Britain, and is for a long distance as perfect as on the day it was laid. The difficulty concerning the second road is: how did it arrive at Blackstone Edge from Manchester? Whitaker (History of Manchester) contended that the missing link (road) passed diagonally through Moston from Ancoats; and then proceeded by way of Chadderton and Royton to Littleborough. He based his theory entirely on place names, freely admitting that no remains of a Roman road had ever been discovered.

W. Thompson Watkin (Roman Lancashire pp. 56, 57) quotes Whitaker (Bk. i ch. v sec. ii): 'Another road of the Romans appears to have been laid from the camp at Manchester, and to have proceeded into Yorkshire; branching probably from the way to Cambodunum (Slack), about Ancoats Lane, and traversing the township obliquely it passed by Street Fold in Moston, Street Bridge in Chatherton, and Street Gate in Ryton, and pointed evidently for Littleborough and Ilkley. And these three appellations ascertain the general direction of its course and supply the wants of any actual remains, or even of any traditional notices concerning it. Leaving Street Fold and the parish, it advanced by Street Bridge and Street Gate, and was lately dug up near Rochdale. About a quarter of a mile to the right of the town, and near the road from Oldham, it was cut through in making a marle pit, and appeared several yards in breadth and deeply gravelled, and upon Blackstone Edge it is intersected as I have mentioned before by the way from Cambodunum to Colania.'

Before giving Watkin's comments, it may be useful to provide a little background. The Saxons used the term 'streat' to describe a paved or metalled road; and, since the only examples of this type of road in existence were Roman, place names such as Street Bridge and Street Field in country areas usually indicate the presence of a Roman road. When Whitaker wrote his History (1771) Moston was in the parish of Manchester. Hence the reference to 'Leaving Street Fold and the parish.' Street Fold is, of course, the old name for the Ben Brierley area. The Street family, which is mentioned in various documents between 1553 and 1624, was of yeoman farming stock. While it is conceivable that Street Fold was named after this family, it is more likely that the family was named after the district. In view of what follows, it may be useful to recall the Roman method of road-building. The ground was dug up; stones were set in the channel thus made; the middle section of the road was raised to permit drainage; and finally gravel was put on top. Simple, but very effective. And now for Watkin:-

'The most singular fact connected with this road is, that no one has ever seen or heard of the portion of it between Manchester and Blackstone Edge from Whitaker's time to the present day. It is true, as Whitaker states, that the names of Street Fold, etc., occur along the route he takes, but even below the surface nothing can be found of the road, unless the remains noticed in the following paragraph form part of it.'

Watkin then quotes from the Manchester City News, 'Notes and Queries' (vol. i p. 19): 'Mr Joseph Ramsbottom writes under date of 21st January, 1878, from Moston, recording a discovery made "in cutting out the foundations for some new houses close to Lightbowne Hall, Moston. . . . When digging out the cellars, at about two feet six inches below the surface, the workmen struck upon the pavement. The road was about four feet wide, of a rather convex surface, being highest in the middle, where the largest boulders had been placed, and there were two layers of stones upon a bed of gravel. Standing in the cellars and looking at the two breasts of stones, one side seemed to run on in a northern direction, with a point or so east, the other ran south, with the same inclination to the west. In the same direction as the latter, for at least some of the distance, the Lightbowns had once had a road to and from their Hall. I do not think it was ever a private road, for in the early part of this century a certain Dr Thorp, from Manchester, used to ride over it once a year regularly for the purpose of keeping it open. But I cannot think that the Lightbown road, being in continual use, could, since the Hall was built, have sunk so far beneath the surrounding level, and am inclined to regard the one just discovered as of a much earlier date."'

There then follows Watkin's verdict: 'Judging of the character of this road as detailed by Mr Ramsbottom, I should certainly be inclined to give a Roman origin to it; but that it is a continuation of the fine road over Blackstone Edge seems almost impossible. It is more like a small road leading to a villa: its width is insufficient for anything else.'

There are several interesting points arising from the above. Lightbowne Hall (demolished in 1965) stood in Kenyon Lane near St Luke's church. The Roman road of Whitaker's surmise would have corresponded to Kenyon Lane - not the re-routed Lane of today, which peters out aimlessly at the bottom of Dean Clough (this is really the continuation of Dean Lane on the Moston side of the

Moston Hall c.1820

railway) - but Kenyon Lane as it was before Lightbowne Road came into existence. The line of the old Kenyon Lane can be seen on the map of 1820, curving round in a southerly direction along the route of the present Lightbowne Road. It was already an ancient road when Lightbowne Hall was built in the middle of the seventeenth century. In a deed of 1455 it is called Saltersgate, and was probably the old road along which salt was conveyed into south Lancashire from the Cheshire wyches or saltworks. According to Canon Raines (quoted in Harland, Mamecestre), all the old roads called Salter Gate or Salter Edge lead in direct lines to the Cheshire salt mines. A glance at the map of 1820 shows how the Moston Saltersgate pointed southwest, eventually linking up via Newton Lane (Oldham Road) with an old road into Cheshire.

All of this makes the location of the Roman find even more intriguing. It occurred near the most ancient avenue into Moston. It lies within a few hundred yards of Moston Hall, site of the oldest known dwelling in the district, the putative tún of Mostún. Recent work on the Dark Ages has stressed the continuity of institutions between the late Roman period and the Old English period. Put simply, this could mean that there were people living in this corner of Moston right down the ages from the end of the Roman occupation (about the year 400) to the twelfth century, when the history of Moston begins to be recorded.

Sometime about the year 668 a holy monk from the abbey of Lastingham in Yorkshire made his way, probably on foot, through Manchester to Lichfield. His name was Chad (or Ceadda), and he had been appointed bishop of the Mercians by Archbishop Theodore of Canterbury. From the newly created see of Lichfield he would journey tirelessly through his huge, sparsely populated diocese, which included the village of Manchester. His missionary zeal and austere manner of life must have contributed to his sudden death in the year 672. His fame, however, lived on in place names such as Chadderton and Cheetham (both meaning Chad's - or Ceadda's - village). Two families, who assumed the names of these places, the Chaddertons and the Chethams, would dominate the Moston scene for five hundred years. Many years hence an Anglican church in New Moston (formerly part of the Chetham-cum-Chadderton territory of Nuthurst) would bear the name of St Chad.

The solitary, brief reference to Manchester in the Domesday Book of William the Conqueror, compiled about 1086, contains two facts of significance for the history of Moston. In its survey of the Hundred of Salford, which was held by King Edward the Confessor (1041-1066), we are informed that in Manchester the church of St Mary and the church of St Michael held a carucate or ploughland, exempt from all taxation except Danegeld. St Mary's was the parish church, and stood on or near the site of the present Cathedral. The medieval parish of Manchester covered some sixty square miles, and included Moston within its most northerly boundary. The church of St Michael was the daughter church, probably situated in Ashton-under-Lyne. The parish church of Ashton has always been dedicated to St Michael. It is referred to in old times as Assheton kirk, thereby showing its Saxon origins. The Saxons used the word kirk (Greek, TO KUPIAKON, the Lord's house; whence kyrk, church) to describe their places of worship. By the late Middle Ages Ashton-under-Lyne had become a separate parish and a sub-manor of Manchester. Some of the earliest references to Moston are in connection with the lords of Ashton. In passing, the ploughland owned by the two churches could well have been that district, near the boundary between the old parishes of Manchester and Ashton, called Kirkmanshulme (Anglo-Saxon, the Priest's Dwelling).

Before we start to thread our way through the early documents relating to Moston, let us disregard the present subdivision of the district into Moston and New Moston; or rather, let us substitute for New Moston (which only got its name in 1851) the ancient and historically important hamlet of Nuthurst whose territory included New Moston. There are as many references to Nuthurst in old charters, deeds and bequests, as there are to Moston. But first, the names: Moston and Nuthurst, originally written Mostún and Notehurst. Mostún (*Mos*, old High German, a bog; *tún*, Anglo-Saxon, a village; hence the village near a peat bog). Notehurst (*Knut*, Anglo-Saxon, or *Noth*, Friesian, pronounced note, a nut; *hurst*, old High German, a wood or sandbank; hence, a grove or bank of hazelnuts). The names are redolent of the tenth century, when this area was brought into the united Saxon kingdom. It was a period of relative peace and stability, made possible by the victory of Alfred the Great (871-901) over the Danes. That king's love of learning and devotion to the Church set the pattern for what was to follow.

During the reign of Alfred's son, Edward the Elder (901-924), who sent Mercian troops to repair and garrison Manchester in 919, and his grandson Athelstan (924-940), and especially during the peaceful period of Edgar (959-975), there was a vigorous restoration of the spiritual and intellectual life of the country. At the centre of it was the revival of monasticism, which had virtually ceased to exist during the Scandinavian invasions. St Dunstan (after whom the first Catholic church in Moston would be named) was the leading figure in founding and refounding many abbeys. With St Oswald and St Aethelwold, he drew up the Regularis Concordia (about 970), a charter for English monasticism, which took into account the great reform movement getting under way on the Continent, especially that most notable development of the Benedictine order, the abbey of Cluny in Burgundy. Founded in 910 by William the Pious, Duke of Aquitaine, among other changes it would substitute for the autonomous abbeys of St Benedict a federation of cells, linked to Cluny and owing obedience directly to the Holy See. Such was Kersal Cell in Salford near the end of the twelfth century. It is in connection with this monastery, founded by Sir Hugh de Byron of Clayton who was also its first monk, that we encounter the Moston family.

The first known inhabitant of Moston assumed the name of the district. Ralph of Moston (Radulfus de Moston) was one of six witnesses named in a bequest of land, made by one Matthew son of Edith, to the Cluniac Benedictines of Kersal Cell. The document, dated between 1190 and 1212, has come down to us in its entirety. Part of it runs in translation:- 'Let all know, present and to come, that I Matthew son of Edith, for the souls of my father and mother and my ancestors, and for the salvation of my own soul and that of my wife, have given and granted and by this my present charter have confirmed to God and the Cluniac order and to the house and monks of Kersal that portion of my land in Audenshaw, between these bounds. . . . . . .' The locality cannot be discovered from the landmarks mentioned. There is appended the seal of Matthew son of Edith, and the signatures of the witnesses. Obviously, Matthew son of Edith hoped to obtain Masses and prayers for himself and his family in return for his rents in Audenshaw.

This Matthew son of Edith was probably one of the Asshetons - Audenshaw is very close to Ashton. Ralph de Moston was in all likelihood a relative (in the next century members of the Moston family held lands in Ashton, Denton and Audenshaw). He resided at Moston Hall. In the little wood behind the Alexian Brothers' Home, known in past times as the Kitchen Clough or Dean Clough, there is a grassy mound. Until forty years ago there stood on this spot the last building to bear the name of Moston Hall. It is still indicated in the latest A to Z map; (in the same edition the footpath by the perimeter fence of the Brothers' Home is called Old Hall Road). The first Moston Hall was of great antiquity, possibly early twelfth century. It was, in all likelihood, a primitive Anglo-Saxon tún (group of buildings) at the rim of a moss, protected by an oaken ring-fence; and it gave the district its name.

Moston and Nuthurst are mentioned explicitly for the first time towards the end of the twelfth century. The two places are linked together by one family, that of Orm of Ashton (son of Ailward). Between 1135 and 1153 Albert Grelley senior, third baron of Manchester, gave to Orm son of Ailward with his daughter Emma in marriage one ploughland in Ashton at a yearly rent of ten shillings. This ploughland could well have been Moston: in charters of 1340 and 1356 Moston is spoken of as lying within the township and parish of Ashton-under-Lyne. In an undated charter (1153-1162) the same Albert Grelley confirmed the grant to Orm's son, Roger, of 'the whole land of Ashton' with various other ploughlands. The death of this Roger, eldest son of Orm, occurred in 1194 or 1195. On 2nd November 1195 his estates in Wrightington, Dalton, Parbold and Moston were parcelled out between his two sons, Roger junior and Orm, and Robert son of Bernard, thegn of Goosnargh. Robert, son of Bernard, inherited Moston.

There was yet another beneficiary in the Last Will and Testament of Roger, son of Orm (son of Ailward). We read that he gave 'to God, St Mary, and the abbey of Cockersand, lands in Nuthurst' (Kuerden's MSS., quoted in Booker, p. 135). So, Moston became the property of Robert son of Bernard; while some of the revenues of Nuthurst went to the Premonstratensian abbey of St Mary of Cockersand, founded as a hospital sometime prior to 1184 by Hugh Garth, who was also its first superior. For some years afterwards in the abbey close by the shore of Morecambe Bay, on the 'bare and windswept flats' between the estuaries of the Lune and the Wyre, the Nobertine Canons would offer Masses and prayers for the soul of Roger, son of Orm (son of Ailward), lord of Moston and Nuthurst. Theyle Cross, mentioned in a deposition dated 1595, may - according to one authority 'perpetuate the former ownership of land in Nuthurst by Cockersand Abbey.' It seems rather fitting that in St

Joseph's Cemetery, Moston, there is a monument to the Right Reverend A. G. Toner, Canon Regular of Premontré, and Titular Abbot of St Mary-of-the-Marsh, Cockersand. The monastery itself was dissolved by Henry VIII in 1538.

Robert, son of Bernard of Goosnargh, did not hold on to his Moston inheritance for long. By the early thirteenth century the whole of Moston was in the hands of Henry de Chetham. This was the beginning of the Chetham dynasty, based on Great Nuthurst Hall, that would last for nearly six hundred and fifty years. Other families - some great, some small - would come and go. The lordship of Manchester would pass from Grelley to La Warre to Mosley, and cease altogether in 1846 when the manorial rights were purchased from Sir Oswald Mosley - before the Chetham power in Moston came to an end. Then, in 1851 the estates of Samuel Chetham Hilton began to be dismembered (fifty seven acres becoming New Moston). T.W. Legh Hilton, the last of the line to reside at Great Nuthurst Hall, about this time moved to Moston Hall. Soon afterwards the two Halls of Nuthurst fell into disrepair, and by the end of the century were in ruins. The name of Nuthurst, so evocative of the ancient past, was to vanish from the map - to reappear fifty or so years later as the name of a minor road linking Moston to New Moston.

Not long after Ralph de Moston witnessed a bequest of land to Kersal Cell, and Roger son of Orm (son of Ailward) disposed of his lands in Moston and Nuthurst to Robert son of Bernard, and Cockersand Abbey - Geoffrey de Trafford received from his father, Richard de Trafford, the manors of Chadderton and Foxdenton; and

thereafter changed his surname to Chadderton. By the year 1260 this Geoffrey de Chadderton had acquired Nuthurst. His sons, Alexander and Roger de Chadderton, are named as freehold tenants of Moston and Nuthurst in a survey of 1320. Between these two dates the Chaddertons had made their home in Little Nuthurst Hall. They would remain there until 1623. So, by the year 1300 we have the Mostons settled in Moston Hall; the Chethams in Great Nuthurst Hall (situated on the west side of the railway line, somewhere between the present Glanton Walk and Enstone Drive, on the Mill Estate); and the Chaddertons in Little Nuthurst Hall (sited between Nuthurst Road, Oakwood Avenue and Greenways: number 148 Nuthurst Road, in the title deeds, is called Little Nuthurst Farm).

The Chethams are called chief lords of Moston and Nuthurst in early records. It is certainly true that the Mostons and the Chaddertons paid them a rent for their lands and buildings. In practice, however, the Chethams do not seem to have interfered in the affairs of Moston Hall and Little Nuthurst Hall. While, for their part, the residents of those two places had a great deal of freedom to dispose of their rented property. It is impossible, with the amount of information at our disposal, to unravel the extremely complicated property settlements of the Moston family. Nevertheless, a serious attempt has been made to present the known facts in a coherent manner. But, first of all, some remarks about feudalism and topography.

Subinfeudation is a clumsy word, but it is a concise description of the complex multi-tiered system of land tenure that developed from William the Conqueror's

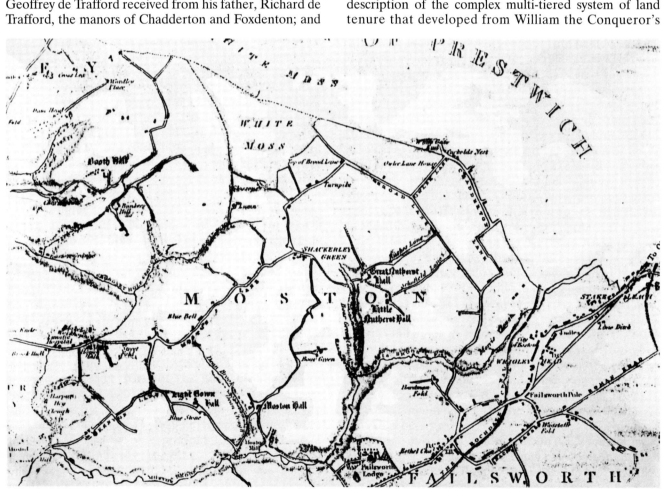

1820 Map of Moston

15

acquisition of all land, except that held by the Church. In the Norman settlement the barons, including the lords of Manchester, held their lands by oath of allegiance to the king. While retaining some lands to themselves as demesne (such was Blackley), they sublet others like Moston and Nuthurst to minor lords - Asshetons and Chethams. These in turn subleased smaller portions to tenant farmers (such as the Chaddertons, Mostons, Shacklocks), who again rented out fields and cottages to the peasantry. At every level fealty was sworn to the immediate overlord. In this way any kind of social advancement was precluded. If you were born a peasant you died a peasant. Moston and Nuthurst are called 'hamlets of Manchester' in 14th century surveys of the manor, and are bound to fulfil certain obligations, e.g. to grind their corn at the mill of the lord on the river Irk. But, apart from taking rents for these outlying districts, there is no evidence that the lords of Manchester showed any interest whatsoever in Moston. Thus, this neck of the woods was allowed to lead a separate existence and acquire its own ambience. Over hundreds of years Moston formed its own personality. It always was - and it still is - different.

An early part of the Moston story concerns the family of Ralph de Moston and its residence, Moston Hall. There seems to be no doubt that the name of the district in its ancient form, Mostún (it is so spelt in documents prior to 1247), refers to a dwelling or group of buildings (tún) in the copse at the back of Arbory Avenue, between St Mary's Road and Lightbowne Road. Before we examine the fortunes of the family, let us think briefly about the whereabouts of the mos (peat bog), which forms the first syllable of its surname. Old authors, such as Booker and Crofton, believed it to be White Moss, which was part of the old Moston township. This explanation has always seemed to me somewhat contrived: White Moss is over a mile away from Moston Hall. To my way of thinking there had to be a peat bog nearer to the Hall; in other words, the mos had to be close by the tún. I think I have found it in the newest portion of Moston Cemetery, the low-lying section starting almost opposite the Blue Bell Hotel and running down to the Dean Brook.

During the First World War, long before the ground was needed for burial purposes, a group of men rented the land from the Cemetery Board for use as allotments. They dug a deep hole, hoping to obtain a supply of water for their gardens. In this enterprise they were very successful - the well never ran dry throughout the history of the allotments, from 1917 until 1955. The water, according to one of the allotment holders, was of a dark peaty colour. This encouraged me to question the head gravedigger of Moston Cemetery about the nature of the soil in this section. Among other facts, he gave me the information I was seeking: seven to eight feet below the surface there is some of the finest peat turf. So, here we have the 'mos' that gave Moston its name. The old inhabitants took away layer after layer of the turf for fuel. The clay, which now covers the area, was probably brought there over a long period of time, part of a large process of reclamation, starting in the late Middle Ages and continuing up to the present.

2

The Tenants of Moston Hall

Strictly speaking the term 'manor' only applies to the estate of the lord of Manchester, of which Moston was a part. But the word is used in old deeds, bequests and rentals to denote the landed property of Moston Hall. With this cautionary note, we are now prepared to meet the Mostons, the Radcliffes, the Shacklocks and other families who resided in the old house in the Dean Clough. After Ralph de Moston witnessed the bequest of Matthew son of Edith about the year 1200 there is silence until 1276 when Richard de Moston (probably a grandson of Ralph) witnessed confirmation of a gift of land to Deane church; he also witnessed a record at York in 1299. We know quite a lot about this member of the family. On 14th May 1301 Thomas Grelley, eighth baron of Manchester, granted to his burgesses the famous Charter whose statutes would - at least in theory - govern Manchester until 23rd October 1838, when the town became incorporated. Among the nine illustrious signatories of this historic document, whose names have come down to us, is Richard de Moston.

How Richard got into the exalted company of Sir John and Sir Richard de Byron, Henry De Trafford, etc., we do not know. He was only a tenant farmer, paying an annual rent of three shillings for the manor of Moston to the lord of Nuthurst. In 1301-2 he made a complaint to the king by writ of Richard Hoghton, late Sheriff of Lancashire, that his common pasture in Nuthurst had been trespassed upon by Geoffrey de Chadderton, who had introduced more than his fair proportion of cattle. From a document of 1309-10 we learn that Alice de Moston was his wife; and from a court settlement of 1404, that he had four sons - William, Richard, Robert and Hugh, and a daughter Emma. In 1310 he put in his claim in a settlement of Moston and Ashton. The last direct reference to him is a most important one. In 1309 Thomas Grelley had transferred the manor of Manchester and the benefices of the churches of Manchester and Ashton to his brother-in-law, Sir John La Warre.

We are indebted to the first of the La Warres for the earliest geographical description of Moston (at least a part of it). In 1315 John La Warre granted to Richard de Moston a part of the waste land, the bounds beginning at the paling of Blackley, following the stream called Doddithokes Clough as far down as Moss Brook, then up to the bounds of Moston as far as the paling up to the head of the stream; together with the Brodehalgh and three acres of waste between it and the hedge of William the Harpur (Harpurhey). The pales of Blackley, often referred to in old documents, were the fencing of stakes enclosing the deer park of the lord of Manchester (Boggart Hole Clough) which extended in a curve from Alkrington in the north to Harpurhey in the south. Eighty acres of land and wood called Le Harpoures-heie were granted in 1327 by the selfsame John La Warre to Adam de Radcliffe and his daughter, Alice de Hulton. Doddithokes Clough would appear to be the ancient name for Harpurhey Clough, which can be seen on the map of 1820 in the present Ashley Lane-Hillier Street area. The section of Moss Brook (Moston Brook) referred to must be Moston Bottoms.

In 1322 Hugh de Moston (Richard's fourth son) possessed twenty five acres of waste land in Denton, which he held from the lord of Manchester. The Mostons, and after them the Radcliffes, maintained their property interests in Denton and Audenshaw for many years. Richard de Moston died before 1325, when we meet for the first time his only daughter, Emma, who was to play a key role in the settlement of his property. In 1325 William de Moston, Richard's eldest son, gave to his sister Emma an unspecified amount of land in Moston. William died soon afterwards without issue; whereupon, Richard his brother, who now had control of the property, gave a third of the manor to William's widow, Lucy de Morley, and the other two thirds to his sister Emma. In 1343 Richard gave to Emma the whole of the manor of Moston. Then, in 1345, we read that Richard made a settlement of all his lands in Moston with remainder (i.e. a future interest in property currently owned by someone else) to Adam, son of Agnes Allimar - also known as Adam de Abney - and John, son of Hugh de Moston. In 1346 Emma granted the manor of Moston to her nephew John (son of Hugh) and his wife Margaret (daughter of Richard de Tyldesley), with remainders to Hugh, Margaret's brother Robert de Tyldesley, and William Mascy of Sale. In the same year Lucy, widow of William de Moston, claimed part of her late husband's estate as dower. The claim was made against John and Margaret de Moston.

Six years later, in Lent 1352, Emma claimed the manor of Moston (except two dwellings, one ploughland, and four acres of pasture) against William de Radcliffe, Robert de Bolton and Margaret his wife (widow of John de Moston), Alice de Radcliffe, and James de Tyldesley. Robert and Margaret, as tenants, answered the claim, stating that the plaintiff's brother Richard had invested her with the property on the understanding that she would restore it to him, with remainders to Adam de Abney and his children, and to John son of Hugh de Moston. Emma did at length settle the manor on her nephew John de Moston, reserving a rent of five marks (a mark was worth two thirds of a pound sterling) for her lifetime. In 1353 Emma granted to John de Radcliffe her life interest in the lands of William de Moston. It would appear that Emma de Moston died in the same year.

In 1354 and 1355 Hugh de Toft and Alice his wife (daughter of Robert de Moston), in right of the latter, claimed against Robert de Bolton and Margaret his wife twelve dwellings and two hundred acres of land (comprising 60 acres of meadow, 80 acres of pasture, and 40 acres of wood; the rest being, in all probability, waste, garden and bog) in Moston by Ashton. The plaintiffs alleged that Emma de Moston pre-deceased Robert de Moston. Hugh de Moston junior (a cousin of Alice) also laid claim to the estate, and did in fact gain control - but not for long. In 1404 Robert, son of Hugh de Toft, recovered the manor of Moston against Hugh de Moston and Alice his wife.

Mention has been made of John de Radcliffe, who obtained the life interests of Emma de Moston in 1353. This was Sir John de Radcliffe the elder. In 1352 and 1353 in a lawsuit he secured from Hugh de Toft and Alice his

Tollhouse at junction of St Mary's Road and Nuthurst Road

wife the reversion of a dwelling, forty acres of land, etc., the property in Ashton-under-Lyne which William de Moston had held. After the death of Emma de Moston one William de Moston (almost certainly a brother of Alice de Toft, and the former tenant of forty acres of land in Ashton), who held lands in Moston for Emma's lifetime, was present and did fealty to John de Radcliffe in court. The same William de Moston is named in a list of Lancashire gentry in the reign of Richard II (1377-99), who had attended a trial decided in favour of Robert le Grosvenor concerning his right to an ancient coat of arms.

The whole manor had come into the possession of the Radcliffe trustees in 1424. A settlement of the manor was made in 1425-6; Sir John de Radcliffe the younger was to hold it for life, the remainder being to James son of Richard de Radcliffe. These were the Radcliffes of Radcliffe. Another branch of the family, the Radcliffes of Ordsall, also had land in Moston: one of them, John de Radcliffe, in 1394 gave his lands there to Henry de Strangeways. From a rental of the estates of the manor of Manchester, dated 1474, it appears that James Radcliffe esquire held the lordship of Moston from the lord of Manchester at an annual rent of six shillings and sixpence. In 1475 Nicholas Hyde of Denton, who claimed a right to the estate, granted to Richard son and heir of William Barlow his manor of Moston, with reversion to Nicholas himself. Richard Barlow in 1483 complained that being in possession of the manor, John Radcliffe of Radcliffe and Richard his son, with many others, had put him out by force. In 1502 Richard Radcliffe esquire died in possession of the manor of Radcliffe, etc., and also of the manor of Moston. Sir John Radcliffe, who died before

1529, had held the manors of Moston, Crumpsall, and other lands in Manchester for an annual payment of ten shillings. In 1522 a rent of 18 pence was paid for Moston by Lord Fitzwalter to John Hopwood, acting on behalf of the Chethams. In the same entry in the Chetham rentals John Radcliffe was bailiff in Moston. It appears that Robert Radcliffe succeeded his father, Sir John. In 1529 this same Robert Radcliffe was created earl of Sussex.

The complexities of the land tenure system called subinfeudation will be seen from what follows. The Chetham rentals continually record the payment of the Moston rent by Lord Fitzwalter and the Earl of Sussex. The Chethams themselves held their lands from the lord of Manchester. The Radcliffes, and after them Lord Fitzwalter and the first and second earls of Sussex (who were Radcliffes, of course), paid six shillings and sixpence to the lord of Manchester and eighteen pence to the Chethams. This measure of independence on the part of the lords of Moston vis-à-vis the Chethams reflected the high social status of the Radcliffes. It was Robert Radcliffe, newly created earl of Sussex and hereditary lord of the manor of Moston, who about 1529 leased lands in the district to the Shacklock family. This heralded the beginning of a new era in the history of Moston Hall - the Radcliffes would fade from the scene; the Shacklocks would stay for a hundred and twenty years.

Before examining these changes at Moston Hall, let us take one more look at the Moston family. It is impossible to ascertain when the family de Moston ceased to reside at Moston Hall. I feel sure that William de Radcliffe, against whom Emma de Moston laid claim to the manor of Moston in 1352, was related to the Mostons by marriage.

18

Also, it looks as though John de Radcliffe senior, who took over Emma's life interests in Moston, was another connection. If this is so, then apart from the short residence of Richard Barlow, continuity of tenure by one family was maintained from the twelfth century until about 1540. Although the Moston family ultimately held its lands from the lord of Manchester, it had strong links with Ashton-under-Lyne.

Earlier we spoke of the lands of William de Moston in Denton and Ashton, which John de Radcliffe the elder wrestled from Hugh de Toft and Alice his wife. In a rent roll of John de Assheton of Ashton-under-Lyne, dated 1380, among the freehold tenants who paid a yearly fine for the use of the mill was the heir of Richard de Moston for his lands in Audenshaw, who paid sixteen pence. This was probably William de Moston. In an old manuscript, formerly in the possession of Sir Ralph Assheton of Middleton (quoted in Corry, History of Lancashire) a list of those paying bench rents includes the following: 'At the first form upon the south side of Assheton kirk, the wife of the heir Henry de Moston.' This could date back to 1332 when a certain Henry de Moston is mentioned in connection with Ashton. The Manchester manor rental in 1473 recorded that Sir John Ashton held the manor of Ashton and Moston. In 1569-70 Ashton parish and the people of Moston made an agreement, whereby Moston had to pay one eighth of a joint tax.

We now return to the succession at Moston Hall. After Robert Radcliffe, first earl of Sussex, made the first grant of land in the district to the Shacklocks about 1529, there is a lull in the affairs of Moston Hall. But, it is the calm before the storm. The preoccupation of Robert, earl of Sussex, with matters of State led him to neglect his manor of Moston. After the ill-fated Pilgrimage of Grace of 1536, a popular rising in the north of England demanding the restoration of well over a hundred monasteries despoiled by Henry VIII (including Lastingham, of which St Chad had been abbot before his elevation to Lichfield); the perfidious monarch pardoned and then butchered the leaders, and anyone remotely connected with the uprising. One of his chief agents in the dastardly and indiscriminate executions that were carried out in the first half of 1537 was the lord of Moston, Robert Radcliffe, earl of Sussex and chief executioner of England. Radcliffe was personally responsible for the summary execution of Abbot Paslew of Whalley and the looting of his Abbey, for which Henry VIII commended him most warmly. He was a man without scruple or mercy; his loyalty to the king greatly increased his already considerable personal wealth. But, he had less than ten more years of life in which to enjoy it. The affairs of Moston must have seemed minuscule to such a man. The lack of any interest on his part was the real cause of the chaos that ensued.

The Shacklocks were establishing themselves indelibly on the Moston scene during the 1530s (their name is perpetuated in Shackliffe Road and Shackerley Green: both names are corruptions of Shacklock). But, the family was split by a bitter power struggle. The feud centred on the rival claims of Robert and Thomas Shacklock and a near relative, Adam Shacklock. In 1542 Robert and Thomas complained in the Duchy court at Lancaster that in the preceding year Robert, earl of Sussex, had made a lease to them, but Richard Shacklock the elder, and his sons, Adam, Hugh and Ellis, had

expelled them. Despite the fact that Robert and Thomas seem to have established their case, there is evidence that in 1543 the earl of Sussex made a lease of land in Moston to Adam Shacklock. In that same year William Radcliffe of Ordsall released his claim in Moston to the Shacklocks (it is not clear which branch of the family). In 1544, after the death of Richard Shacklock, Robert and Thomas were again in court at Lancaster; this time they claimed that forcible entry had been made by Margaret widow of Richard, Ellis her son, and others. Yet again, in 1546, Robert and Thomas Shacklock were plaintiffs at Lancaster in a cause against Hugh Shacklock and others over a disputed title to a dwelling and lands, held by lease from Robert earl of Sussex.

A short time before 1547 Henry Radcliffe, second earl of Sussex, sold the tenure of the manor of Moston to John Reddish. In 1547 John Reddish sold the tenancy of Moston Hall to Robert and Thomas Shacklock, and another part of the estate to the Bowkers. To Geoffrey and Oliver Bowker John Reddish sold twenty six acres of the manor, and to Nicholas Bowker he sold twenty acres. The Bowkers (the name comes from the practice of 'bowking', i.e. washing and bleaching linen, which was carried out on the banks of local rivers and streams) have a twofold claim to fame. First, we owe them one of those tantalising glimpses into the Moston of far-off times. In 1418 Thomas La Warre, lord of Manchester, owned a house, and sixty acres of land adjoining, called Brideshagh next to Boukerlegh within the hamlet of Moston late in the tenure of Thomas le Bouker.

The boundaries of this property are given as follows (it is interesting to try locating the places mentioned):- on the south at the gate at the side of a lane (Moston Lane?) which leads from the common pasture of Theyle moor (the southeast part of White Moss) to the vill of Manchester, and thence following a hedge between Brideshagh and a parcel of land of Moston now in the tenure of Robert Shacklock (in 1524 Richard Shacklock, who had made a garden on the waste, agreed to give a bunch of leeks to each of the owners of Nuthurst. This would explain why Shackerley Green is in Nuthurst. See the map of 1820) to the common pasture of Theyle moor, and following the pasture to the pales of Blackley, and following the pales to a hedge between Brideshagh and the dwelling late of John de Jonesse in Moston, and following the hedge to the first-named lane (opposite to Hough Hall?) and following the lane to the said gate, together with common of pasture on Theyle moor and common of turbary there, with free ingress and egress for digging, drying, and carrying turves. The second claim to fame of the Bowker family derives from its residence, Bowker Hall, which was prior to 1418 the dwelling of Thomas le Bouker next to Boukerlegh, and was still standing roughly on the site of the present North Manchester High School for Girls at the end of the 19th century. It is generally agreed among old writers that the local dialect pronunciation of Bowker Hall, which in time was applied to the nearby clough or hollow (the former deer park of the Grelleys), is the origin of 'Boggart Hole' Clough.

There is little more on record concerning the Bowkers. Oliver Bowker, late of Moston, died in 1565, leaving a son and heir Edward, of lawful age. Edward Bowker purchased a dwelling and land in Moston from George

Bowker in 1567. Edward died in 1585-6, leaving a son Geoffrey, eighteen years old. The Bowker property in Moston at this time was held of John Lacy (the West family - lords de la Warre - sold the manor of Manchester in 1578 to John Lacy, citizen and clothworker of London, who, seventeen years later, sold it to Nicholas Mosley, citizen and alderman of London). Nicholas Bowker of Harpurhey and Jane his wife in 1572 sold lands in Moston to Robert Shacklock.

Mention of a Shacklock brings us back to the tenancy of Moston Hall. Before we continue the turbulent tale of the Shacklocks, it is necessary to note the final act of the Radcliffe saga. Although keeping in the background, Henry Radcliffe, second earl of Sussex, continued in possession of the manor of Moston (the Shacklocks lived in the Hall) until his death in 1557, after which his interest appears to have passed to another branch of the family. There is no further mention of his direct heirs in connection with the Moston estate. In 1568 Sir William Radcliffe, a relative, was in possession of the manor of Ordsall and of lands in Moston. The Moston property is mentioned in later inquests of Sir John Radcliffe his son (1589), and Sir Alexander Radcliffe his grandson (1599), both of Ordsall. Gradually, the interests of the Radcliffes ceased entirely, their estate passing into the hands of numerous small proprietors.

Meanwhile, back at Moston Hall, in 1551, five years after Robert and Thomas Shacklock had taken Hugh Shacklock and others to the Duchy court at Lancaster; Thomas Shacklock was back in the same court, this time as defendant, in a suit brought against him by Edmund Assheton and others, tenants of Nuthurst, for having interrupted the right of way to the Manchester market. Thomas Shacklock died at the end of 1570, leaving a son and heir Robert, of full age. Robert Shacklock, Thomas' partner in litigation, died in 1588, leaving behind a son and heir Edward, of full age. This Edward was married to Alice Cudworth, daughter of Ralph Cudworth of Werneth, and sister to Margaret, wife of James Chetham of Nuthurst. There is a rather pathetic episode connected with this Edward Shacklock. A relative of his, who was also his tenant, Thomas Shacklock, died early in 1610. In his will he is described as a chapman (trader). To his son Robert Shacklock he gives all his estate and interest in one close or parcel of ground in Moston, called The Marled Earth, entreating his 'loving cousin', Edward Shacklock, to be a kind kinsman to his son Robert, and to renew the lease on the property for a hundred years. Thomas states in his will that Edward had promised to do this twenty two years previously, on the condition that he (Thomas) make suitable repairs to the house. He goes on to say that he had spent at least £40 on repairs to the premises. We do not know whether Edward renewed the lease. Thomas' goods and chattels were valued at £46.15.2. Eight years later, Edward Shacklock, the 'loving cousin' of Thomas, died (1618) leaving a son and heir John, aged twenty two.

This John Shacklock, who came to be called the elder, made a conditional conveyance of Howgate and other lands in 1628, the remainders being to his son and heir John the younger, another son Edward, and Daniel brother of John the elder. John the younger died before 1649, in which year Edward is described as son and heir apparent. The Shacklock family in residence at Moston

Moston Hall c.1875

20

Hall in 1655 comprised John the elder and his wife Mary (nee Radcliffe); Edward and his wife Margaret (nee Entwisle). Two sisters of Edward, Elizabeth and Mary, are also mentioned in a conveyance of 1655. On 28th December 1663 Edward Shacklock sold the Moston estate to Edward Chetham of Smedley. Margaret, the widow of Edward Shacklock, made a claim for £500 against the estate; but Edward Chetham, the purchaser, refused to discharge it until certain deeds were surrendered to him. In 1669 the £500 were paid. Moston Hall was now the possession of a branch of the Chethams, which would soon acquire Nuthurst.

This is a suitable moment to interrupt the catalogue of tenants of Moston Hall. Before we embark upon a similar exercise in regard to the other Halls of Moston and Nuthurst let us pause to make some necessary observations. Behind the romantic, foreign-sounding names and the lofty talk of estates and pedigrees, there lurks continually the spectre of a bleak, largely infertile terrain. Up to the middle of the thirteenth century this area was a wilderness of forest, peat bog and moorland waste. Even the lords of Moston and Nuthurst had to be content with the most basic standard of living. While the peasants - cottars, living in tied cottages (one of these was still standing in the last century); socmen tenants farming often less than one acre of land - had to struggle to survive. The threat of starvation was never absent. Undernourishment, lack of hygiene (overcrowding, inadequate drainage) and ignorance of medicine contributed to high infant mortality, premature ageing, suffering and distress. And, worst of all, there was the pestilence that could decimate the population. During the outbreak of bubonic plague, known as the Black Death (1347-50), twenty million people died in Europe - a higher toll of human destruction than that exacted by the Second World War. As a result, fear abounded; and, hand in hand with fear, went superstition.

There is evidence in this locality of medieval attempts at reclamation: assarting (deforestation), and 'conquering' the marshland (drying it out by means of sand and marl). We have already mentioned the peat bog that gave Moston the first part of its name, and how it subsequently disappeared from sight and memory. In 1840 Messrs Jones and Gould undertook reclamation work in the Alkrington part of White Moss and in Moston and Chadderton. One of the most interesting facts connected with these operations was the discovery made on the Moss. The peat was from four to ten feet deep. First of all, the diggers uncovered a basin of rich marl over sand. Then, nearby they unearthed many tree trunks and huge branches - mostly oaks, beeches, alders, firs, and one or two fine yews; some were partly charred. One oak was twelve feet in circumference and was traced for fifteen yards. The trees were found some six feet below the surface. Here is proof of a thirteenth or fourteenth century attempt to reclaim the land for cultivation from the ancient, paludial forest. Such attempts were in vain. In a chart of Moston and White Moss, dated 1556, we find the legend, 'A white moss that nothing can grow upon.'

Only a small area of Moston was ever under the plough (the vegetable crops on White Moss belong to a much later period). In the late Middle Ages, before the introduction of potatoes, lettuce and tomatoes, there were probably only some thirty five acres given over to cereal crops such as oats, barley, wheat and rye. Oats were fed to horses; oatmeal was used for porridge and bread (the staple diet). Barley and rye provided cattle fodder; the former also being used for brewing ale - large amounts were drunk daily, perhaps on average a gallon per person! Because of the climate and the texture of the soil, wheat would not grow in sufficient quality and quantity to be a viable proposition. We know that Richard Shacklock, who had made a garden in the waste, in 1524 agreed to give a bunch of leeks to each of the owners of Nuthurst. Along with leeks, he would have grown onions, peas, beans and vetches (the last two were often baked into bread), and perhaps garlic. Meat was rarely seen on the table of poor people - and then it would be mutton, seldom beef, chicken or pork. Bread and cheese (occasionally butter was available), washed down with milk or water or ale, constituted the peasant's most frequent meal. He would also eat nuts and hedge fruits. Pottage, a sort of pease pudding based on oats, would also come around with monotonous regularity.

This area was primarily pastoral. In 1322 Blackley alone had pasture for two hundred and forty cattle and the same number of deer. Moston was always, up to some sixty years ago, mostly meadow land - pasture for beef and dairy cattle. In medieval times the land lacked fertiliser; it was also furrowed by streams and dotted about with ponds (as late as the Census Report of 1901 seven acres of Moston were inland water; but the Ordnance Survey map of 1893 shows that 80% of this was five man-made reservoirs). Sheep would have been more in evidence, occasionally goats. There was plenty of pannage for pigs in the numerous woods - pig farming has always been the mainstay of smallholders in this part of the world. Only the well-to-do owned a horse.

An important insight into social customs involving Moston and Nuthurst in feudal times is gained from the surveys of the manor of Manchester, dated 1320 and 1322. Grelley's Charter of 1301 obliged the burgesses of Manchester to grind their corn and malt at the mill of the lord on the river Irk, and to bake their bread at his oven close by. The manorial extents or surveys of twenty years later restate the obligation, and specify tenants and hamlets outside the vill of Manchester to whom the obligation also applies. So, for example, in the 1320 survey Alexander de Chadderton and Roger his brother are freehold tenants of Moston and Nuthurst 'by homage and fealty . . . and they ought to grind.' In both surveys the singular privilege of the lord of Moston (at the time perhaps one of the Asshetons) is mentioned. Here is the more concise version of the 1322 extent: 'There is there the mill of Manchester, running by the stream of Irk, worth £10 (rateable value), at which all the burgesses and all the tenants of Manchester, with the hamlets of Ardwick, Openshaw, Crumpsall, Moston, Nuthurst, Gotherswicke, and Ancoats, ought to grind. They grind to the sixteenth grain, except the lord of Moston, who is hopper-free to the twentieth grain.'

A few words of explanation: the law then required vassals to grind their corn at the lord's mill, for which soke or privilege they paid him a multure (grinding fee), a tax in kind. At first the toll was entirely at the discretion of the lord of the manor; but later legislation restricted the tax (at first in kind, later in money) according to the custom of the land and the force of the river. In the case of the mill of

Manchester during this period the burgesses and other tenants had to hand over the sixteenth filling upwards of the hopper (a funnel-shaped chamber) to the lord of the manor. The lord of Moston, however, for some reason we cannot discover, only surrendered the twentieth hopperful. Nuthurst was not included in the privilege. The obligation to grind continued binding upon the tenants of the manor until the year 1758 (during the sixteenth century ownership of the mill of Manchester, with the right to multure, was transferred to the Grammar School), when, after much litigation, the monopoly was abolished except for the grinding of malt.

A point of some interest in this regard: about 1834 John Collinson and George Simpson had taken over the lease of a glue factory on the west side of Monsall Lane and converted it into a brewery. The height of Mr Simpson's ambition at that time was to brew five barrels of ale a week, a target he soon exceeded. In 1858 the partners built new premises on the east side of Monsall Lane (at that time outside the Manchester township) in order to avoid the necessity of sending their malt to be ground at the mill of the Grammar School. After Mr Simpson's death in 1862 his sons, Joseph and George, carried on the business in Monsall Lane until 1865, when Mr H.C.F. Wilson in partnership with Mr W. Philpot bought the brewery. Mr Philpot died of hydrophobia (rabies) two or three years later. This was the genesis of the mighty Wilsons Brewery.

There is one more practice related to Moston and Nuthurst that we must mention. The 1322 extent tells us that there was a certain bailiff, the lord's sergeant, sworn to him to ride about and superintend his territory, and to pay to the lord the rents of the outside tenants; that the said bailiff, called the 'Grith-Sergeant' or keeper of the peace, had to be sustained - himself, a boy and a horse, and his four under-bailiffs - by (among others) the tenants of Moston, Nuthurst, Hulme near Alport, and Heaton Norris. Elsewhere we read: 'They shall find for the said chief sergeant, when he shall come, bread, ale and victuals, and other things necessary according to the season; and for his boy and four sub-bailiffs, such food as they provide in the household; and provender for his horse.'

3

The Chethams of Great Nuthurst Hall

Immediately to the north of Moston, across a wooded ravine that for centuries acted as the natural boundary, lay the hamlet of Nuthurst. It housed two families of note, the Chethams and the Chaddertons, whose histories intertwined (sometimes disconcertingly) down the years. Before we look at the inhabitants, however, let us first consider that ravine: its location, significance, and how it disappeared. Writing in 1907, H.T. Crofton had this to say about the topography of Moston: 'Its natural features are that from Moston Brook four cloughs or ravines run northwards; one on the west called Harpurhey Clough, running upwards from Moston Bottoms, one about midway called Dean Clough, and further east there are two close together, of which the westerly is called Boar Green Clough and leads to Great Nuthurst Hall, and to the east of the last mentioned clough Moston Brook is called Morris brook in Morris Clough.'

Long before Crofton wrote this description Harpurhey Clough (known in the fourteenth century as Doddithokes Clough) had disappeared in the urban sprawl of the late nineteenth century. The stream that flowed through it into Moston Brook was the traditional boundary between Moston and Harpurhey. Preparatory to building houses in the area, a culvert was made for the stream; and Hall Street (now Hillier Street) was built along the same alignment. Thus Hall Street became the boundary. John Ward says that when the stream was in spate the culvert could not carry it, and it had to be diverted through the original Old Loom public house.

The Dean Clough, landscaped, and protected against housing development by the terms of Sir Edward Tootal Broadhurst's gift, is now part of Broadhurst Park. In this picturesque dell stood Moston Hall. We shall have something to say about Moston Brook and Morris Clough in another place. For the moment let us consider the rest of Crofton's account. He is clearly mistaken in positing two separate cloughs, one leading to Great Nuthurst Hall and the other to Little Nuthurst Hall. The reason for his confusion (he obviously had not consulted the map of 1820) is that Boar Green Clough disappeared about the middle of the nineteenth century. A glance at that map shows that Boar Green Clough ran up to a point just west of Great Nuthurst Hall, skirting Little Nuthurst Hall on the way. A map of 1838, showing the projected railway from Miles Platting to Middleton (it was not completed until the following year), helps us to locate Boar Green Clough with some precision. It stretched from St Matthew's Playing Fields across the railway and the Fairway, and eventually met up with Moston Brook at the back of Hoylake Close.

Now we shall attempt to answer the question: whatever happened to Boar Green Clough? It is surely more than coincidence that the disappearance of the Clough occurred about the time that the railway track was being laid across it. More importantly, in 1840 Shaft Number One of Moston Pit (326 yards deep) was sunk where Woodstock Road describes a right-angled bend, near Nuthurst Bridge. Ten years later Shaft Number Two (336 yards deep) was sunk at the head of the Clough (immediately to the west of Moston Mill). In my opinion, the displaced earth and slag from these workings obliterated Boar Green Clough from the face of Moston; or rather, from Moston and Nuthurst; because the removal of this natural division marked the end of the distinction between the two hamlets, and the extinction of Nuthurst as a separate entity. There is something at once sad and yet fitting about this; because I am convinced that Boar Green Clough was the original 'grove of hazelnuts' denoted by the name Nuthurst. Just for the record, Boar Green House (seen on the map of 1820 to the northeast of Moston Hall) was only demolished in 1937 to make way for the expansion of the new Ferranti Radio Works. It can be seen on an aerial photograph, taken in 1935, a drab farmhouse backing onto the railway behind the last row of houses in Woodstock Road. Its only claim upon our attention is its name, reminding us of the distant past.

Just under a mile to the northeast of Moston Hall stood the two halls of Nuthurst: Great Nuthurst Hall, home of the Chethams; and Little Nuthurst Hall, occupied for centuries by the Chaddertons. Both have disappeared without a trace, unless Little Nuthurst Farm, 148 Nuthurst Road, is a part of the Little Nuthurst Hall group of buildings. Booker (Ancient Chapel of Blackley, pp. 136 and 137) has a description of them as they were about 1854. In view of the importance of these two families, I here reproduce it verbatim:-

'A few yards to the west of the Lancashire and Yorkshire line of railway stands Great Nuthurst Hall, an irregular pile of brick, without much pretension to antiquity. It claims no particular notice if we except an antiquated gable still remaining at the east end, evidently much older than the main structure of which it now forms a part, and apparently the only existing remains of a former building occupying the site of the present edifice. This gable is in the ordinary style of the old timber houses - a strong framework of oak, plaided with dark heavy beams of the same material, and the spaces filled in with a rough plaster formed of rushes, mud, and clay. The woodwork, though clearly of great antiquity, is still in a remarkable state of preservation. At a field's length from Great Nuthurst, and on the opposite side of the railway, is Little Nuthurst Hall, which is rapidly disappearing under the combined efforts of time and modern innovation. The only remaining portion of the old hall is interesting from the curious and rare examples of ornamental plaster-work which it exhibits. The mode of construction appears to have been the same as in the generality of half-timbered houses, laths nailed to a framework of oak, and coated with plaster: but here, instead of the woodwork remaining exposed, as is ordinarily the case, the whole is covered with mortar, stippled over, and studded with a curious four-leaved conical flower, in its parts not unlike the dog-tooth peculiar to the thirteenth century, with this exception, that the latter embellishment invariably consists of a number linked together and usually serving as an enrichment to a moulding, whilst in the present instance the flower is unconnected, forming an ornament complete in itself. There are also some other specimens of ornamentation in plaster still remaining. With the exception of that portion of the old mansion just alluded to, Little Nuthurst Hall is of comparatively modern date,

Great Nuthurst Hall c.1880

constructed of brick, and in its outward appearance presenting nothing worthy of observation.'

Booker then proceeded to rhapsodise about the families of distinction which had graced the Moston scene; although he admitted to knowing very little of them. Thanks to the Victoria History of Lancashire, published in 1911, we are in a more fortunate position. Early in the thirteenth century Robert son of Bernard, who had inherited Moston from Roger son of Orm (son of Ailward), disposed of all of it to Henry de Chetham. A short time later Henry de Chetham granted Nuthurst to Thomas de Eccles, whose brother William about 1260 transferred it to Geoffrey son of Richard de Trafford. This Geoffrey, upon receiving from his father the manors of Chadderton and Foxdenton some years previously, had changed his surname to Chadderton, and so may be considered the patriarch of the Chadderton family. Sir Geoffrey de Chetham, as chief lord of Moston and a witness to the grant of 1260, had to be paid a rent of thirteen pence. We know that Geoffrey de Chetham died before 1275; because in that year his widow Margery claimed dower of twenty acres in Moston and Chadderton against Geoffrey de Chadderton. The Chetham land in Ashton, mentioned in 1278, probably refers to Moston.

In 1320 Alexander and Roger, sons of Geoffrey de Chadderton, held Moston and Nuthurst of the lord of Manchester by homage and fealty and a rent of ten shillings. About this time we are informed that the moieties or half shares of the estate were settled on the Chetham and Chadderton families, by now residing in the two halls of Nuthurst. There is further mention of Alexander and Roger being in possession of the lands of Geoffrey de Chadderton in 1340. In 1345 the two sons of Geoffrey de Chadderton defended their right to certain land against Richard de Moston, who claimed as heir of William de Moston his brother. In 1340 Roger, son of Geoffrey de Chadderton, made a will settling his lands in Moston upon his son Roger, with remainders to younger sons - Geoffrey, John, Henry, Robert and Richard. There was a limitation to male heirs in each case. The other son of Geoffrey de Chadderton, Alexander, in 1356 granted to John de Chetham and Alice his wife all his dwellings and lands in the hamlet of Moston in the town of Ashton, together with the rent of three shillings due from the lord of Moston.

A few words concerning John de Chetham might be inserted here. He is mentioned in 1331 as landowner in Butterworth, and in 1332 as resident in Crompton. In 1335 he settled land in Butterworth on his son Richard, with remainders to other sons, Robert and Roger. Another son, Adam, is mentioned in settlements of land elsewhere in 1342. There then occurs something mysterious: a Thomas de Chetham, described as son and heir of John de Chetham, was defendant in a lawsuit in 1382. It appears that subsequently Thomas de Chetham was killed by his neighbour, Thomas de Chadderton - how, we do not know. His son, John de Chetham, was a minor; but came into possession of his property in 1404. The mystery surrounding the above violent episode is compounded by the following event. In 1412 John, son of Thomas de Chetham, granted to Ellis, son of John de Chadderton, all his lands in Nuthurst for the term of thirty years at a peppercorn (nominal) rent. John Chetham in 1413 made a settlement of lands in Crompton, Ashton and elsewhere, with remainder to his son James. Nine years later John Chetham was still alive. His son James in 1440 married as his second wife, Margery daughter of John Langley; James was still alive in 1475. In 1466 a grant was made by William Heaton to Thomas Chetham, son and heir apparent of James, on his marriage with William's daughter Elizabeth. A son Nicholas is mentioned in 1496.

By an agreement between James Chetham and another son, Thomas, in 1468 the latter received Nuthurst and Sidgreaves, paying £4 a year to his father; James, the father, also had eighteen pence, a moiety of the free rent of Moston. Thomas Chetham, who died in 1503, was found to have held his share of Nuthurst of the earl of Derby. He held a dwelling, thirty four acres of land (ploughland?), six acres of meadow, two hundred acres of pasture, and sixty acres of wood in Nuthurst, together with lands and dwellings in other places. During the lifetime of Thomas Chetham (1440-1503) the Theyle Moor litigation began. It continued in one form or another for over a century. The value of this dispute is twofold: first, it throws light on the social conditions then prevailing in Moston and Nuthurst; but, more important, it brings to life in vivid fashion the personalities of the people involved.

Although Thomas Chetham and his descendents down till 1614 held their share of Nuthurst from the earls of Derby, they being the mesne or intermediate landlords; in practice, the mesne lordship was ignored, and the Chethams paid their rents directly to the lord of Manchester. John Chetham, Thomas' son, in 1487 married Margery daughter of Ellis Prestwich. John died in 1515. His son and heir, Thomas, was twenty six when his father died. He married Elizabeth daughter of John Hopwood. According to a series of rentals from 1520 to 1546, Nuthurst seems to have been almost entirely in the hands of the Chethams. There was one under-tenant in 1520 who paid three shillings and four pence; and in 1524 a second tenant is mentioned, paying two shillings. There has already been a reference to Richard Shacklock's garden in the waste in 1524, and the rent he paid in leeks to each of the owners of Nuthurst. The Thomas Chetham, who obtained the tenure of Great Nuthurst Hall in 1515, died in 1546, leaving the estate to his son John. By his will, dated 1573, John left to his wife Isabel his mansion house of Nuthurst with lands and dwelling in Crompton. The widow married William Radcliffe. The son of John and Isabel Chetham, Henry, was twenty two years old when his father died in 1573.

Four years later, while riding through a stream at

Pedigree of Chetham of Nuthurst

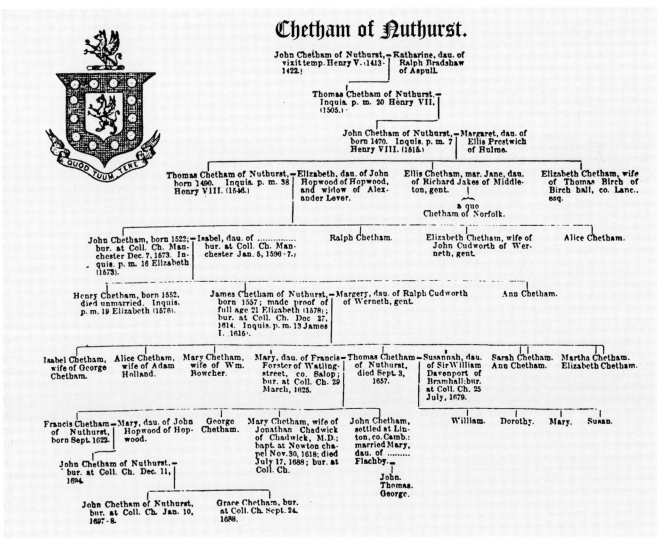

Middleton, Henry was drowned. James, his brother and heir, was twenty years of age at the time of the tragic accident; so his mother Isabel was granted the wardship. In 1591, after Isabel had married William Radcliffe a settlement of the hall of Nuthurst was made. Not long afterwards Isabel Radcliffe (formerly Chetham) died. Her will is dated 3rd January 1596. James Chetham had succeeded to the inheritance upon reaching his majority a short time after the death of his brother Henry by drowning. James managed the affairs of Great Nuthurst Hall until his death in 1614. His son and heir, Thomas, was under sixteen years of age; consequently, he was placed under the guardianship of his mother, Margery Chetham, by order of the king.

By his will dated 31st January 1613 James Chetham of Nuthurst in the County of Lancaster, gentleman, desired that all his lands, tenements, and hereditaments be divided into three equal parts. The first portion shall be and remain unto Margery Chetham, his wife, for and during the term of her natural life. It consists of 'these several parts and portions of his capital messuage called Nuthurst, and these closes, fields, and parcels of lands, being parcels of the demesne lands appertaining to the same, and hereafter particularly expressed - that is to wit, the Kitchen, the Lower house, the Dene house, and all the rest of the New building, as well below as above the New barn, with the cowhouse adjoining to the same, the Kilne, and the Water corn mill, together with the suit and multure belonging thereunto, with one Garden, and the Orchard and Croft, and The Great Copthorn Hill, The Little Copthorn Hill, The Six Acre, The Five Acre, and all the Sidgreaves, and all these messuages and tenements in Nuthurst, in the several occupations of Robert Ogden, Thomas Mellor, George Wyrrall, William Travis, Hugh Kemp, Richard Hill, Isabel Jackson, widow, and Katherine Jackson, widow, etc.'

'And one other third part of his said messuages, etc., shall be and remain unto Thomas Chetham, his son and heir apparent, for and until such times as he shall accomplish the age of twenty-one years; that is to wit, the Hall, the Parlour, two chambers over the parlour, and all the old buildings adjoining the Kitchen, the one long-slated Barn, with two cowhouses adjoining upon either end of the said barn, one other Bay to lay in hay, and one cowhouse under the same, one Stable, with two little chambers adjoining to the end thereof, the great Archeshawe, the meadow thereunto adjoining, the three Pyncrofts, with the woodlands thereunto belonging, the Rysshie field, the Blackarne, etc.'

'The other third part, that is the Four Acre, with parcel of land called the Rysshes adjoining the said Four Acre, and one other parcel of land called the Roughe hey, adjoining to the Meyrediche, and also adjoining unto Thomas Whittycar his new marled close, one other meadow at the back of the garden, one other parcel of land called the Intach, and one meadow lying at the back of the Orchard, and also one close, and now ffeyed to be marled, adjoining to the ground of Hugh Kemp, and the same Turf moss or Rowmes as are now enclosed, and the rent of all the said Rowmes belonging to him, the said James Chetham, and also several messuages and tenements in Crompton, and also the issues and profits, setting and letting, of "one cole myne" commonly called and known by the name of Lenardyne, and with liberty to

set down more shafts, and to dig and mine for the finding and getting of coals, shall be and remain to his executors, for and towards the payments of his debts, and for the education, advancement, and preferment of Sarah, Martha, Ann, and Elizabeth Chetham, his daughters, for and until they shall have severally received the sum of forty pounds apiece, etc.'

From the Clowes Deeds we learn that John Chetham had built a mill on Moston Brook at Boar Clough, together with a mill dam, soon after his accession to the lordship of Nuthurst in 1546. This John Chetham in 1572, the year before his death, bought up the rights of Edmund Chadderton of Nuthurst in a watercourse from Thealmore down and away by the (Little Nuthurst) hall, which E. Chadderton then inhabited, and so forward by Moss Brook. This watercourse was assuredly the stream that flowed down through Boar Green Clough and into Moston Brook. So we can locate the corn mill which James Chetham bequeathed to his wife Margery in 1613. Obviously, the monopoly on the grinding of corn that belonged de jure to the lord of Manchester was de facto being eroded by the existence of the mill on the brook. Maybe it was a special privilege accorded to Nuthurst, along the lines of the privilege granted to Moston (but denied to Nuthurst) over two hundred years previously.

Mention of the Great Copthorn Hill and the Little Copthorn Hill in the first part of James Chetham's will likewise enables us to locate the places referred to with some precision. In a deed dated 12th April 1573 'the New Close in Nuthurst' is mentioned; and then in one dated 19th April 1586 we come across 'a close called Le Copthorne hill, in Nuthurst, containing by estimation 12 acres, and another, called Le Newe Marled Earth, in Nuthurst, containing by estimation 6 acres.' It would appear that Copthorn Hill was in fact a close, twelve acres in extent. Where was it? Charles Roeder (some Moston Folk-Lore, 1907) states that Copthorn Hill, in Nuthurst, is the highest point of the township of Moston. In 1575 the Theyle Moor rioters pulled up a great gate at Hartley Shawe, in Nuthurst, and carried it to Copthorn Hill, 'a place of very great height,' and made of three of the largest pieces one pair of gallows (on which they threatened to hang all who contradicted them).

H.T. Crofton carried out a lot of research into the Theyle Moor litigation. He is of the opinion that Theyle Moor was the southeast part of White Moss. The references to Copthorn Hill (that is, the Great Copthorn) in connection with Theyle Moor would seem to site it in the vicinity of White Moss. Now the highest point in Moston (and Manchester, for that matter) at 364 ft 8 ins above sea level is, according to the Ordnance Survey Map of 1848, close to the present Gardeners Arms Hotel. In my opinion the spot at which Lightbowne Road breasts the crown of the hill is the Great Copthorn Hill. John Ward (Moston Characters at Work, p. 175) mentions 'the second coal-pit shaft sunk in Moston, the one in what is called the Kop-thorn.' This is Shaft Number Two of Moston Pit, situated immediately to the west of Moston Mill. So, it would seem that the twelve acre Copthorn Close included the summit of Lightbowne Road and the area about the Mill. The Little Copthorn Hill, in my estimation, is that mound behind Moston Mill which forms the highest part of Pleasington Drive.

The 'Rysshie field' mentioned in the second part of

James Chetham's will was almost certainly in the vicinity of Rushes Lane, seen on the map of 1820 leading from Great Nuthurst Hall (Mill Estate) to that section of Broad Lane now called Moston Lane East, between Hollinwood Avenue and Broadway. Rushes Gate Farm stood on the eastern side of the railway at the back of Dunsley Avenue and Heyford Avenue up till some fifty years ago. I like to think that the rushes used in the wattle and daub walls of the original Great Nuthurst Hall were gathered in the Rushie Field that was situated in this area. We may well have in the third part of the will, in the section dealing with 'one cole myne' commonly called by the name of Lenardyne, the first reference to coal mining in Moston.

After the death of James Chetham in 1614, as we have remarked earlier, the estate was in the hands of his widow Margery for some five years, until their son Thomas came of age. During the Civil War Thomas fought for the Parliamentary cause. As a captain of Infantry, he took part in the defence of Manchester in 1642. He was appointed a commissioner two years later. Upon his death in 1657 he was succeeded by his son Francis. This Francis caused a pedigree to be recorded in 1664. Three pedigrees of the Chetham family were entered in that year: Chetham of Cheetham; Chetham of Nuthurst; and Chetham of Turton. All three branches of the family claimed descent from the Chadderton family, according to Booker (Ancient Chapel of Blackley, p. 148), who argues from the absence of a mark of filiation on the Nuthurst coat of arms, that the Chethams of Nuthurst were the oldest line. This is a moot point. Despite the rather tortuous argument from heraldic devices, and some wishful thinking, Booker was unable to establish an ancestral link between the Chethams and the Chaddertons.

Soon after Francis Chetham had put the Chetham genealogy on record he proceeded to squander the family fortune and mortgaged Nuthurst. He died without issue in 1678. The process of dissolution was carried on by his younger brother and heir, John Chetham of Linton in Cambridgeshire, who, after encumbering the estate still further sold it in 1692 to Edward Chetham of Manchester, son of Edward Chetham of Smedley. The purchaser became known as Edward Chetham of Nuthurst, according to the inscription on his tomb in the Collegiate church. Upon his death in 1714 he was succeeded by his only son, another Edward, upon whom as the last male heir of the family devolved the entire estates of the Chethams, including Moston Hall and the two Halls of Nuthurst. The last of the Chetham men died unmarried and intestate in 1769. By a partition deed, dated 31st October 1770, the extensive estates of the family were shared between his sisters - Alice, widow of Adam Bland; and Mary, wife of Samuel Clowes the younger.

Nuthurst and Moston became the property of Mary Clowes. She died in 1775. In her will Nuthurst was given to James Hilton, son of her daughter Mary, who had married Samuel Hilton of Pennington. So the Moston and Nuthurst property of the Chethams was conveyed to the Hiltons. By his will, dated 16th January 1793 (proved at Chester 1st March 1803), James Hilton bequeathed all his estate real and personal to his eldest son, Samuel Chetham Hilton esquire. The new lord of Nuthurst was high sheriff of the county of Lancaster in 1811. By his marriage to Martha, daughter of Samuel Clowes (whose

family owned the Broughton estate), he had several children; one of whom, T. W. Legh Hilton, inherited the Nuthurst estate on the death of his father in 1835. By his will, dated 5th March 1831 (proved at Chester 11th May 1835), Samuel Chetham Hilton bequeathed his estate to certain trustees, directing that they should sell off all his real estate with convenient speed.

Even though parcels of land were sold from time to time, in 1851 the trustees of Samuel Chetham Hilton were still in possession of an estate of 620 acres (half the entire township of Moston - Nuthurst having been absorbed into Moston), including Great Nuthurst Hall, Little Nuthurst Hall, and Moston Hall. Sometime about 1851 the last descendant of the Chethams moved out of Great Nuthurst Hall. In 1854 T. W. Legh Hilton, son and successor of Samuel Chetham Hilton, was residing at Moston Hall. According to the Census Enumerators' List of 1871, Great Nuthurst Hall was occupied by Samuel Shawcross, who farmed thirty acres of land. There is nothing on the Ordnance Survey Map of 1893 to indicate the situation of the ancestral home of the Chethams of Nuthurst.

The Chethams had purchased Moston Hall from the Shacklock family in 1663. There is no further record of residents in the Hall until 1841. In that year, according to the census taken by Miss Mary Taylor, John Slingsby was living there with his wife, four children, and five servants. Slingsby was a farmer and cattle dealer. During Slingsby's time at Moston Hall we have the first mention of the Moston Farmers' Rent Dinner, then held at John Smith's beer house, Moston Mill, opposite the lane leading into the Hall. After T. W. Legh Hilton (known to the locals as Squire Hilton) came to the Hall in the early 1850s the dinner was held in the Hall. John Ward (Moston Characters at Play, pp 168 - 174) describes the proceedings. The squire's tenants were invited to the dinner on the occasion of paying their rents. Most of them found it expedient to attend the dinner, even though they were charged the then exorbitant price of two shillings and sixpence for their victuals. They came (two from each farm, one from each cottage) to eat roast beef, roast mutton and plum pudding. Home-brewed ale was the only drink available - at extra cost. The entertainment that followed this feast was supplied by the guests themselves. So they were at least spared the expense of paying artistes.

How long John Slingsby stayed at Moston Hall is not known, but Ward asserts that he made a considerable fortune out of his activities as farmer, cattle breeder and butcher. As we have seen Squire Hilton (T. W. Legh Hilton) was in residence in 1854. His stay cannot have lasted very long, perhaps fifteen years. After his departure Moston Hall was for a few years in the hands of a banker called Sam Brook. With the departure of Squire Hilton the Moston Rent Dinner came to an end. According to the Census List of 1871 Moston Hall Farm, together with sixty four acres of land, was in the possession of James and Elizabeth Marshall. A pig farmer by name of Dixon seems to have been the last occupant. After 'Piggy' Dixon's time the old Hall stood derelict and forlorn for a few years. It was an exciting place for children to play: the whole area was supposed to be haunted.

4

The Chaddertons of Little Nuthurst Hall

The early years of the Chaddertons in Nuthurst have already been reviewed - from the time (c. 1260) when William de Eccles conveyed the territory to Geoffrey de Chadderton (formerly Trafford) down till 1356 when Alexander de Chadderton, his son, granted to John de Chetham and his wife Alice all his dwellings and lands in the hamlet of Moston in the town of Ashton. As mentioned previously, in 1340 Roger the other son of Geoffrey de Chadderton made a will settling his lands in Moston upon his son Roger, with remainders to younger sons - Geoffrey, John, Robert and Richard. Then there occurred the mysterious death of Thomas de Chetham, son and heir of John de Chetham, at the hand of his neighbour Thomas de Chadderton (sometime between 1382 and 1404). The assailant must have been one of the Chaddertons of Chadderton; I can find no trace of a Thomas de Chadderton in Nuthurst during this period. There are no inquests relating to the Chaddertons, nor was any pedigree recorded. So, we shall have to make do with what scant information is available. In 1412 John de Chetham granted to Ellis, son of John de Chadderton, all his lands in Nuthurst for the term of thirty years at a nominal rent. An insight into the social customs of the time is obtained from a record of 1446. In that year Geoffrey son of Ellis de Chadderton, then under fourteen years of age, was contracted to marry Alice daughter of Richard Chorlton, and had an estate settled on him.

The details of this estate provide another tantalising glimpse into the Moston of old. The bounds began at one and a half acres near a ditch by the west part of Boothclough, and so southwards to Theyle Moor and Moss Brook, to the lower part of Smallclough, to the Newearth, and between Hencroft and the Newearth to Theyle Moor and so back to the start. We shall have occasion to discuss Theyle Moor in some detail later. Moss Brook is Moston Brook. H. T. Crofton thought that Booth Clough was a ravine running eastwardly from near the meeting point of Moston, Alkrington and Chadderton, near which there stood a boundary mark in 1556 called the 'Bothe Holyn'. Ellis de Chadderton made a further grant of lands in the hamlet of Moston in 1455, the bounds beginning at Saltersgate (Kenyon Lane), following the water of Mose-broke (Moston Brook) towards the east as far as the boundary between Ellis Chadderton and John Chetham (Boar Green Clough), and so as far as unto le Theyle-more by metes and bounds (in an irregular line), and then descending towards the west as far as a ditch and hedge as far as unto Mose-broke, and so as far as to Saltersgate, with an acre and a half of land lying next to the same ditch and hedge.

Geoffrey Chadderton was in possession of Nuthurst in 1483. The pedigree given in Booker (Ancient Chapel of Blackley, p. 147) is incomplete and misleading. I have attempted to reconstruct it in the light of later research. Geoffrey Chadderton was succeeded by a son Edmund who married Margaret Cliffe. Among their children were Edmund, George and William. The first named,

Edmund, took over Little Nuthurst Hall prior to 1529. He was to play a leading role in the dispute over Theyle Moor. In 1537 Edmund Chadderton, together with John Chetham, had a lease of the tithes of Moston. George Chadderton, who had married Jane Warren of Poynton after 1529, in 1552 made a settlement of his estates in Nuthurst and Ashton. Edmund in 1573 confirmed to Henry Chetham a sale made to his father, John Chetham, of the New Close in Nuthurst, then occupied for life by Margaret, grandmother of Edmund. The will of Edmund Chadderton of Nuthurst, dated 1588 and proved in 1589, names Isabel his wife, Edmund his son and heir, son Edmund's 'dear uncle and good lord' the Bishop of Chester, and others. From an inventory of Nathan Jenkinson of Little Nuthurst Hall, dated 1637, we learn that the house had a room called 'the Bishop's chamber.'

William Chadderton, Warden of Manchester, Bishop of Chester and later of Lincoln, was born at Little Nuthurst Hall about 1535, the youngest son of Edmund Chadderton and Margaret Cliffe his wife. Baptised a Roman Catholic, rising to eminence in the Church of England, he was a paradigm of the successful Reformation cleric. Details of his early education are lacking. He graduated in Arts at Queen's college, Cambridge, and became a Fellow of Christ's college. In 1567 he was appointed Margaret Professor of Divinity; and in the same year he became a Prebendary of Westminster. Preferments followed in quick succession:- 1568 elected President of Queen's college, appointed Archdeacon of York, nominated as chaplain to Robert Dudley, earl of Leicester; 1569 succeeded to Regius Professorship of Divinity in the university of Cambridge; 1573 installed Prebendary of York and preferred to a stall at Southwell; 1578, through the interest of the earl of Leicester, created Bishop of Chester; then, in 1579 elected Warden of Manchester college and made an ecclesiastical commissioner for Lancashire and Cheshire. This last appointment led to his taking up residence in Manchester.

Booker tells us that 'to his superintendence were committed the children of numerous families in Manchester and the neighbourhood, and of others even from distant parts of the country, for the more effectual stemming the progress of popery, in conformity with the orders of Elizabeth and her council.' On 5th April 1595, having resigned the wardenship of Manchester, he was translated to the see of Lincoln. William Chadderton, D.D., held this office until his death in 1608. He has been described as a 'learned man and liberal, given to hospitality, and a more frequent preacher and baptiser than other bishops of his time.' His only daughter, Joan, by his wife Katherine Revell of London, married Sir Richard Brooke of Norton, Cheshire. Roger Parker, the bishop's nephew (son of his sister Elizabeth Chadderton, who married Robert Parker of Browsholme, Lancashire), was, through his uncle's influence, advanced to the deanery of Chester.

So far I have presented the profile of Dr William Chadderton given by an admiring Anglican clergyman, Revd John Booker (Ancient Chapel of Blackley, pp. 145, 146), which lists his attainments; glosses over his activities in 'stemming the progress of popery;' and, finally, characterises him (in Hollingworth's words) as 'a learned man and liberal, given to hospitality, and a more frequent preacher and baptiser than other bishops of his time.' Another, altogether different, picture of Dr Chadderton is painted by John O'Dea (The Story of the Old Faith in Manchester, 1910, pp. 52, 56 ff.). In order to preserve the purity of doctrine of the Church of England and to suppress Roman Catholics and other dissenters, Elizabeth I appointed forty four Ecclesiastical Commissioners. These were invested with plenary powers to extirpate 'recusants' and 'heretics' by 'all efficacious means whatever, including even torture and imprisonment, and to punish the delinquents at their own pleasure and discretion.' The Queen's Ecclesiastical Commissioners for the north of England were the Earl of Shrewsbury, the Earl of Derby, the Earl of Northumberland, the Archbishop of York, and the Bishop of Chester. Here is O'Dea's account of the Bishop:

"The Bishop of Chester at this time was William Chadderton, D.D., a native of Nuthurst, near Moston, Manchester. He had been brought up at Cambridge, where he was a fellow of Christ's College.

He was appointed Chaplain to the notorious Dudley, Earl of Leicester, the leman of Elizabeth, and the murderer of Amy Robsart. He would not enter into the bonds of matrimony until he had consulted, and besought the advice of his patron, the Earl. He must have profited by the advice he received from his cynical patron, for preaching a wedding sermon himself at Cambridge, it is said that he made use of the following curious comparison:-

"The choice of a wife is full of hazard, not unlike to a man groping for one fish in a barrowful of serpents. If he 'scape harm of the snakes, and light on the fish, he may be thought fortunate: yet, let him not boast, for perhaps it may be but an eel."

Dr Chadderton was also the Warden of Manchester Church. "His wardenship," Dr Hibbert Ware, a Protestant himself, writes, "is greatly sullied by the persecutions which took place against the Catholics, whose refusal to acknowledge the Queen's (spiritual) supremacy was considered treason against the throne of England. They were stigmatised under the name of Recusants. By the force of the Act passed against Catholics, recusants were liable to fines and imprisonment."

In June, 1580, the Lords and others in Council represented to Henry Hastings, Earl of Huntingdon, Lord President of the North, that many gentlemen and others in Lancashire had fallen away to the Popish Religion, and it behoved them, therefore, to proceed more strictly against the gentry who had led to the defection of others.

Prompt attention was paid to this order. Small fines were at first imposed for non-attendance, then larger mulcts. These proving ineffective, the principal recusants were ordered to be imprisoned in Halton Castle in Cheshire.

In 1581 the Queen expressed her determination "to proceed more roundly against the Catholics." In a letter dated 28th May, 1581, in order to secure uniformity of religion, she enjoined the Bishop of Chester (William Chadderton) to examine what recusants he had in his diocese, and to send in their names to the custodes rotulorum and justices of the peace, that they might be

Brief Pedigree of Chadderton of Nuthurst

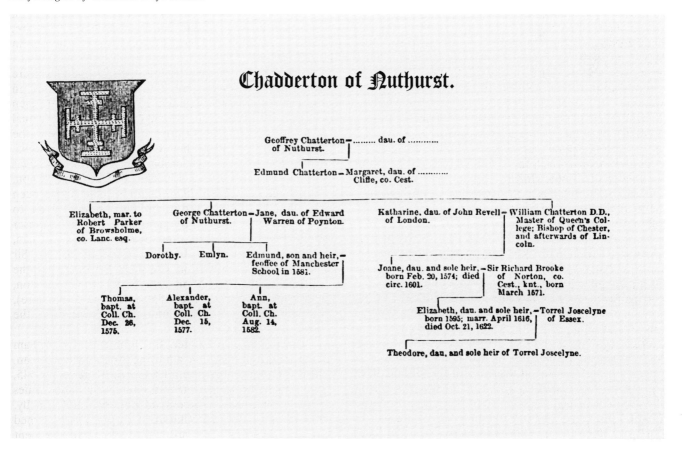

Sandford of Nuthurst.

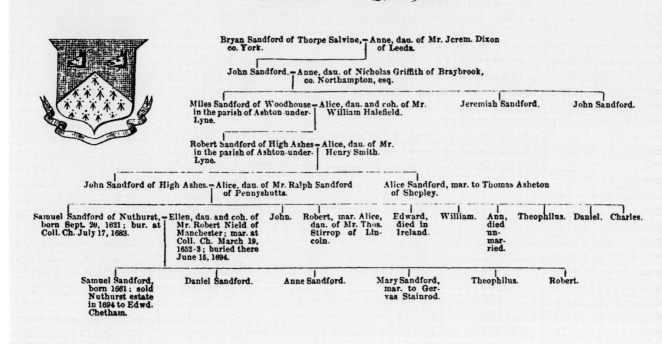

Bryan Sandford of Thorpe Salvine, — Anne, dau. of Mr. Jerem. Dixon
co. York. | of Leeds.

John Sandford. — Anne, dau. of Nicholas Griffith of Braybrook,
| co. Northampton, esq.

Miles Sandford of Woodhouse — Alice, dau. and coh. of Mr.   Jeremiah Sandford.   John Sandford.
in the parish of Ashton-under- | William Halefield.
Lyne.

Robert Sandford of High Ashes — Alice, dau. of Mr.
in the parish of Ashton-under- | Henry Smith.
Lyne.

John Sandford of High Ashes. — Alice, dau. of Mr. Ralph Sandford   Alice Sandford, mar. to Thomas Asheton
| of Pennyshutts.   of Shepley.

Samuel Sandford of Nuthurst, — Ellen, dau. and coh. of   John.   Robert, mar. Alice,   Edward,   William.   Ann,   Theophilus. Daniel. Charles.
born Sept. 20, 1621; bur. at | Mr. Robert Nield of   dau. of Mr. Thos.   died in   died
Coll. Ch. July 17, 1683. | Manchester; mar. at   Stirrop of Lin-   Ireland.   un-
| Coll. Ch. March 19,   coln.   mar-
| 1652-3; buried there   ried.
| June 15, 1694.

Samuel Sandford,   Daniel Sandford.   Anne Sandford.   Mary Sandford,   Theophilus.   Robert.
born 1661; sold   mar. to Ger-
Nuthurst estate   vas Stainrod.
in 1694 to Edwd.
Chetham.

Pedigree of Sandford of Nuthurst

indicted at the next sessions.

Further, the Parliament enacted that "any person reconciling another to the See of Rome should be punished as a traitor, and the person so reconciled incur misprision of treason; saying Mass was to be punished by a fine of 200 marks; hearing it, by a fine of 100 marks, with in each case, a year's imprisonment; absence from church was to be punished by a fine of £20 a month, and if continued a year, two sureties of £200 each were to be given for future good behaviour. All schoolmasters were to be licensed by the Bishop of the Diocese, or suffer a year's imprisonment, and persons employing them to be fined £10 a month."

In 1581 Bishop Chadderton decided to quit Chester and settle altogether in Manchester, in order to cooperate the more coveniently with his fellow Commissioner, the Earl of Derby, who had a residence in Aldport Park.

In order to suit the convenience of the resident Commissioners, it was resolved to remove the recusants who were confined in Halton Castle, Cheshire, to Manchester. It was thought, too, that by doing this, the prison service might be worked more economically, for then there would be but one keeper required and one diet, one guard and one chaplain for all. At this time the Bishop computed that there were 2,442 recusants in his Diocese, but the probability is that there were very many more. The prison accommodation of the Dungeon on Salford Bridge was altogether inadequate for the numbers who were dragged from Cheshire in the wake of the Bishop. They had, therefore, to shut up a number of the prisoners in Radcliffe Hall (near the site of the present Cross Street Chapel). But even this, in addition to the Dungeon, did not prove sufficient, so a third prison had to be erected in Hunt's Bank. This was named the New Fleet, and it was here that the greatest proportion of the prisoners were confined.

The prison had not been opened many weeks before it claimed its first victim, for we read that in August, 1581, "Richard Smyth, an oulde prieste, died in prison in the Fleet for relygion."

In January, 1584, it was noted the following persons were in prison in Manchester for the Faith:- 1 Knight, 10 gentlemen, 12 priests, 3 schoolmasters, 7 husbandmen, 4 widows, and 2 spinsters.

The sufferings of several of the recusants in Manchester were now drawing to a close . . . . On 22nd March, 1584, an order was received from the Queen's Council, in which it was stated that "there being several Popish priests now prisoners at Manchester for preventing the Queen's subjects from their allegiance, it was thought good that they should be tried for the same, in terrorem, at the next Assizes." ' This concludes the quotation from O'Dea. Bishop Chadderton also had within his jurisdiction the Salford gaol. Here in 1583 died Thurstan Arrowsmith, a yeoman of Haydock and grandfather of the martyr St Edmund Arrowsmith. He had been severely tortured for refusing to abjure the Catholic Faith by Robert Worsley, the Warden of the New Fleet and collaborator of Dr Chadderton. Three of the recusants were taken from the New Fleet in 1584 to be hanged, drawn and quartered - Father James Bell and John Finch, yeoman, at Lancaster; James Leybourne, Esq., according to tradition at Knot Mill. Their heads, after being boiled in tar, were impaled on the tower of Manchester Collegiate Church.

During the fifteen years of his wardenry William Chadderton displayed unflagging zeal and determination in tracking down and punishing Roman Catholics who refused to conform to the Established Church. Not content, however, with incarcerating and torturing adults (in the latter activity he worked closely with Worsley, the Keeper); William Chadderton had the children of recusant parents quarantined and indoctrinated in the truths of the Reformed Church and the errors of Popery. It would seem that Bishop Chadderton ('one of the most unscrupulous of Elizabeth's new-fangled Superintendents,' O'Dea calls him) was only moderately successful in his attempts to reform Catholics, young and old alike. In a document entitled 'The Manifold Enormities of the Papists,' compiled in 1590 (five years before Bishop Chadderton left Manchester for Lincoln), several Protestant ministers complained that those papists who 'seemed to have reformed came seldom to church, and when they did, they withdrew to the farthest parts, they said their own private prayers "most with crossings and knocking of their breasts, and sometimes with beads closely handelled . . . . . The youth, both of the gentry and the common sort, were nursed up in Poperie by many Popish schoolmasters fostered in gentlemen's houses and other places." ' (O'Dea, The Old Faith in Manchester, p. 55). On that reactionary note we leave the career of the 'liberal' Dr William Chadderton, the luminary of Little Nuthurst Hall.

In 1623 Edmund Chadderton, son of Edmund and Isabel Chadderton and nephew of Bishop Chadderton, sold his estate to John Holcroft of Lymehurst. In a deed of 1625/6 Edmund Chadderton is described as of Wentbridge in Kirk Smeaton, Yorkshire. A few years later John Holcroft sold Little Nuthurst Hall to Nathan and Samuel Jenkinson, sons of Robert Jenkinson alias Wilson of Failsworth. Edmund Chadderton confirmed the sale in 1629. In 1630 Samuel Jenkinson and Elizabeth his wife released their right in Nuthurst to Nathan Jenkinson. The following year Nathan and Samuel Jenkinson of Moston and Thomas Chetham of Nuthurst, gentlemen, refused knighthood, paying £10 composition. Nathan Jenkinson died in 1637. By his will, dated 28th July 1637, he left his estate in Nuthurst and Failsworth to his wife Alice until his son Robert should come of age. The inventory taken at his death showed goods and chattels worth £557. His residence of Little Nuthurst Hall contained, among others, the following apartments: the Lady Chamber, the Clock Chamber, the Bishop's Chamber, the Great Chamber, the Study, the Little Parlour, the Chamber over the Hall.

Robert Jenkinson, son of Nathan and Alice, described as of Nuthurst, died in 1654. His son William Jenkinson sold Little Nuthurst Hall in 1662/3 to Samuel Sandford, who was in possession in 1664. The will of Samuel Sandford of Little Nuthurst (son of John Sandford of High Ashes and his wife Alice), made in 1683 and proved in 1684, mentions Ellen his wife, Samuel his son and wife Mary, and other sons - Theophilus, Robert and Daniel. Samuel the son sold Little Nuthurst Hall and estate in 1694 to George Chetham of Smedley, his brother Daniel Sandford of London, silkman, concurring in the sale. Edward Chetham of Nuthurst was the sole owner in 1698. The Census Enumerators' List of 1871 informs us that Little Nuthurst Hall was occupied by five families. The deeds of number 148 Nuthurst Road use the title 'Little Nuthurst Farm' to describe the property, which is probably a part of the Little Nuthurst Hall messuage where Edmund Chadderton was besieged by the Theyle Moor rioters.

5

The Theyle Moor Dispute

Theyle Moor was a waste or common pasture, some six hundred acres in area, a third of which was claimed by the two lords of Nuthurst; the other two thirds being the property of the lords of Chadderton and Alkrington. On the south side it stretched from White Moss to Moston Brook. The other boundaries are not known; but White Gate, Hollinwood and a place called Fox Holes (perhaps Foxdenton) are mentioned in various testimonies. It would appear that less than seventy acres of the portion owned by Edmund Chadderton and Thomas Chetham in 1526 were within the parish of Manchester. This should be borne in mind in all that follows. For, while Messrs Scholes and Whitehead may seem the villains and certainly adopted a belligerent stance towards the owners of Great and Little Nuthurst Halls, the latter were deeply resented as land-grabbers and trespassers.

The Theyle Moor dispute is important for several reasons. First, it is a valuable source of information concerning the locality; secondly, it gives us a rare insight into the life style and social customs of the inhabitants of Moston, Nuthurst and Chadderton; thirdly, its boisterous episodes bring characters and events from the past into dramatic focus. Starting during the lifetime of Thomas Chetham of Nuthurst (c. 1440 to 1503) the Theyle Moor litigation continued in one form or another for a century. It was pursued in every variety of action - criminal, civil and ecclesiastical. Among the numerous documents in the Clowes muniment chests, which relate to the various claims and counterclaims, one is of very special interest. It is a chart of Theyle Moor, dated 1556, showing the division of the Moor between Nuthurst in Manchester parish and Chadderton in Oldham parish. We are indebted to H. T. Crofton for the recovery of this singular document, the earliest known cartographical representation of the Moston area. His comments on it are worthy of inclusion in this account as illustrating the problems encountered by the historian in trying to reclaim the past.

'The most interesting of all these documents is a map, styled "A Platt or Carde," that is a chart. There are two copies, both on sheepskin, and dated 1556. They are, unfortunately, in such a state of mouldiness, creasing, dirt, and faded ink that it is impracticable to make a facsimile which would be legible. The writing is in all directions, and is upside down in places, so it has been deemed more convenient to prepare a sketch copy, which preserves the delineation, but adjusts the writing uniformly, and distinguishes what appear to be very erratic annotations made possibly by counsel in the course of the case, and within square brackets are given my own attempts at identification. The lettering of the original, with regard to the Alkrington boundary, has required the north to be inconveniently kept at the bottom of the map.' The sketch is reproduced elsewhere in the book.

A full account of the century-long litigation would be beyond the scope of this work, concerned as it is only with Moston and Nuthurst. During the fifteenth and sixteenth

centuries there was much Moss litigation in southeast Lancashire. In 1433 Ashton Moss was disputed by Sir John de Ashton and Sir John de Byron; about 1515 Cockey Moor in Ainsworth was in dispute between Richard Assheton of Middleton and the Lords of Radcliffe; and in 1552 Hathershaw, near Rochdale, was the centre of a dispute between Sir John Byron and the King's tenants at Crompton.

There were three phases to the Theyle Moor litigation. The first was ecclesiastical - concerned with tithes of animals, which gave birth to young on the moor; the second was manorial - relating to pasturing rights: whether animals could range over the whole moss, or must be kept within their own parish or manor; the third had to do with rights of turbary, enclosure, and tithes on an area near to the Nuthurst-Chadderton border, called the Equal. Before entering into the discussion of who had rights in Theyle Moor we need to make some remarks about the place itself that was the bone of contention. Booker (Ancient Chapel of Blackley, pp. 135, 136) asserted that Theyle Moor, Nuthurst Waste and Hale Moss are one and the same piece of ground, which 'consists of the tract of land, bordering on Failsworth, which is enclosed between the Lancashire and Yorkshire Railway and the Rochdale Canal.' Crofton (supported by the evidence of the Chart of 1556) rejects this view. According to the latter, the real Theyle Moor was the southeast part of White Moss. All the evidence adduced by Crofton (none of which Booker had to hand in 1854) points to this conclusion.

The earliest mention of Theyle Moor is in a deed of 1418. According to this document, Thomas La Warre, lord of Manchester, owned a dwelling, and sixty acres of land adjoining, called Brideshagh next Boukerlegh within the hamlet of Moston late in the tenure of Thomas le Bouker, the bounds of which began on the south at the gate at the side of a lane (Moston Lane?) which leads from the common pasture of Theyle moor to the vill of Manchester, and thence following a hedge between Brideshagh and a parcel of land of Moston now in the tenure of Robert Shacklock to the common pasture of Theyle moor, and following the pasture to the pales of Blackley, and following the pales to a hedge between Brideshagh and the dwelling late of John de Jones in Moston, and following the hedge to the first-named land and following the lane to the said gate, together with common of pasture on Theyle moor and common of turbary there, with free ingress and egress for digging, drying and carrying turves.

If we take Boukerlegh to be the vicinity of North Manchester High School for Girls, the parcel of land now in the tenure of Robert Shacklock to be Shackerly Green, and the pales of Blackley Park (Boggart Hole Clough) to run from near the White Walk by the back of the Girls' High School; then we shall have a rough idea of the whereabouts of Theyle Moor. The Moor is again mentioned in a settlement dated 5th November 1446. This relates to messuages (houses with outbuildings and land attached) in Moston, and goes a long way to proving that Theyle Moor lay between the meeting point of Moston, Alkrington and Chadderton, and Moston Brook in Morris Clough (see map of 1820). It tells us that the messuages began by the west part of Booth Clough (in my view, the continuation of Boggart Hole Clough to the

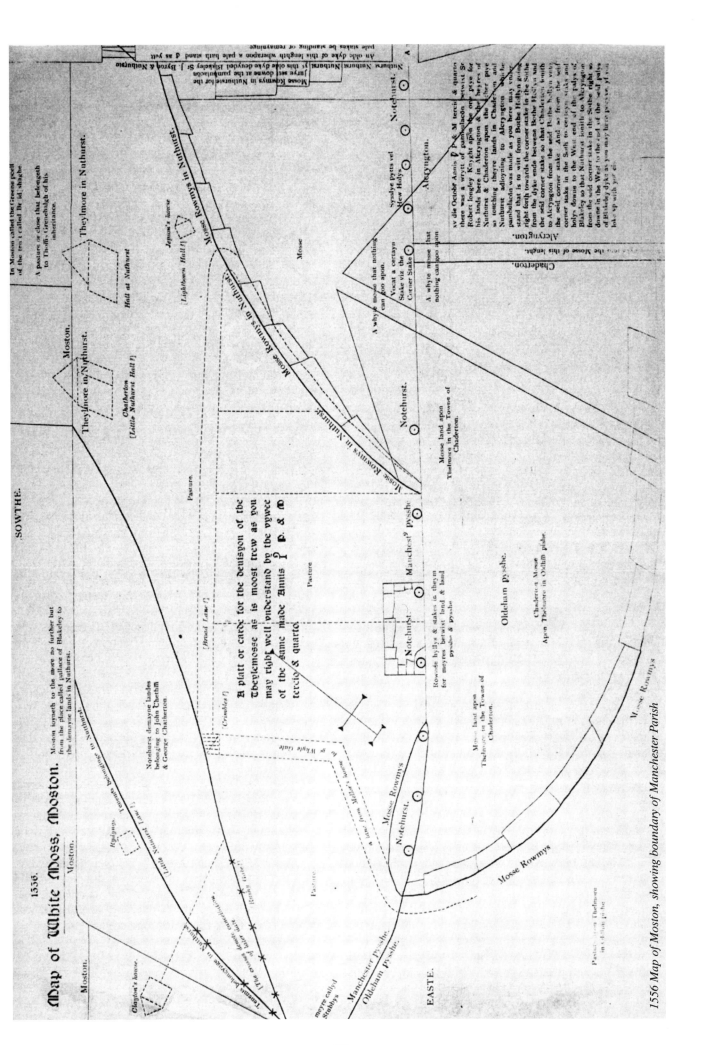

1556 Map of Moston, showing boundary of Manchester Parish

33

north, running roughly parallel to Moston Lane), and so towards the southeast towards the Theyle moor unto Moss Brook.

In a memorandum of 1500-1550, headed 'The Boundary which separates Theyle Moor', and which is obviously an extract from a document no longer extant, we read that the boundary followed Stubbs (near Failsworth) to part of Red Brook unto Moss Brook, and thence going between Nuthurst and Nuthurst Moss as far as unto Le Bradshaw (Bradshaw Fold?), and thence following the pales of Blackley as far as Leghles Byrche and Hugh walle (High or View Holes?) and thence Sissele Pitts as far as east side of Copthorne Hill, and as far as fox holes (perhaps Foxdenton) and thence Le Stubbes. Leghles Byrche, according to Crofton, was on the Alkrington border at the meeting point with the pales of Blackley. The Chart of 1556 would seem to suggest that there was little to distinguish Sissele Pitts from Hugh Holes; the use of the Latin word 'vel' suggests that one district encroached upon another, as for example Barnes Green and Blackley. Likewise, Red Brook is a part of Moston Brook near the present Broadway. John Worrall's deposition of 1595 is spot on: 'Red Brook in the clay alias Moss Brook'.

Enough has been said to locate Theyle Moor with some precision. Certainly from the fourteenth century it was common pasture with common of turbary. Before the mining of coal the principal fuel was peat turf (as indeed it still is in Ireland). Common of turbary, or the right to cut peat for fuel on a common waste, had been enjoyed by the people of Moston on Theyle Moor from time immemorial. This right to gather turf on Theyle Moor - or at least that part of it known as the Equal - was challenged by the lords of Chadderton. During this, the third phase of the litigation, in 1595 it was declared that the inhabitants of Moston 'do get their living only by occupying and making white (i.e. bleaching) linen yarn, which doth require very much fire to the use thereof, and have none other kind of fire or fuel for their necessary burning, nor never had, but only such as they have used yearly to get in and upon the said waste.'

The central point at issue in the Theyle Moor litigation was the claim by the lords of Nuthurst (the Chethams and Chaddertons) to ownership of a substantial part of the waste. The owners of Chadderton (Radcliffe, Standish and Assheton) contested this claim, and asserted their right to intercommon all over the moor. As early as 1501-2 Thomas Chetham recorded the names of the men who had assaulted him in his own house and had torn down his hedge on the Friday after the Epiphany of Our Lord. Theyle Moor is described in a letter dated 28th March (1529?) as a 'wet mosse grounde that nothing may goo apon'. In the same year, 1529, Edmund Chadderton, one of the joint owners of the Nuthurst rights in Theyle Moor, claimed that his grandfather, Geoffrey Chadderton, had been in possession of a moiety of the waste ground of Nuthurst, 'in a place called Stubbes in the southeast part of Theyle Moor, and so to a great hill in the moss northward, and from the hill to an old dyke, and from the old dyke by some hills over the White Moss to the pales of Blackley, to a place called lyless byrche.' While there was general agreement about the boundaries of Manchester, Prestwich and Oldham parishes, there was dissent on both sides as to the division of Theyle Moor between the interested parties. And this despite the fact that with the consent of both parties of Chadderton and Nuthurst writs of perambulation had been issued by the court of chancery on two occasions prior to 1529, in order that deputations from both sides might determine their boundaries.

From the pleadings we learn that some time before 1526 Theyle Moor had been divided into three parts, the lords of Chadderton, Alkrington and Nuthurst each having one part. The lord of Chadderton had been Sir John Radcliffe; and in 1526 Ralph Standish, Edmund Assheton of Chadderton, and Thomas Radcliffe of Foxdenton, were heirs to two hundred acres of Theyle Moor. They were not content with this acreage, which was anyway simply a pleader's rough estimate; and they claimed that all the moor was theirs for the purpose of grazing cattle in common. Their tenants, Nicholas Whitehead and William Scholes, put their cattle and sheep on the moor in dispute. Then began the mayhem, which would continue sporadically for three years. On 20th May 1526 the lords of Nuthurst, Edmund Chadderton and Thomas Chetham, chased the beasts and sheep (of Whitehead and Scholes) from the moor and with dogs worried them and killed several sheep, and again on Monday in Passion week, 6th April, 1526, with three persons (a pleader's number for technical purposes) riotously drove the beasts pasturing upon the moor from the same.

The same day Whitehead and Scholes with two hundred persons and above 'came to the moor and chased all the beasts and cattle of Edmund and Thomas to the side of the moor and all day long kept their cattle from the same whereupon hastely labour was made to Mr Richard Assheton of Middleton then being next Justice of the Peace to come and see for the King's peace. And he sent his credable servants William Steel and Roger Kirkman and came himself, and found twenty or thirty boys and wenches, sons and daughters to the tenants, sat watching the cattle, and the boys and maydes brought the cattle and at the house of Ralph Werall adjoining to the waste standing, shouting and crying, and cast up their caps off their heads, and making great noise, and saying come out hoores and thieves.' Then two of the servants to Chetham and Chadderton 'were taken by the hair of the head, and cast to the earth, and their clothes over their heads, and sore stricken that the blood ran from their bodies.'

On 4th April 1527, about eight o'clock in the morning, Thomas Radcliffe of Chadderton, gentleman, John son of Edmund Tetlow, Ralph Cowper of Chadderton, husbandman, John Smethurst of Chadderton, husbandman, with other wrongdoers to the number of thirty, whose names were unknown, assembled on the waste of Nuthurst, in the hamlet of Moston and within the vill of Assheton, riotously, and drove off the animals of Thomas Chetham and Edmund Chadderton, gentlemen, which were feeding there according to ancestral custom.

On 20th April in the same year Robert, Thomas and Henry Shacklock, Nicholas Jackson, Edward and Anthony Bowker, John Sondeforthe, Thomas Become senior and junior, James Baresleye, Thomas Platt, Richard and George Street, William and Thomas Sydall, Oswald Mosley, John Schofield, Ralph Radley and Roger Pendleton, 'upon the sound of a horn arrayed with arms with sixteen other unknown persons assembled on Theyle moor, and beat and wounded the servants and tenants of Edmund Chadderton and James Chetham, and five days later, being the feast of St Mark the Evangelist, with seven score other unknown persons, in the time of divine service upon the moor assembled, arrayed with bows, arrows, bills, staves, swords and daggers, having with them a bagpiper of name unknown, at whose piping the disordered persons in most devilish dancing spent that time which they ought to have spent in being at divine service, and Edmund Chadderton, in most neighbourly wise, advised them to give over piping and dancing and repair to divine service, to do which they utterly refused, whereupon Chadderton endeavoured to apprehend the piper, and called upon the others to aid in conveying him as a rogue to the next constable or justice of the peace, but they not only refused but assaulted Edmund, and put him in peril of his life, and took the piper from him, and did continue dancing and piping all the day long.'

On 6th April 1528 Standish, Assheton and Radcliffe, with William Scholes, Nicholas Whitehead, Thomas Cowper and Geoffrey Whiteacre (another writ lists a further eighteen names) all of Chadderton with about forty unknown persons, with swords, bucklers, bows and arrows, and other weapons, assembled riotously, and drove off the cattle of Chetham and Chadderton, and put in a great number of their own cattle, upon which Richard Assheton of Middleton one of the King's justices of the peace, came and commanded them to appear at Manchester before him and other justices, where they were bound to keep the peace.

On 27th, 28th and 29th May, 1528, Nicholas Whitehead and William Scholes, with many other tenants and inhabitants of the town of Chadderton, drove all the horses and mares and other cattle beside a place called Holyn-wood and another place called North-wood, with divers horses and mares to the number of twenty four beasts and above of another parish, and brought them upon the part of Theyle moor belonging to Edmund Chadderton and Thomas Chetham, and there kept them at their pleasure.

There was a hearing before the commissioners in Manchester on 22nd October 1530. It would appear to have been inconclusive. The edited depositions in Crofton contribute nothing to our knowledge of the case. The chart of 1556 would seem to mark a significant step forward in reconciling the opposing parties. There was, however, the outstanding difference regarding the tract of land called The Equal. About 1594 an alteration in the boundary between the estates of Chadderton and Nuthurst near the Stubbs (close to White Gate End) was agreed upon by staking out of the Manchester part of Theyle Moor a plot called 'The Equal.' This was done 'to make Mr Assheton and others their parts in Oldham parish, in quantity and quality (equal) with the portions of James Chetham and Edmund Chadderton of Nuthurst' (Clowes Evidences). This alteration of private ownership would seem to explain the peculiar indentation which Chadderton makes into New Moston, following the line Welbeck Avenue, Hollinwood Avenue, Moston Lane East, Scholes Drive.

The simple device of allocating part of the Nuthurst territory to the lords of Chadderton brought to an end the century-long Theyle Moor dispute, which had entailed numerous lawsuits and many rowdy episodes. Rights of pasture and turbary were life and death issues for many ordinary people. Unable to resort to legal proceedings, they made their own protests against what they considered the usurpation of their land rights. In 1575 the Theyle Moor rioters pulled up a great gate at Hartley Shaw in Nuthurst and carried it to Copthorne Hill, 'a place of very great height,' and made of three of the largest pieces 'one pair of gallows (on which they threatened to hang all who contradicted them) and the residue of the gate hewed in small pieces.' They also pulled down James Hill's gate, and carried it 'unto a place of great height on the moor,' and hewed it into small pieces, and took six wheelbarrows of Jeffre Hull's turves to Copthorne Hill, 'and cut them in pieces, and Nicholas Nicholson in great bravery said they would repair thither again, and would have better cheer, and he would bring wine with him.' An indictment about the same date charges Nicholas Jepson and Nicholas Nicholson with coming to Theyle moor with 'bigis' (two-horsed carts) and erecting a bridge there. In other proceedings of the same date 'John Rosterne said he would be pulled in pieces with wild horses rather than confess anything concerning the pulling or casting down of a ditch upon Theyle moor.' On that defiant note we leave the Theyle Moor dispute.

In the wake of such stirring events it may seem like bathos to return immediately to mundane details of topography. But the Theyle Moor litigation is a unique source of information regarding the locality. Trying to relate place names in the Moston of hundreds of years ago to their modern counterparts can easily become an obsession. The portion of Moston (or rather, Nuthurst) in old records whose whereabouts most baffles historians of the district is Sidgreaves. It is often mentioned. By an agreement between James Chetham and Thomas his son in 1468 the latter received Nuthurst and Sidgreaves, paying £4 a year to his father. In his will dated 31st January 1613 James Chetham bequeathed to his wife Margery, among other properties, 'all the Sidgreaves.' The Clowes deeds record that in 1670 Jonathan Chadwick gave it to James Scholes, and nine years later James Scholes the younger of Oldham gave it to Thomas Stevenson. Then in 1684 Robert Stevenson of Tetlow gave it to Alexander Davie. Finally, we read, it was granted in 1693-4 by John Chetham of Nuthurst and John his son to Mary Davie and others. So where was Sidgreaves?

In 1529 a complaint mentions boundaries comprising 'a place called Stubbs in the southeast part of Theyle Moor, and so to a great hill (Theyle Hill or the Equal?) in the moor northward.' Crofton states more than once that Stubbs lay on the eastern side of the Equal, in the northeast corner of Moston. Perhaps, writing in 1907, he had evidence for the fact. The answer to the question of the location of Sidgreaves is provided by the deposition of John Worrall (1595). He is describing the bounds of Manchester and Oldham parishes, as beginning on the south 'at Red Brook in the clay alias Moss Brook (surely Morris Clough, that section of Moston Brook near Broadway), and so goes up straight northward between Stubbings (east of White Gate End) and Sidgreaves, whereof Stubbings is in Oldham parish and Sidgreaves is in Manchester parish.' This would make Sidgreaves the area of New Moston bounded at present by Chauncy Road, Belgrave Road, Northfield Road, and then by a beeline to Moston Lane East near Scholes Drive, and back by Moston Lane East to the Failsworth boundary.

6

The Jepsons and Lightbownes

Once again we are indebted to John Booker (Ancient Chapel of Blackley) for a description of an old hall of Moston, this time Lightbowne Hall which stood in Kenyon Lane near its junction with Lightbowne Road. Up until its demolition in 1965 the hall had served as the rectory of St Luke's church; prior to this it had fulfilled a similar role for the mother parish of St Mary, until the new rectory was built in Broadhurst Park (now the North Manchester Music Centre). It seems likely that the first house on the site in Kenyon Lane was built by one of the Jepsons, perhaps Adam Jepson. The substantial building that stood there for three hundred years was probably the work of James Lightbowne the second, who lived in Moston from 1639 until 1664. Here is Booker's description of it as it was in 1854:-

'Lightbowne Hall, to the eye of the casual observer, presents in its external appearance but few features of attraction; it is only upon a more close examination that anything of an antiquated character can be discovered, the outer walls being covered with whitewash, which at once conceals its beauties and its defects. It is of two stories, constructed entirely of brick, with mullions, quoins, and window-dressings of stone. The upper windows have been modernised, but those in the basement story still preserve their original form - squareheaded, divided into lights by substantial mullions, moulded, and crossed by transoms, protected with a label continued as a moulding. The general arrangement of the house seems in the course of years to have undergone considerable changes, the main front having formerly extended some distance beyond its present limits; whilst at the rear additions have from time to time been made, to meet the requirements of successive occupants. The interior still preserves much of its ancient character, notwithstanding the altered purposes to which many of its apartments are now applied - still exhibiting its original oak-panelling untouched by the sacrilegious brush of the painter, and spared as yet the too frequent infliction of whitewash. On the ground floor is an apartment of considerable dimensions also wainscoted, lighted originally by four windows, one of which has been blocked up. The ceiling is of plaster, intersected by oak beams moulded at the angles.' Such was the old hall where it seems Oliver Cromwell was a visitor. A horse-mounting stone, reputed to have been used by Cromwell when Lightbowne was in the hands of the Roundheads, was taken from St Luke's to St Mary's churchyard in 1969. This is all that remains of Lightbowne Hall.

The earliest member of the Jepson family of whom we have any record is Ralph Jepson of Moston, who died in 1560 or 1561. He left a son Nicholas, of full age, as his heir. Nicholas died in 1595. By his will, dated 13th June 1595, he gave to his wife a third of his possessions for the term of her natural life. All the rest and residue (together with the wife's portion, on her death) he bequeathed to his son Robert. Among other provisions he wills that Robert shall pay £60 to his (Robert's) younger brother John, the transaction to take place 'upon the feast day of St Michael the Archangel which shall be in the year of our Lord one thousand and six hundred, at or in the south porch of the parish church of Manchester.' Nicholas' goods and chattels were valued at £133.

Robert Jepson did not long survive his father, dying in 1601. He left a son and heir Adam, nine years old. Robert had held two dwellings and land in Moston of Sir Nicholas Mosley at an annual rent of eighteen shillings. Adam, his eldest son and successor, is described as of Chorlton Row in Manchester, where he carried on business as a dealer in cotton yarns. He held on to his Moston inheritance, residing there part of the time, and doing a bit of farming. In 1619 he married Jane Holland of Eccles, by whom he had seven daughters. When he died in 1632 he left his Moston estate to his eldest daughter Jane, only twelve years of age. The inventory of Adam Jepson's goods, valued at £610, mentions the shop at Manchester and the yarn chamber. Seven years after her father's death, in 1639, Jane Jepson married James Lightbowne of Manchester, the future owner and occupant of the estate in Moston which came to bear his name.

The Lightbowne family came from Bolton. James Lightbowne senior, a successful tradesman in Manchester married Eleanor Kenyon by whom he had three sons and four daughters. His second son James married Jane Jepson, heiress of Adam Jepson of Moston, and took up residence in the Jepson home. It was probably within the next ten years that he rebuilt the old house, known from then onwards as Lightbowne Hall. Kenyon Lane must have got its name about this time, being named after his mother's family. In 1656 the Manchester Jury found 'that Mr James Lightbowne is possessed of certain lands situate and lying in Moston, which were given by the last will and testament of Adam Jepson of Moston to his daughter Jane, now wife to Mr James Lightbowne,' and he was summoned to do his suit and service. By this year he had purchased lands in Moston from Lawrence Lomax and Richard Ashworth. James Lightbowne was a woollen draper in Manchester, having his own fulling mill in Blackley. By his marriage to Jane Jepson he had four sons and two daughters. His sudden death in late 1664 is thus described by his friend Henry Newcome: 'We went out but on Saturday and returned on Monday, and I found my friend Mr James Lightbowne dead; who fell violently ill on Saturday night, and died on Sabbath day night. I was much startled with the providence and affected.'

By his will, dated 6th November 1664, James Lightbowne left his Moston estate (except Street Fold, which was held by assignment from Henry Hardman) to his eldest son James, who was also to have chambers in Gray's Inn. The fulling mill in Blackley and the house in Manchester became the property of a younger son Samuel. James Lightbowne junior was only eighteen in 1664. He graduated at Oxford in 1672, becoming a barrister and bencher of Gray's Inn. In 1681 he was a steward of the Manchester Court; and in 1696 he was appointed a feoffee, or member of the governing body, of the Grammar School. He continued to reside at Lightbowne Hall - to which he brought his bride Elizabeth Hough in 1679 - until his death in or before 1699. His son, yet another James, succeeded him. This James Lightbowne was possibly the last bearer of the family

Inside Lightbowne Hall

Lightbowne of Moston and Manchester

(*From the MS. Collections of the late Mr. John Palmer.*)

James Lightbowne = Eleanor, dau. of ....
of Manchester, | remarried at Coll. Ch. Jan. 30,
bur. at Coll. Ch. | 162¾, to John Dawson ; bur.
April 2, 1621. | there May 8, 1640.

Lydia Lightbowne, bapt. at Coll. Ch. April 18, 1620 ; bur. there April 7, 1621.

James Lightbowne, of Manchester, draper ; bur. at Coll. Ch. Nov. 9, 1664. = **Jane,** dau. and heiress of Adam Jepson of Moston ; bapt. born 1614 ; at Eccles Feb. 13, 1619-20 ; mar. at Coll. Ch. May 14, 1639 ; bur. there July 21, 1662.

Ann Lightbowne, mar. to Thos. Minshull of Manchester, apothecary. From whom the M'shulls of Chorlton. Bur. at Coll. Ch. Dec. 24, 1669.

Nathaniel Lightbowne, bapt. at Coll. Ch. Dec. 21, 1617.

John Lightbowne, of Salford, esq. Bencher of Gray's Inn, the friend & correspondent of Humphrey Chetham ; mar. at Coll. Ch. Nov. 16, 1643, Elizabeth, dau. of Mr. William Lever of Kersall ; bur. at Coll. Ch. Dec. 23, 1667.

Lightbowne, wife of Mr. Thos. Bacon.

Lightbowne, wife of Mr. Joseph Worden.

Elizabeth Lightbowne, bapt. at Coll. Ch. July 16, 1644 ; mar. at Coll. Ch. Dec. 26, 1665, to Thos. Dickinson.

James Lightbowne, of Moston, bapt. at Coll. Ch. July 5, 1646 ; a feoffee of the Manchester Grammar School.

Samuel Lightbowne, of Manchester, woollen draper ; bapt. at Coll. Ch. Feb. 4, 1648-9 ; mar. at Coll. Ch. Jan. 29, 1679-80, Eliz. Booth ; bur. there Nov. 6, 1697.

John Lightbowne, of Manchester, linen draper ; bapt. at Coll. Ch. July 13, 1651 ; died in St. Mary's Gate ; bur. at Coll. Ch. Aug. 30, 1711. = **Alice,** dau. of William Page of Manchester, draper ; bapt. at Coll. Ch. Feb. 16, 165⅘ ; mar. there Dec. 11, 1673 ; bur. there Feb. 8, 1709 - 10.

Mary Lightbowne.

Adam Lightbowne.

Mary, dau. of .... Bowker ; mar. at Coll. Ch. May 25, 1710 ; bur. there Oct. 25, 1727. = **James** Lightbowne, bapt. at Coll. Ch. May 30, 1686 ; died Sep. 30, 1747. = **Margaret,** dau. of .... died March 9, 1765 ; bur. at Coll. Ch.

Elizabeth Lightbowne, bapt. at Coll. Ch. July 29, 1677.

William Lightbowne, bapt. at Coll. Ch. May 6, 1683.

Hannah, dau. of .... Roscow ; mar. at Coll. Ch. Feb. 10, 172¾. = **Thomas** Lightbowne, bapt. at Coll. Ch. Nov. 2, 1690 ; bur. there June 11, 1732. = **Mary,** dau. of......... Greenwood. mar. at Coll. Ch. Jan. 6, 1712-13 ; bur. there Nov. 20, 1728.

James Lightbowne, bapt. at Coll. Ch. Dec. 27, 1734 ; bur. there March 12, 1734 - 5.

Elizabeth Lightbowne, bapt. at Coll. Ch. May 19, 1737 ; bur. there May 14, 1738.

Eleanor Lightbowne, bapt. at Coll. Ch. 1735 ; bur. there Nov. 7, 1743.

Ann Lightbowne, bapt. at Coll. Ch. Nov. 30, 1733 ; bur. there Oct. 21, 1745.

Sarah Lightbowne, bapt. at Coll. Ch. Aug. 2, 1713.

John Lightbowne, bapt. at Coll. Ch. April 7, 1715.

Thomas Lightbowne, of Manchester, engraver ; bapt. at Coll. Ch. July 7, 1717 ; bur. there April 2, 1775. = **Mary,** dau. of ... . born 1722 ; bur. at Coll. Ch. Jan. 11, 1797.

Ann Lightbowne, bapt. at Coll. Ch. Nov. 8, 1719.

Joseph Lightbowne, bapt. at Coll. Ch. Feb. 25, 1721 - 2 ; bur. Nov. 8, 1722.

Joseph Lightbowne, bapt. at Coll. Ch. Nov. 10, 1723 ; mar. there Sept. 10, 1753, Mary Longshaw.

Mary Lightbowne, bapt. at Coll. Ch. April 20, 1746 ; bur. there June 1, 1746.

James Lightbowne, bapt. at Coll. Ch. Feb. 18, 1747 - 8 ; bur. there March 8, 1747 - 8.

Mary Lightbowne, bapt. at Coll. Ch. July 6, 1761.

Charles Lightbowne, of Manchester, engraver. = **Margaret,** dau. of .... Bayley ; mar. at Coll. Ch. Sept. 11, 1767.

Mary Lightbowne, bapt. at Coll. Ch. Nov. 8, 1767.

Thomas Lightbowne, bapt. at Coll. Ch. June 18, 1769.

Margaret Lightbowne, bapt. at Coll. Ch. Feb. 17, 1771 ; mar there Feb. 21, 1796 ; died June 3, 1838. = **Thomas** Worthington, of Manchester, merchant.

James Lightbowne, bapt. at Coll. Ch. May 17, 1772.

Ann Lightbowne, bapt. at Coll. Ch. May 15, 1774.

Charles Lightbowne, bapt. at Coll. Ch. June 16, 1776.

Joseph Lightbowne, bapt. at Coll. Ch. Aug. 16, 1778.

John Lightbowne, bapt. at Coll. Ch. Nov. 5, 1780 ; died Sep. 18, 1808 ; a partner of Thos. Worthington.

Elizabeth, bapt. at St. Ann's Ch. Manchester, Nov. 25, 1796.

John, bapt. at St. Ann's Ch. Manchester, June 15, 1798.

Thomas, bapt. at St. Ann's Ch. Manchester, Octob. 2, 1799.

Pedigree of Lightbowne of Moston and Manchester

name to live in the Hall. He died without issue in 1738. A sister Elizabeth, wife of John Illingworth of Manchester, was heir to the Hall. It seems, however, that she never lived there. In her will, dated 14th December 1759, she is described as of Queen Square, Westminster, widow.

In her will Elizabeth Illingworth bequeathed Lightbowne Hall to her daughter Zenobia Ann, widow of Benjamin Bowker, after whose death it was to go to three granddaughters - Ann Bowker (Mrs George Bolton), Elizabeth Bowker (Mrs Lewis Mathias), and Maria Bowker (Mrs Robert Haly). Maria alone survived her husband; and in 1800 she and her sisters' heirs sold the Lightbowne estate to Samuel Taylor. One William Cross seems to have been the sitting tenant, and was to remain in residence. The details of the deal are interesting. For the sum of £9,000 Samuel Taylor purchased Lightbowne Hall with fifty eight acres of land belonging to it; the pew in the Collegiate Church and the pew in the chapel of Newton; several parcels of land with the houses thereon, known as Wilson's tenement, Chadderton's tenement, the Lum estate, in all eighty one acres, together with the public house known as the Blue Bell Inn. The Lightbowne Hall estate remained intact in the possession of the Taylor family until Samuel Taylor of Eccleston, grandson of the purchaser, sold Bluestone Farm (twenty four acres) in 1831 to Joseph Bleakley of Ardwick. Then in 1848 Samuely Taylor disposed of Lightbowne Hall itself, together with fifty nine acres, to the same Joseph Bleakley.

Among the principal landowners of Moston in 1851 we find Joseph Bleakley (Lightbowne Hall estate, etc.) owning one hundred and six acres. John Ward (Moston Characters at Work, pp. 193 - 195) quotes from an auctioneer's catalogue of a sale of lands in Moston, which took place on 20th August 1850 at the Palatine Hotel, Manchester. According to this catalogue, Joseph Bleakley of Lightbowne Hall acquired five lots at a total cost of £1,900, comprising some thirteen acres of prime building land adjoining Moston Lane and extending from Harpurhey to the Blue Bell Public House, including the site of Moston Lane School. St Mary's school was built in 1844, and St Mary's church in 1869. Lightbowne Hall was acquired by the dean and canons of Manchester as the rectory of the new parish at some time subsequent to 1851. A secret chamber, said to be a priest's hiding hole, was opened up as a dressing room by the first rector, Revd Thomas Wolstencroft.

Lightbowne Hall c. 1954

7

Hough Hall

Hough Hall, standing in Hough Hall Road behind Moston Lane School, is the most historic building in Moston. It is a large two storeyed timber and plaster farmhouse of the Tudor period. While it conforms to no known design, it is nevertheless extremely attractive in its sturdy eccentricity, and a most valuable relic of the past. Belonging to the latter half of the sixteenth century, it gets its name from the Hough family (spelt Halgh in old records). Valentine Halgh in 1613 purchased the hall and lands in Moston from Richard Assheton of Middleton. The Asshetons had inherited it from the Radcliffes of Ordsall, with whom they were connected by marriage. The house may originally have been built for Hugh Shacklock, whose family received a grant of land in Moston from Robert Radcliffe, the first earl of Sussex, about 1529. The registers of Manchester Collegiate Church (later the Cathedral) contain frequent references to the Halgh family. It had associations with Blackley.

By indenture of 14th March 1629 Robert Halgh, son and heir apparent of Valentine Halgh of Moston, conveyed to Robert Maden of Hopwood all those several closes or parcels of land situate and lying in Moston, known as the Great Stake Field, the New Close, the Long Shutt, the Burnt Acre, the Hollow Meadow, and the Yarn Croft. During the Civil War this Robert Halgh espoused the Royalist cause, and had his estate sequestered. Claiming the benefit of the Truro Articles of 1646, he paid two sums of money (in 1648 and 1653) by way of composition, and finally had his lands restored to him. By his will, dated 30th March 1678, Robert Halgh bequeathed his lands, messuages, tenements, etc., situate in Moston, to John Dawson alias Halgh, his illegitimate son. John Dawson in 1685 sold the hall and estate to James Lightbowne of Lightbowne Hall.

Hough Hall soon afterwards passed into the possession of the Minshulls of Chorlton. James Lightbowne's aunt, Ann Lightbowne, had married Thomas Minshull of Manchester, apothecary, some years previously. Evidently, an agreement was reached between James Lightbowne and his Chorlton cousins; and by the early years of the eighteenth century Hough Hall was occupied by the Minshulls. One member of this family was Elizabeth Minshull, who became the third wife of the poet John Milton.

In 1769 the marriage took place in the Collegiate Church of Mrs Barbara Minshull of Chorlton Hall, widow of an apothecary who had left her a substantial fortune, and Cornet Roger Aytoun of the Marquis of Lothian's regiment of dragoons. The bride, aged sixty five, was the owner of Hough Hall estate, which she made over to her husband many years her junior. Roger Aytoun, better known as 'Spanking Roger', would later be a hero of the British defence of Gibraltar against the Spanish and rise to high military rank. The new owner of Hough Hall was a tall, handsome Scot of dissolute character, who was so drunk on his wedding day that he had to be held up by his friends during the service. He deserted his wife within a

Hough Hall c. 1890

39

Hough Hall today

week of their marriage; and squandered his wife's fortune with such rapidity that only five years later Chorlton Hall, Garratt Hall and Hough Hall, with their respective demesnes, had to be sold to pay his debts. The purchaser of Hough Hall in 1774 was Samuel Taylor, who would acquire Lightbowne Hall twenty six years later. In 1841 the tenant was Thomas Thorp, a farmer who lived in the Hall with his wife, two daughters, one grandchild, one son-in-law, and one servant.

About 1880 the owner, Samuel Taylor of Eccleston, through his representatives, sold Hough Hall to two brothers Robert and John Ward, successful textile manufacturers and merchants, who had been born in a tiny cottage off Kenyon Lane. Robert Ward and his family lived in the Hall and expended a great deal of time and money in restoring the old place. After Robert Ward's death in 1904 his wife remained in residence until after 1911. Doctor Moore, who had taken over Doctor Sankey's general practice on Sankey Brow, moved his surgery into Hough Hall. Since then it has changed hands several times and has been used for various purposes - a sanitary ware storehouse, a coal yard, a factory for making lipsticks. At present it is used primarily for the storage and distribution of calor gas. The present owner of the Hall, Mrs Joan Clough, spent a large sum of money in restoring the fabric of the building. Parties of schoolchildren visit the Hall, with the proprietor's permission. In 1973 the Hough Hall Festival was staged, with various floats (including a Rush Cart) parading through the streets of Moston.

It has been conjectured that Street Fold, the central area of Moston, was named after the Street family, which lived in the locality four hundred years ago. Arguably, of course, it might have been the other way round, with the family being named after the district. Little is known of the Streets. In 1553 one William Street was defendant in a suit in the Duchy of Lancaster court entered against him by William Cade and Margaret his wife, the latter being the executrix of Ralph Standish deceased. The dispute concerned a title to tithes of corn and grain in Newton, Moston and Crumpsall. George Street of Moston, possibly a son of William Street, died in 1588 holding a messuage and land, which he had in 1586 settled on himself and his wife Isabel for life and then on Cecily Ogden, a daughter of Richard Ogden of Moston - later married to Robert Kenyon. George Street's heir was his brother Richard, then forty years of age. Richard Street died in 1592, his next of kin being his son William then a minor, who came of age in 1597. This William was ordered by the Manchester Jury to come in and do his suit and service in 1600. A last mention of the family comes in 1624. In that year John Booth purchased a messuage and lands in Moston from William and John Street.

8

The Taylor Family and Moston House

The first mention of the Taylor family, which was to make a notable contribution to the Moston scene, comes in 1774 when one Samuel Taylor esquire purchased Hough Hall with its twenty six acres of land. In 1776 this Samuel Taylor built Moston House on the site of the present Margaret Ashton Sixth Form College (formerly Harpurhey High School for Girls) to be his Manchester residence. It must have been an imposing house, with large reception rooms on the ground floor and eighteen bedrooms. Around Samuel Taylor's mansion were thirteen acres of beautifully laid out gardens, lawns and wooded dells. There were also eight hothouses, two summerhouses, a vinery, a coalhouse, a lake, extensive stables, and kennels for a pack of hounds. In 1800 Samuel Taylor of Moston, as he was then called, bought Lightbowne Hall estate. The following year the master of Moston House died. By his will, dated 10th October 1801, Samuel Taylor bequeathed all his freehold estates situate in Moston and Blackley to his wife Mary and her assignees for the term of her natural life, and after her death to his son Samuel Taylor and his male heirs. Mrs Mary Taylor, widow and heir of Samuel Taylor, died on 17th November 1802; whereupon her son, another Samuel Taylor, according to the terms of his father's will, took over all the estates.

The new owner of Moston House was Colonel Samuel Taylor of the Manchester and Salford Rifle Regiment of Volunteers, who was also a magistrate. In February 1807 the Grand Lodge of the Loyal Orange Institution of England was established at the Star Hotel, Deansgate. On this occasion Colonel Taylor of Moston was elected Grand Master of the Orangemen of Great Britain, a post he was to hold until his death in 1820, when he was succeeded by His Royal Highness Frederick Duke of York and Albany. Colonel Taylor would frequently ride to hounds over the fields of Harpurhey and Moston. The dirt road, leading from St George's Road (later Rochdale Road) to Moston House, was for years known as Taylors' Lane. The Colonel Taylor Orange Lodge of Blackley was still thriving in 1892. There is a beautiful white marble plaque in Manchester Cathedral, inscribed as follows:-

Sacred to the Memory
of
Samuel Taylor Esqre
of Moston & Eccleston
in the county of Lancaster;
One of His Majesty's Justices of the Peace;
and LIEUT: COLONEL of the Manchester & Salford
Rifle Regiment of Volunteers:
He was a man of warm and generous Feelings;
of unblemished Honour and Integrity;
and with a most ardent Spirit of Loyalty.
He maintained through Life
a firm independence of Character.
He died October 23rd 1820, aged 48 years.

Colonel Taylor was succeeded by his son, Samuel Taylor of Eccleston. In 1837 this the third Samuel Taylor to be connected with Moston, and the last to live at Moston House, made the first of several gifts of land to the Church of England, which have earned him a place of honour in the annals of several local churches. On 10th July 1837 the foundation stone of Christ Church, Harpurhey, was laid by Edward Andrew esquire, the owner of the Harpurhey Hall estate. The site for the new church, 2,413 square yards in extent, was donated jointly by Miss Andrew of Green Mount and Samuel Taylor of Eccleston. Consecrated on 24th September 1838, the new church was designed to serve not only the people of Harpurhey, but also the deprived Anglicans of Moston, who had been forced to travel to All Saints, Newton Heath, or farther afield. Henceforth Taylors' Lane would be known as Church Lane.

About this time Samuel Taylor sold Moston House to Malcolm Ross, who was in residence in 1841. Although Samuel Taylor had left Moston (Booker, Ancient Chapel of Blackley, gives his address in 1853 as Ibbotsholme in the county of Cumberland), his benefactions to the area did not cease. In 1844 a school was built in Moston for the Church of England. The site, including a small field adjoining, was given by Samuel Taylor. Twenty five years later the new church of St Mary was built in this field, another portion being allocated for a graveyard. Taylor had sold Bluestone Farm with twenty four acres to Joseph Bleakley in 1831, and then in 1848 he sold Lightbowne Hall with fifty nine acres to the same client. But, even after disposing of so much land, Samuel Taylor of Eccleston was still in possession of one hundred and six acres of Moston in 1852. In 1874 he sold fourteen acres of this to the Salford diocesan trustees for use as a Catholic cemetery. The representatives of Samuel Taylor in 1880 sold Hough Hall estate to Robert Ward. When Samuel Taylor of Eccleston died in 1881 his remaining property passed to his son, Samuel Taylor of Birkdault near Ulverston.

We have touched upon the property dealings of three generations of Taylor men bearing the name Samuel. But, probably, the Taylors of Moston will be best remembered for a female member of the family. Mary Taylor, daughter of Colonel Samuel Taylor, probably took up residence at Crofters House (now Harpurhey Dogs' Home) before Moston House was sold by her brother Samuel Taylor of Eccleston during the 1830s. A friend and student of John Dalton, formulator of the Atomic theory, who left her £100 in his will, Miss Taylor in 1841 commissioned her manservant John Robinson to take a census of Moston. According to this survey there were one hundred and twenty five dwellings in the township, housing six hundred and seventy two men, women and children. There were fifty six handloom weavers; thirty seven farmers; five bricksetters; five dyers, and only one collier. Food and drink were provided by two provision merchants and three retailers of beer, one of whom was also licensed to sell wines and spirits. There were, however, two dealers in 'hush whiskey.' Only four persons travelled outside the township to work.

A few words about Miss Mary Taylor. As a child she had suffered much from a respiratory ailment. On medical advice she went to live in Switzerland, where she quickly recuperated. By adhering to a strict regimen in eating and exercising she was enabled to lead a full and active life, finally dying in her ninety third year. Botanist, philanthropist, social historian, she was universally respected. During her lifetime Manchester emerged from its servitude to the lord of the manor to become a great industrial city. Moston, from being a rural township with a few hundred inhabitants, developed into a suburb of Manchester with a population in excess of ten thousand. The daughter of the first Grand Master of the Orange Lodge (formed to uphold the Protestant supremacy over Roman Catholics) lived just long enough to see her father's residence at Moston House converted into a Catholic Convent.

According to Mary Taylor's Census of 1841 Malcolm Ross and his wife with their two children were living at Moston house. Ross was a wealthy businessman and keen gardener. During his stay at Moston House great attention was paid to the cultivation of the grounds and the care of horses and hounds. Moston House cottage, in the yard of Moston House, in 1841 housed the head gardener, James Greenwood, with his wife and child. Malcolm Ross was associated with the landscaping of Queens Park. In the early 1870s Ross had been followed as owner of Moston House by George Milner, a manufacturer of calico and a well known author. As President of the Manchester Literary Club, he entertained some of the leading writers of the day at Moston House. In his 'Country Pleasures' George Milner has preserved some interesting items of local folklore. Charles Roeder (Some Moston Folklore, 1907) gives an old prayer, which Milner claims was recited nightly by an old lady in Moston as recently as 1878:-

Fro' o' mak o' witches an' wizarts an' weasel skin,
An o' mak o' feaw black things 'ut creepen up deytches
Wi' great lung tails - may the Lord deliver us.

Soon after 1881 Moston House became the home of John McKenna, the owner of a local brewery, B. J. McKenna Ltd of Harpurhey - better known as McKenna's Vaults, and later of the Derby Inn (The Top Derby). McKenna neglected the fabric of Moston House; and it required extensive repairs to be carried out over several months before the new owners could move in. At the end of 1888 the Daughters of the Cross, a religious congregation founded in Liege fifty five years previously by Marie Therese Haze, took over Moston House. The Sisters came with a twofold object: to teach in the recently opened Mount Carmel School; and to establish a home for thirty orphan girls, hitherto cared for by the Presentation nuns of Livesey Street, Collyhurst, on behalf of the Salford diocesan Rescue Society. Some background material on the Daughters of the Cross is necessary to show how they came to be in Moston, and why they were eminently suitable for the tasks they were asked to perform.

Mother Marie Therese Haze was encouraged to found her Order in secret. Belgium was under anti-Catholic rule from Holland, and Religious Orders were proscribed. The whole of Europe was in chaos as a result of the Napoleonic wars. The Sisters were soon being hailed by the people and the authorities for their work in the educational field. Their services were requested and willingly given in caring for the poor, orphans, prisoners, fallen women (their record of conversion and rehabilitation was extraordinarily high), nursing the sick in general and cholera victims in particular. In Germany the Daughters of the Cross were to become national heroines. In two wars (Prussia-Austria, and Franco-Prussian) they formed front line medical corps, ministering to the wounded and dying under fire. In the second and much longer conflict forty two Sisters were decorated with the Iron Cross for protecting the helpless wounded. Incidentally, forty five years later Daughters of the Cross (some of them Belgian) would be looking after wounded Belgian soldiers in the grounds of Blackley Park Convent.

The expulsion of the Sisters from Germany during Bismark's Kulturkampf persecution of the Catholic Church (he later rescinded the order under pressure from other German states) widened the Sisters' apostolate. They had already set up missions in India (1862); and in 1863 they had come to England to work in a women's prison. But, their work in England was to be mainly nursing and teaching (at present they run three hospitals and an epileptic colony in this country, in addition to their educational work). The first foundation of the Daughters of the Cross in the north of England was in Bury. Bishop Herbert Vaughan (later Cardinal Archbishop of Westminster) had a lot of German and Belgian priests in his diocese. These had brought his attention to the spectacular success which had attended the social work of the Daughters of the Cross on the Continent. The Parish Priest of Mount Carmel, Blackley, Father Vermeulen was a Belgian. He was anxious to have the Sisters in his new school, opened in 1871. In addition. Bishop Vaughan was eager to have the Sisters take charge of an orphanage for thirty girls under the patronage of St Brigid.

Sister Iphigenie, at that time Superior in Bury and about to become the first Provincial of the Daughters of the Cross in England, negotiated the purchase of Moston House. The sale was concluded in late 1887 or early 1888; but for nearly a year a caretaker and his wife and family were in residence while alterations and repairs were made. Incidentally, two of the caretaker's daughters later joined the Order, and served in it for many years. Their names in religion were Sister Bonaventure and Sister Edwardine. Accommodation had to be built for the orphans. Old kennels and stables were demolished to make room for dormitories and classrooms. A chapel was erected, with a small sacristy - its walls lined with carved wood panels. The chapel was connected with the house by a covered way. The chaplain had his own house nearby. Sister Mary Electa was the first Superior at Moston House. In 1892 she was succeeded as Reverend Mother by Sister Ambrosine. Sister Mary Electa was recalled to Liege, where she died the following year. At first the nuns were either Belgian or German (later on at Blackley Park there would be a Russian member of the Community, Sister Olga); but English and Irish girls soon flocked to become Daughters of the Cross. Father Schuster, the new parish priest of Mount Carmel, was German; the predominantly German Alexian Brothers were only a mile and a half away; so the Sisters from Germany and Belgium would be made to feel at home.

Moston House was invaded by a small army of nuns towards the end of 1888. There was a lot of work to be done before the orphans could be received. They seem to

Old house in Moston Bottoms

have arrived in the latter part of 1890. On 4th March 1889 two Sisters had begun duty in Mount Carmel Schools; they were Sister Elphege, headmistress, and Sister Austine, assistant. The average attendance for the whole school at the time - boys, girls and infants - was one hundred and fifty one. By the end of the year it had risen to two hundred. As standards rapidly improved so numbers increased; consequently by November 1893 a total of three hundred was reached. The Infants became a separate department. Sister de Pazzi, transferred from Bury, became Head of the new Infant School in December 1894. Numbers continued to grow. Sister de Pazzi was moved to the Mixed Department in January 1896; while Sister Mary Regina took over the Infants, where she was joined in 1896 by Sister Mary Sigibert.

The orphans were certainly in residence at Moston House by the beginning of 1891. Sister Austine, who was to mother them at first, was already teaching in Mount Carmel. The terms of the legacy which endowed the orphanage dictated that it be known as St Brigid's, and that the girls wear green uniforms and 'poke' bonnets. Although old-fashioned in 1891, the 'poke' bonnet had never really gone out of style; in 1897 it came back into fashion with the celebration of Queen Victoria's Diamond Jubilee. So the orphans of St Brigid's Convent, Moston House, did not look dowdy in their nonetheless quaint headdress. They were taken to Mount Carmel School daily, walking both ways. Sandwiches were provided for lunch. Hot tea was supplied by arrangement with the Farm Yard Hotel just across the road from the school.

Every year the orphans walked as a group in the parish Whit Procession. The Procession followed a two mile route from Mount Carmel church to Moston House, where Benediction of the Blessed Sacrament was celebrated. It then returned to the Clough, near the present Mount Carmel Social Centre, where the orphans were regaled with milk and buns. There were also the traditional orphans' concerts at Shrovetide. During Sister Ambrosine's time as Superior (1892-98) the number of girls in the orphanage reached its highest total of thirty three. Most of them were trained for domestic service, and many found work in the neighbourhood. Some were suitable for further education. Miss Joanna Leary, one of the orphans, went on to college and in 1898 she was in charge of Standard II in Mount Carmel School. Several of the orphanage girls became nuns, either with the Daughters of the Cross or other Orders.

The Sisters founded a Boarding School at Moston House in 1892, in response to requests from many local residents. Numbers grew so rapidly that by 1896 more room was urgently needed. A large house on the other side of Church Lane was purchased, and the orphans moved into it. The chickens went too, under the care of Sister Justina; for the new house had a lovely garden and conservatory in which the children played. Behind the house was a ravine, deep and mysterious (known as the Throstle Glen), a magical place to explore on half holidays. Very soon there were sixty boarders at Moston House. The curriculum was extensive. The most modern teaching techniques from the Continent were employed. 1903 was the peak period of Moston House. Nearly one hundred children were cared for by a staff of twenty nuns. There was also the farm. Sister Justina minded the hens,

Plaque on old house in Moston Bottoms

and looked after the eleven acre garden at Moston House, plus the large garden across the lane. Sister Alberta tended the pigs, milked the cows, baked the bread, and churned the butter. During World War II Sister Alberta was growing potatoes and cabbages in a part of the playground at Blackley Park. In addition to teaching in Mount Carmel Schools, the Sisters took charge of a large group of Children of Mary, looked after the sacristy, visited the sick, and gave religious instruction. Many girls joined the Order through their contact with the Sisters at Moston House.

Sometime between 1896 and Sister Elphege leaving Moston House there was a period when she and Sister Austine went to teach in St Edmund's, Miles Platting. It was too great a distance for the arrangement to last. There were also two Sisters who conducted a similar exercise with regard to St Peter's School in Middleton during 1896, walking there and back. There was a resident chaplain at Moston House from 1889 until the house closed in 1910. Father Maguire, one time curate at Mount Carmel but later in poor health, was in charge for some time. Then Father Peter Baetings a Dutch priest, Father Fitzpatrick, and Dr Kelly (who came to Moston House so that the country air might restore his health); these were some of the priests who served the spiritual needs of the Sisters and children of the orphanage and boarding school. A Father Holohan was nursed by the Sisters during his last illness.

Father Schuster died in 1898. He was succeeded by Father Robert Hayes, who saw the new church of Mount Carmel built in 1907. There was a movement afoot to create a new Catholic parish in Moston, which was to materialise in 1911. Father Hayes, a very strong-minded man, wanted the Sisters within easy reach of church and schools. Two large houses. The Laurels and Tudor

House, were up for sale. They stood almost midway between Mount Carmel church and schools, with ample space for expansion. After consultation with Liege and Carshalton (the headquarters of the English province), it was decided to transfer the convent and boarding school from Moston House to the new premises, which became known as Blackley Park Convent - they now house St Joseph's Social Centre and Mount Carmel Social Club. Moston House was sold to the Manchester Education Committee. After some years it was demolished to make way for a new Girls' High School. The orphanage was transferred to the Cross and Passion nuns at the Crescent, Salford. I discovered most of this information when I visited the Daughters of the Cross in their Convent on Rochdale Road at the top of Valentine Brow.

A passage in Wentworth (History and Annals of Blackley, 1892, p. 210) had led me to approach the Sisters for further information. Writing at a time when there was strong Nonconformist agitation to abolish all government aid to voluntary schools, Wentworth, a non-Catholic, had this to say about the Daughters of the Cross in Mount Carmel School: "The government reports speak well for the discipline maintained in the schools, and for their efficiency in other respects. At my brief visit I became very much impressed with the exceptional intelligence of the headmistress, who answered my questions with frank courtesy and dignified condescension. I was given to understand that the children taught in this school are not the children of Roman Catholic parents exclusively and that no violence is done to the consciences of the most sensitive of Protestant parents.' Many non-Catholics in Moston today, who were educated or whose children were educated by the Daughters of the Cross, will bear witness to the truth of this last statement. The Sisters endeavoured to serve the whole community, regardless of creed.

9

The People and the Land

City dwellers in general have a tendency to idealise the countryside. Charles Roeder ('Some Moston Folklore') wrote in idyllic fashion of Moston. I shall give three passages, and append brief comments of my own. Under the heading 'MOSTON IN FORMER TIMES' he writes:

'The township of Moston, covering about 1,297 acres, now absorbed into Greater Manchester, situate 3½ miles northeast of the city, stretching over an elevated country (250 feet above sea-level), of which Copthorne Hill, in Nuthurst, is the highest point, forms one of those ancient outlying parts of the parish of Manchester which by its lonely situation was little in contact with the mediaeval manor of Mamecestre. It was skirted on its western side by one of Grelle's deer parks of Blakeley, seven miles in circuit, and one of its deer-leaps runs up Boggart Hole Clough. Oak, ash, hazel, alder, willow, briar and bramble, holly, gorse, and heather abounded; formerly foxes, weasels, and adders were common. On the south and east flowed Moston Brook; on the west lay the clough and the extensive mossland which swept up round the northern limits. The undulating ground gave rise to many small wooded dingles and cloughs and rills, and the tablelands were occupied by the large heathery moors on which the inhabitants drove their cattle for grazing and dug their turf.'

This account should be compared with the description of Moston in 1858 by John Higson, which I have included at the end of the chapter. Roeder was indebted for much of his information to Thomas Lancashire of Bacup Brow, the sage of Moston. A section dealing with old cottages in Moston is of special interest. Under the title 'THE OLD INHABITANTS' Roeder writes: 'In early feudal times the lords of Moston had attached to and scattered about their little hall-steads a small cluster of villeins, cottars, and bordars, who looked after their cattle and farming and things domestic. These in course of time developed into yeomen and husbandmen. None of their cots are now to be seen; Mr Lancashire knew one near the Lily Pit and another at Mal Garden in the Boggart Hole Clough. These thatched huts were called patten or parren and made of raddle and daub, that is, with hazelsticks, mortar, and clay; they were very low, having their little pile of peat at the side. . . . . . . The old Clough Top farmhouse, also of raddle and daub, he always took for the place where one of the ancient foresters of the deer park lived.' It seems that Lancashire remembered these medieval shacks being still inhabited in the early part of the nineteenth century. John Ward describes a cottage near Streetfold, which was scarcely an improvement on the antiquated dwellings by the Lily Pit and Mal Garden.

The third extract from Roeder is a purple passage, which serves as an excellent introduction to this chapter on the social conditions of working class people in Moston from time immemorial until the middle of the nineteenth century. Here is Roeder:-

'We perceive . . . . that the Moston people were mainly given to agriculture and weaving. Their habits and mode of life were quite simple, their pleasures and amusements few. They had their wakes, morris dancers, and rushcarts, their pace-egging, and carol singing at Christmas, and led a very quiet existence. Their vernacular dialect retained some peculiarities of its own, and in the Blue Bell Inn or the few beer houses they discussed, when at leisure, the events of the day. They were fond of a little fowling, hunting, and fishing. Like all more or less isolated communities who follow few and mainly manual vocations, they were rather clannish, keeping to and marrying among themselves. Progress of new ideas went at a slow pace, and old superstitions, beliefs, and customs had a tough life. They peopled their brooks, pits, lanes, and cloughs, with all sorts of boggarts, fairies, and imps. They dreaded the dark night, and few ventured to go abroad at midnight. The moans and shrieks in the cloughs and dingles, and the soughs which swept over moor and moss, made them quake with apprehension in their lonely homes. Underneath certain bridges they saw lurking water-sprites. At the Platting, a little watercourse which found its way into the Kitchen Clough, the belated often fell in with a boggart, which assumed the shape of a cow, lying down beside the Platting, which, when once kicked at by a couple of farmers, uttered an unearthly penetrating low, but made no resistance; it was a phantom cow into which a boggart, or buggane, had changed himself, a being which even now troubles the old manx peasantry considerably at night.

Then, again, the east end of Boggart Hole Clough was haunted with the nut-man, that used to shriek terribly at times as it flitted among the hazel bushes, and continued the great bugbear of all children. To the same clough the young people came to gather silently the seed of the Saint John's fern on the eve of St John's Day to gain the affections of their unyielding damsels. A lonely farmhouse at the bottom of this clough had its bar-gaist, a lonely creature enough, who would render many good services to the occupants. One of the pits harboured an uncanny evil spirit and was called the Devil's pit.' Roeder then catalogues the legends of Moston: the spirit hunter of Hough Hall; the fairy spade of Moston Hall; Old Bess's Ghost, connected with Moss Gate Farm. To these I would add the legend of the headless horseman, of Civil War origin.

It is hard to know who is the more credulous in these matters - the ignorant, unlettered peasant, with his great store of folk memory, regaling the studious visitor from the city with often repeated (perhaps half believed) stories of the supernatural: or the dude professor, taking shorthand notes, and buying rounds of drinks to be told spooky stories, which he knows to be local variations of well known legends. Anyway, the Moston versions, as may be seen from the example given, are not very exciting.

The poor people of Moston, according to a deposition of 1595, 'do get their living only by occupying and making white linen yarn, which doth require very much fire to the use thereof, and have none other kind of fire or fuel for their necessary burning, nor never had, but only such as they have used yearly to get in and upon the said waste.' Behind the simple statement that 'bowking' or linen bleaching had been the sole means of sustenance for the cottagers of Nuthurst and Moston over a period of years lies the ever present fear of exclusion from the waste (in this case, Theyle Moor). Having no land of their own, they had their 'crofts' in the waste for spreading out linen cloth in the sun (in Lancashire dialect the word 'croft' has this restricted meaning). In addition, they cultivated small vegetable plots in the waste. I sense in this pathetic utterance the hopelessness of the Moston peasant in the face of the Chethams and Chaddertons and, ranged behind them, the magistrates with their officers. The feudal system, which kept him downtrodden and illiterate, would last for another two hundred and fifty years.

Booker (Ancient Chapel of Blackley, p. 142) tells us that in 1689 the sum of £20, given by the will of Elizabeth Chetham, was set aside for the promotion of religious education among poor children in Moston and Newton 'until they can read the English Bible, and no longer.' In 1854 the £20 (plus interest) were still in the hands of trustees. Ward (Moston Characters at Work, p. 44) is scathing: 'Although Moston could for a great number of years boast of five old Halls, yet they did not seem to have had much influence for good, so far as finding labour for the people, or giving them either secular or religious knowledge.'

For many years the population of Moston was sparse; the value of land and property in the township was low. In 1665 there were twenty three ratepayers in Moston. The total rate collected for the six months ending 25th November of that year was eight pounds, seventeen shillings and seven pence halfpenny. According to the land tax of 1692 the annual value of real property in Moston was a hundred and ninety six pounds, two shillings and eleven pence. Population growth was slow up until 1841, after which it gathered momentum. In 1774 there were eighty houses occupied by five hundred and sixty three persons. In 1801 ninety one houses; six hundred and eight inhabitants. In 1831 one hundred and eleven houses; six hundred and fifteen inhabitants. So, in the fifty seven years from 1774 until 1831 the population of Moston increased by only fifty two. Thereafter the rate of increase was at first sure and steady, then spectacular.

As we have seen from Mary Taylor's census of 1841, Moston had one hundred and twenty seven houses with six hundred and seventy two residents. Ward (Moston Characters at Play, p. 23) gives the following population statistics:- 1851 - 904; 1861 - 1,200; 1871 - 1,660; 1881 - 3,465; 1891 - 5,179; 1901 - 11,897. By comparison with the fifty seven years prior to 1831 and their population increase of only fifty two, a similar period from 1841 onwards shows an increase of some ten thousand. Ward's explanation of the huge increase as 'owing to the growth of Manchester trade' is a bland generalisation. We shall offer a diagnosis of the main factors in due course.

While Colonel Samuel Taylor went about his many activities as a public figure, dividing his leisure time between his two Moston properties (Moston House and Crofters House) and the country residence at Eccleston. appalling events took place at Manchester, in which the Colonel - as soldier and magistrate - must have played some part. On 13th June 1812 at Lancaster eight persons were executed for their parts in the Manchester food riots of the previous April: four men for mill burning, three for breaking into a house to obtain food; and a woman for stealing some potatoes at Bank Top. We do not know what role Colonel Taylor played in these events. As a

Moston Lane, near 'The Ginnel' c. 1912

magistrate he would subscribe to such draconian measures; he may indeed have referred the cases to Lancaster. There can be no doubt that he was closely involved in the events of 15th August 1819. In the early hours of that day information reached the authorities in Manchester that large crowds were assembling on the moor four miles outside the city known as White Moss. In fact between fourteen and fifteen hundred men were mustered on the Moss by 4 a.m. on this particular Sunday morning, busily engaged in forming companies and drilling.

That such a loyal and public spirited man as Colonel Samuel Taylor, whose land at one point adjoined the Moss, could be in ignorance of these happenings is unthinkable. The magistrates sent out two spies, Shawcross and Murray, to obtain information. Again, we do not know who sent these men; but whoever it was knew the area intimately, and could direct the secret agents. Messrs Shawcross and Murray, wandering across the wild moorland in the dark, blundered into a trap. According to Aston's Metrical Records, p. 75, (quoted by Ward, Moston Characters at Work, p. 42) they were lucky to escape with their lives; they did, however, receive a severe beating. The drilling referred to above consisted of nothing more sinister than marshalling the crowds in companies to maintain order, and thus enable the maximum number to get into St Peter's Fields in Manchester for a great rally on the following day. This particular contingent was from Middleton. It was led by Samuel Bamford, mill worker, social reformer, journalist and poet. Bamford was to spend the last fourteen years of his life in Moston. His neighbour in Hall Street would be Ben Brierley, the Failsworth born dialect poet and playwright.

The next day, 16th August 1819, Bamford joined the radical speaker Henry Hunt on the platform to address an orderly gathering of eighty thousand men, women and children. The various speakers called for reforms in the inhuman laws of the time, which condemned millions to a life of poverty, wretchedness, tyranny and injustice. The Lancashire and Cheshire magistrates (was Samuel Taylor among them?), enraged by the airing of such sentiments and their rapturous reception by the huge crowd, sent in the Manchester Yeomanry to seize 'revolutionary' banners. When these raw troops failed in their objective the magistrates sent in the 15th Hussars and the Cheshire Yeomanry to quell the 'riot'. Eleven people were killed and five hundred injured in the ensuing melee, which became known derisively as 'Peterloo'. The Manchester magistrates received a letter of congratulations from the Home Secretary, Viscount Sidmouth. Colonel Taylor of Moston died the following year. He is handsomely commemorated in Manchester Cathedral. Orator Hunt and Samuel Bamford were sentenced to two years and one year respectively in prison for 'conspiracy to alter the legal frame of government and constitution of these realms and with meeting tumultuously at Manchester.'

Of course, a public conspiracy is a contradiction in terms. Authoritarian government had been utterly discredited. Public indignation accelerated political and social reform. Cobden, the apostle of Free Trade, blamed the manorial system of Manchester for the outrageous behaviour of the magistrates at Peterloo. In 1837, when summoned to attend the Court Leet as a juror, he saw things as they really were. 'What in the world does all this mean?' he demanded. 'Is it that in this great town of Manchester we are still living under the feudal system? . . . . I will put an end to this thing. We will get a charter of incorporation for Manchester.' Incorporation as a Borough came in 1838. Six years previously Manchester had obtained parliamentary representation. In 1846 the manorial rights were purchased from Sir Oswald Mosley. The payment - to be made in instalments - would cover a period of forty eight years. During this period Manchester became a city (1853) and Moston became its suburb (1890).

Near despair led the masses to assemble in St Peter's Fields. Manchester saw some of the worst evils of the industrial revolution. Engels was on hand to record them in his 'Condition of the Working Classes in England' (1844). The lot of the slum dwellers was indeed abject. The case of Moston was different. The concentration of land ownership in the hands of a few families and inaccessibility from Manchester (the township became obscured from view behind the marshalling yards of Newton Heath) probably account for the fact that manufacturing industry only touched the periphery of Moston. The first three factories situated in Moston were marginal. An inscription on a cottage in Moston Bottoms (near the Harpurhey boundary) still exists, commemorating the first factory in the township. The inscription in Latin reads:-

Hanc Domum 1713
Condebant Molam 1714
Homo Viviscit Tunc
Fabricat Mox
Occumbit

The passable translation beneath it states: "This house was built in 1713 and the mill in 1714. Man lives, builds and soon passes away.' The wadding mill referred to in the inscription was a place of sweated labour, according to Ward (Moston Characters at Play, p. 189). When John Ward and Thomas Lancashire tried to trace the boundary of Moston in 1879 the old mill lay in ruins.

The Moston Mill Print and Dye Works, standing near the present junction of Williams Road and St Mary's Road, was the second factory in Moston. It is on the map of 1820. In the Census Lists of 1871 and 1881 we find Thomas Barlow, Cloth Printer and Dyer, with his wife Mary in residence at Moston Mill. The mill is shown on the Ordnance Survey Map of 1893. I have met an old lady who knew it in this century, and who referred to the mill lodge as 'Barlus' Lodge.' Between 1820 and 1848 the third factory in Moston, Dean Brook Dyeworks, was built near the confluence of Dean Brook and Moston Brook. It was a skein or yarn dyehouse. Here John Ward worked for a short time at the age of sixteen. Part of the site was in Newton Heath, and a proportion of the rates levied on the bleach works was paid to the Newton Heath authorities. In 1911 Ward recorded: 'it is now utterly gone.' These three enterprises constituted the whole Moston industrial scene until the late nineteenth century. Even after that we can number the industrial concerns in the township on the fingers of two hands.

In themselves these projects do not explain the increase in the Moston population that occurred in the middle of the nineteenth century. But their presence on the border with Newton Heath points to the real cause of the increase; for Newton Heath at the beginning of the last century was becoming a large industrial complex. Many of the work force in the mills and locomotive carriage and wagon works came to live in Moston. In the early part of the seventeenth century industrial Manchester found new occupations for farmers and cottagers in the surrounding townships. So, in Moston a large class of handloom linen websters or weavers grew up among the tenantry. Then, with the decline in the linen trade in the eighteenth century the Moston people took keenly to cotton weaving. In 1825 the Newton Silk Mill started to operate. Monsall had its Silk Dyeworks soon afterwards. Taylors, silk manufacturers, of Newton Heath, put out much handloom weaving in the district.

This particular cottage industry was of relatively short duration - about fifty years. It was demanding work. The quality controllers - 'cutlookers' they were called - rejected any piece of silk that was flawed in the least degree. The pay was very poor, considering the amount of labour and expertise involved. John Ward (Moston Characters at Play, p. 160) gives us an important item of information. A weaver, by name Robert Glossop, before the Oldham magistrates on a charge of drunkeness, was asked by the presiding magistrate what he did for a living and how much he earned. Glossop replied: 'I get 6s. for weaving 75 yard - that is not so damned much a yard, is it old man?' There was laughter in court, and the case was dismissed. Wards comments: '75 yards of Sarsnet, woven by hand for 6s., a week's work, was not much to laugh at with Robert.' It is not easy to date episodes in Ward's books. But, it would appear that this incident occurred about 1850. Sarsnet (or Sarcenet) was a fine soft silk fabric used for clothing, ribbons, etc. In the companion volume, Moston Characters at Work, on page 189, Ward sums up this particular Moston cottage industry: 'Whatever anyone may say about handloom silk weaving being a nice clean occupation, and bewailing its having died out, they cannot know much about it or they would never wish it to be revived. It is a clean calling certainly, and compels those who work in it to have soft, smooth hands and clean teeth; but it has many drawbacks which have to be reckoned with. It cannot possibly compete with power looms, and even before power looms had got to such perfection, it was an ill-paid and starving occupation. I never heard of anyone who had got away from it wanting to return.'

The most potent factor in the sudden and continuing increase of the Moston population after 1841 was the opening of an important rail link through the township in 1839. As early as 1825 there had been talk of a railway between Manchester and Leeds. But it was only with the successful opening of the Liverpool and Manchester Railway in 1830 that the project was taken seriously. George Stephenson, whose locomotive the 'Rocket' pioneered this the first scheduled passenger train service in the world, was appointed as engineer to survey the route of the proposed Manchester-Leeds line. After much discussion and considerable opposition from the proprietors of the Rochdale Canal, whose interests were threatened, the decision was made to go ahead and the necessary Parliamentary Bills were passed. Stephenson's route, though somewhat circuitous, would save the

shareholders of the Lancashire and Yorkshire Railway a lot of money. The Manchester terminus for the first five years was Miles Platting. It was not until 1844 that a terminus to link up with the Liverpool-Manchester line was opened at Hunts Bank. From this new station, the largest in the country and the first to be named after Queen Victoria, there was a very steep incline to Miles Platting. Since steam locomotion was in its infancy, it was necessary to use cable haulage to assist the ascent from Victoria.

Then there commenced the first section of the Manchester to Leeds railway, started in 1837 and completed in 1839, from Miles Platting to Littleborough. This is the railway line which runs through Moston. It drove a deep furrow between the two ancient Halls of Nuthurst, and helped to obliterate Boar Green Clough, the boundary between Moston and Nuthurst. Twelve years later it would become for most practical purposes the dividing line between Moston and New Moston. O.S. Nock (The Lancashire & Yorkshire Railway, p. 23) describes this section of the line in lyrical style: 'Once past Miles Platting the train enters upon George Stephenson's splendidly engineered route, on a uniformly ascending gradient of about 1 in 155 and a magnificent alignment.' In the wake of the Manchester-Leeds Railway would come the locomotive carriage works of Newton Heath. Many men came to live in Moston and to work at Newton Heath Loco. A good number lived in houses owned by the Railway Company - at first the Lancashire and Yorkshire, later the L.M.S. The Carriage Works continued to provide employment for many in the district until their closure in the early 1930s. The operation of railway timetables depended upon the electric telegraph. Booker (Ancient Chapel of Blackley, p. 138) informs us that 'The wires of the Electric Telegraph company run through the township (i.e. Moston), and were in 1852 rated for the relief of the poor, the first assessment ever made in the United Kingdom on that description of property.'

There were genuinely poor people in Moston throughout the years. Although John Ward, that stern upholder of the Protestant work ethic, has harsh things to say about workshy residents of Moston, he admits that the stop-start nature of their employment as handloom weavers was largely to blame. 'They had so much enforced idleness that it became habitual, hence they spent more than half their time in the fields and everyone who could scrape up money for a gun got one; and those who had not the fortune to possess a gun, knitted nets with which they dragged the ponds for fish.' (Moston Characters at Work, pp. 189, 190). He describes the Blackley Workhouse, which stood on Sankey Brow near the border with Moston: 'a very plain looking building, having the appearance of a county prison in the old days. This was the Workhouse (it was closed and pulled down when the Swinton schools were built. Whole families were kept in it, and the children were sent to Blackley National School. I am speaking here of my own recollection, as far back as 1840.' (Moston Characters at Work, p. 47). In fact, the Swinton Schools were opened in February 1846; but the Blackley Workhouse was still standing in March 1848 (see Plan of Moston, 1848). I prefer to think that the Blackley Workhouse remained in use until 1855, when the new Manchester Workhouse (Springfield) was built to relieve pressure on

Strangeways. On 13th April 1850 Moston and Blackley united with other townships on the north side of Manchester in the Prestwich Union for the joint administration of the laws for the relief of the poor. The Blackley Lunatic Asylum (also seen on the Plan of 1848), which stood lower down Moston Lane near the present Goodman Street and Cobden Street, probably closed down in 1851. In that year the new County Asylum, with accommodation for five hundred patients, opened in Prestwich.

In 1844, so Ward informs us, 'the Church of England had commenced a Sunday School in a cottage in Kenyon Lane, and they had given relief in kind to the poor people, who made application.' (Moston Characters at Work, p. 104). Trade in general and silk weaving in particular were in a very depressed state. At a public meeting of unemployed handloom weavers on 30th July 1841 an appeal was made to the merchants, manufacturers, and gentry of Manchester and its vicinity. It reads as follows: 'Gentlemen, - The present crisis in the manufacturing districts bears heavily on the industrial portion of the community, but more especially on the unfortunate hand-loom weaver, whose miserable pittance, when fully employed, is scarcely sufficient to procure him the common necessities of life, which is so plainly seen in his miserable appearance and half-starved complexion. But, gentlemen, how must it be when at a period like this the hand-loom weaver can find no employment, - his hungry wife and starving children looking up to him for bread, and has none to give them?' Undoubtedly, Moston would have been represented at this meeting; and the address from which we have quoted would describe the situation in the township. Ward describes the cottages in which the handloom weavers of Moston plied their precarious trade.

With reference to a house which stood a little to the east of Streetfold, he writes: "These ancient looking buildings have a very picturesque appearance and look well on canvas, but further than that, they are for the most part, poor, inconvenient and unhealthy dwellings, - like some other ancient institutions, - they do well to infuse some people with a little amount of sentiment, and recall past times which sensible men are thankful enough have passed away and for ever. Many of these were hot beds of fever and rheumatism without any attempt at drainage, except into the sink, and with scarce a particle of ventilation, except that which came in at the doorway, or some broken pane of glass, which happily when broken, was a long time before it was repaired. The repair, for the most part, that had to serve was a piece of paper plastered over the hole, as if to keep out the health-giving element so necessary to a robust state of body. Most of these dwellers in low thatched houses, that I have noticed, have a sallow and sickly complexion, and their general movements wanting in both grace and vigour.' (Moston Characters at Play, p. 84).

Small wonder the poor wretches 'spent more than half their time in the fields' by way of escape from such noisome hovels. John Ward, author of 'Moston Characters at Play' (1905) and 'Moston Characters at Work' (1911), was born in a cottage in Kenyon Lane. In the second book he describes the family connection with the fustian trade through F. & A. Pershouse of Bread Street, Manchester. Fustian was a tough fabric of linen

Broad Lane Railway Bridge c. 1915

and cotton, used by the working class as an inexpensive alternative to wool. Unhindered by the restrictions on the wool trade, the Manchester fustian masters put out a lot of work to the cottagers in the locality. The firm of Robert Ward & Co. (in which three Ward brothers were directors - James, Robert and John) owned a row of two-up-two-down cottages in Moston Lane opposite Moston Lane School. In the early years of this century these cottages housed a number of the Ward family workpeople, employed as fustian cutters.

A comparison between two mid-nineteenth century surveys of Moston will help us to chart the development of the township in terms of housing. The Ordnance Survey of 1848 gives the area of Moston as 1,297 acres. Another survey of 1851 (quoted in Booker, pp. 138, 139) has the surface area as 1,271 acres, divided as follows: 1,100 acres of arable, meadow and pasture land; 131 acres of woods and plantations; and 40 acres of moors and waste land. The discrepancy between the two surveys can be explained by the fact that the Ordnance Survey included built-up areas. Subtracting the second total from the first, and allowing for gaps in what was after all piecemeal and unplanned housing development, we have a built-up area of some twenty six acres. Most of this was on the south side of the township. If the population growth in the southeast part of Moston was due to its proximity to Newton Heath; then, equally, the urbanisation of the southwest portion was the result of Blackley's industrial growth and the consequent movement of working people into the area.

The industrialisation of Newton Heath preceded that of Blackley because of the better road link between Manchester and Oldham; which again was due to the importance of Oldham as a textile and later textile machinery centre. By contrast, practically all commercial traffic between Manchester and Rochdale was via Moston and Middleton, and after 1804 by the Rochdale Canal. Up until 1804 St George's Road, the first stage of the Manchester to Rochdale road, only reached as far as the junction with Moston Lane. The Middleton Turnpike extension through Blackley was opened in 1804. But it was several years before there was a good road through to Middleton. With improved communication between Blackley and the town centre came much factory development in the hitherto sleepy hollow, a large part of which soon became an industrial slum - in stark contrast with picturesque Boggart Hole Clough, the old hunting ground of the Grelleys, which had remained virtually unaltered down the centuries.

Even before 1664 James Lightbowne had owned a fulling mill in Blackley. About the beginning of the nineteenth century the Delaunays, reputedly emigrés from the French Revolution, established their Turkey red dyeworks in the village. Levenstein's Chemical Works (1840), Morgan's Match Works, and several mills, drew workers out from Manchester. Blackley village was always just that - a village, with the fields only two hundred yards away from Market Street; no urban sprawl here. The new wave of workers would settle for the most part in Harpurhey and Barnes Green. Along Rochdale Road from Queens Park (acquired by Manchester in 1846. John Ward as a youth worked on the landscaping) as far as Boggart Hole Clough there was good flat land, ideal for housing purposes. Of the three Institutions in

Blackley only the Boys' Reformatory (closed down in 1905) was near the village. The Lunatic Asylum and the Workhouse were built on Moston Lane near the border with Moston, then a very lonely place. How lonely it was can be gauged from these words of John Ward (he is talking of the period around 1818): 'No conveyance of any kind passed through the village, and seldom was a stranger seen walking through the lanes: and then he was an object of wonderment.' (Moston Characters at Work, p.44).

The area near the junction of St George's Road, the Turnpike Road and Moston Lane, was known as Three Lane Ends until in the 1820s a character called John Barnes, licensee of the first public house in the area (the Printers Arms, later named the Farm Yard) stamped his personality on it. Thereafter it became known as Barnes Green. Ward tells us: 'In those days there were horse races at Barnes Green during Blackley Wakes. The course was from Barnes Green to almost opposite where Hall Street begins in Moston, and it took a sweep round the fields; all the land was then open fields.' (Moston Characters at Work, p. 102). Great numbers of people from the terrible slums of Manchester soon settled in the Moston Lane area and found employment in the village (there were also several dyeworks in Harpurhey). The housing was dense by today's standards - square mile after square mile of terraced housing, without bathrooms and with only outdoor toilets. But it was paradise to the people from the town slums. Cardwell's Rope Works (established in 1845), which stood between Gill Street and Clough Road, and Sankey's Soap Works, built on or near the site of the old Workhouse about 1860, found employment for a small number of local people. The housing spread inexorably to Brass Knob Street (Ashley Lane). On the west side of Moston Lane it became difficult to trace the boundary between Moston and Blackley.

Industry was the key to the development of the southern area of Moston. Politics would account for the opening up of the northeastern part. New Moston, as it came to be called, was the brainchild of a local businessman, Elijah Dixon of Newton Heath, who was alive to the opportunities presented by the recent parliamentary Reform Act. The Act of 1832 did away with the Pocket and Rotten Boroughs, created constituencies in the new towns, and extended the franchise in the boroughs to householders rated at £10 or more. In the counties the forty-shilling freeholder retained the vote; and for the first time £10 copyholders and £50 leaseholders joined the electorate. The upper middle classes had most to gain from the new Act. Elijah Dixon was quick to realise the implications and to exploit the possibilities. Before we examine his scheme, which would secure voting rights in the county for himself and a wide circle of friends, a word about the man behind it. John Ward (Moston Characters at Work, p. 176) calls him 'the well-known Elijah Dixon (the originator of the firm of Dixon, Sons & Evans, of Newton Heath).' While H. T. Crofton (A History of Newton Chapelry, vol. II, pp. 1, 2), in describing a large brick building in Newton Heath, has this to say: "This house was occupied in 1862 by Elijah Dixon, of the firm of Dixon, Nightingale & Co., whose extensive works for manufacturing chemical lights, matches, and pill boxes were contiguous.' The transaction

Nuthurst Railway Bridge c. 1915

is described succinctly by Booker (Ancient Chapel of Blackley, pp. 139, 140):-

'In January, 1850, a society designated "The Manchester Bridgewater Freehold Land Society" was organised in Manchester, having for its object the formation of one common fund by the united weekly payments of its members, and with the proceeds of such subscription the purchase of a tract of eligible building land to be divided into allotments and possessed by the several members, each of whom would thus obtain a freehold qualification as a county voter. Moston was selected as the arena for the society's experiment.

By indenture dated March 6th, 1851, the trustees of the late Samuel Chetham Hilton, esquire, conveyed to Elijah Dixon, William Ricketts, and James Gaskell (representing the society) 57 statute acres of land for which the sum of £2,900 was paid to the aforesaid trustees. To the tract of land thus purchased they gave the name "New Moston," and having redeemed the land-tax and made a good approach (twelve yards wide) to the estate, they entered into contracts for making sewers and streets, which are to be completed during the present year. The total cost of the undertaking, including purchase-money, will be about £8,000. The number of allotments is 230.' The streets of the hamlet of New Moston at first bore the names of leading members of the Bridgewater Land Society: Jones Street (Eastwood Road), Dixon Street (Belgrave Road), Ricketts Street (Parkfield Road), etc. Ward says that for the most part the owners of the houses came to live in them. But, as we have seen, in 1862 Elijah Dixon was still residing next to his factory in Newton Heath. As a venture into real estate the Bridgewater

Freehold Land Society was an undoubted success. Further Reform Acts and amalgamation with Manchester rendered it a political anachronism. A sketch map of 1859, entitled 'Plan of Freehold Estate called New Moston' shows a hamlet, consisting of three farms, some half-a-dozen scattered houses, and a few cottages, roughly corresponding in area to the old district of Sidgreaves which is first mentioned in 1468. It remained a small enclave in the northeast corner of Moston, linked mainly with Failsworth, until after the First World War.

It might seem to some readers that a rural area like Moston should be considered primarily in agrarian terms. The truth of the matter is that without their cottage crafts the peasants would have starved. They had no stake in the land. The owners of the fields and woods, which surrounded them, often lived at a distance. The neglected farmland presented a dreary spectacle to one traveller in the last century. The following account is taken from 'Moston and White Moss' by H. T. Crofton (pp. 41 - 43):-

'On March 13th, 1858, an article entitled "A Glance at Middleton," by the late John Higson, appeared in a local newspaper. In it he described how after passing Moston Hall, on his way to Alkrington Hall, he kept for some time along an uninteresting lane to a footpath leading off on the left through some desolate looking fields, where the hedgerows were deformed, with dwarfish misshapen trees, and antediluvian rails apparently rescued from the moss. The grey sward betrayed the poverty of the soil. Next he passed through a farmstead (Shackerley Green?) round which the surface of the country was broken into gentle knolls with but few habitations, and a stream margined with alders and willows slowly trickled, and a coalpit shaft or two (on the northeast) to complete the landscape. The grass was knotty or tufty, and the farmer was burning it off, as too acrid for his cattle. Hereabouts Mr Higson came to the White Moss of cheerless aspect. To the right a stunted tree or two and a couple of factory chimneys alone broke the horizon. The dykes and drains yielded a rusty scum or sediment of chalybeated tint. The name White Moss, Mr Higson remarked, may have originated in the cotton rush, which has given rise to the local simile, "as white as mosscrop," or from the peat near the surface being lighter coloured than elsewhere in the neighbourhood, or from the white herbage on the reclaimed parts indicating the lightness of the soil. Nearly all the moss was in tillage, and in a central situation was the farmhouse (Moss Farm, in Alkrington), occupying a "deavely" (lonely) site. On the left lay a small part of the moss in its original state. Passing to the left, over a moss stream and across a field, Mr Higson entered an occupation lane, and soon afterwards exchanged it for broad fields, till he came to the highway close to Alkrington Hall.'

The traditional boundary between Blackley and Moston was the pales or paling of Blackley, an ancient fence which ran down the eastern side of Grelley's deer park (Boggart Hole Clough). Perhaps the 'antediluvian rails apparently rescued from the moss' were the remains of this fence. Crofton quotes Booker (Ancient Chapel of Blackley, p. 8 note): 'about 1834 "in digging a deep trench on the confines of Blackley and Moston (north of Lum Farm?), the better to define the limits of the respective townships, the remains of this park fence were discovered buried deep in the moss land, which is there of considerable extent. The wood bore a close resemblance in colour and grain to the bog-oak of Ireland." ' The

forlorn landscape, described by John Higson in 1858, was not enhanced by the headgear, boilerhouses and workshops of the new Moston Colliery, not to mention the slag heaps that were beginning to appear. But, all was not gloom.

On 6th October 1869 St Mary's, the new Anglican parish church of Moston, built at a cost of £2,500, was consecrated by James Prince-Lee, first bishop of Manchester. The church authorities had selected a central site for the first Anglican church in the township, but one that was lonely enough. Situated roughly midway between Moston Hall and the two Halls of Nuthurst, it was enclosed on the north side by the mine workings. The area was sparsely populated - just the odd farmhouse or cottage dotted about. A dirt road wound its way along the front of the cottage school, church and graveyard, then headed north through the colliery. The first section of this road from Moston Lane to the graveyard was Coalpit Road, the second section that ran up through Nuthurst was Coalpit Lane

There was no rectory. Lightbowne Hall served as a rectory until 1910 when St Luke's church was built. The old St Mary's rectory, now the North Manchester Music Centre, was built in the same year. The first rector of St Mary's, Revd John Goodwin, held services in the cottage school while the church was being built (Ward, Moston Characters at Play, p. 139). Across the road from the graveyard, at what was to become the junction of St Mary's Road and Nuthurst Road, stood a tollhouse. John Ward has this to say of it: 'There has been a little one-storied cottage, built after the coal-pit was sunk, and when that road was cut for the convenience of the colliery. It was used long as a toll bar - in fact it was built for that purpose.' (Moston Characters at Play, p. 165).

10

Moston Pit

In his will, dated 31st January 1613, James Chetham of Nuthurst left in the hands of his executors for the payment of his debts and the benefit of his four daughters 'the issues and profits, setting and letting, of one coal mine, commonly called and known by the name of Lenardyne, and with liberty to set down more shaft or shafts, and to dig and mine for the finding and getting of coals.' We cannot be sure of the whereabouts of the Lenardyne coal mine. But, the reference to shaft mining in this area at such an early date is of special interest. The coal mining industry was still in its infancy.

Near the end of the sixteenth century shafts were being sunk to depths of 70 to 120 feet. The coal was worked out from the base of the shaft. There was very little propping and no attempt at artificial ventilation. At the first sign of the roof collapsing the shaft was abandoned. Coal was shovelled into circular baskets called corves and placed on wooden sleds, which were dragged to the shaft bottom. Then it was wound to the surface by horse drawn gins. This method continued until deeper shafts were sunk about 1800. The sinking of the first shaft of Moston Colliery in 1840 to a depth of just less than 1000 feet would seem to imply considerable drilling in this area prior to that date. The evidence suggests that even while rights of turbary were being disputed during the last phase of the Theyle Moor litigation (about 1595) shafts were being dug and coal was being mined in Moston.

The Plan of the Township of Moston, based on the Ordnance Survey Map of 31st March 1848, shows three coalpits. Let us dispose of one of them immediately. The 1848 Plan has a coalpit slightly to the northeast of Moston Hall, on the opposite side of what is now St Mary's road. A map of 1890, however, shows the same site labelled 'Old Brickfield.' There is no record of a coal mine in the vicinity of the present Dresden Street and Shelley Street. I suggest that the cartographer when copying out the names of locations mistook claypit for coalpit; in which case the pit on that site was the source of clay for the brick works. We also need to clarify the numbering of the other pits on the Plan of 1848.

Shaft number one of Moston Colliery was sunk in 1840 near Nuthurst Railway Bridge, where Woodstock Road now bends sharply to run parallel to the railway. Shaft number two was sunk about 1850 on the site of the 'Old Coal Pit', shown on the Plan. Confusion prevails to this day concerning the numbering of shafts one and two. Former employees of Moston Pit reverse the above order. I follow the National Coal Board Plan of the Colliery (see No. 1); John Ward (Moston Characters at Work, p. 175), who says the second shaft was in the Kop-thorn; and an article from the Oldham Chronicle, dated 18th March 1961, whose author J. Beckett appears to have had access to Platt Brothers' records.

The cause of the mix-up would seem to be twofold: first, there was a coal mine on the site of number two shaft for many years before that particular shaft. The fact that it is called the 'Old Coal Pit' in 1848 is indicative of its antiquity. Secondly, shaft number one is the nearer of the two to the new shafts (three and four); so it was quite natural that over a long period of time people assumed it was number two. Both Ward and Beckett are consistent in their accounts of the floods of 1876 and 1884, the former insisting that number two was flooded; the latter that two was flooded before one. These details are consonant with the fact that the source of the flooding, White Moss, was nearer to number two shaft in the Copthorn, close to the present Moston Mill.

It was not by accident that deep shaft coal mining came to Moston immediately after the completion of the railway through the township in 1839; nor was it fortuitous that the first shaft was sunk some thirty yards away from the railway line near Nuthurst Bridge. George Stephenson, the engineer of this rail route, was the son of a colliery engineer and had started his career by building locomotives for colliery tram-loads at Killingworth between 1814 and 1817. The steam engines used in manufacture and locomotion depended upon coal: the expanding coal industry relied upon steam for pumping, winding and transport. The mutual interests of rail transport and coal mining shaped the decision, made while the railway was being constructed, to sink shaft number one (326 yards deep) close to the permanent way. The decision to sink shaft number two (336 yards deep) on or near the site of the old pit in the Copthorn was made in the light of ten years' experience of drilling from number one.

The earliest seams to be exploited were underneath White Moss; and that way lay trouble. H. T. Crofton thought that the 'white' of White Moss might have been a corruption of 'wet.' Theyle Moor, a part of which lay in the southeast part of White Moss, in 1529 was described as a 'wet moss ground that nothing can grow upon.' In January 1614 there was a great eruption of water on White Moss, and the torrent flowed down into Boggart Hole Clough. From the beginning the old Moston Colliery was beset by flooding. Despite this recurring problem, there is no record of any death from drowning; although there were several narrow escapes. The risks, it would seem, were outweighed by the rewards. The Moston coalfield, with its combination of quantity and quality, had tremendous potential. That potential had not gone unnoticed. On 1st January 1874 Platt Brothers & Co. Ltd of Oldham, in conjunction with the Railway Steel & Plant Co. and the Broughton Copper Co. of Manchester, acquired the lease of Moston Colliery.

The firm of Platt Brothers was the prime mover in the transaction. Founded in 1821 by Henry Platt of Dobcross, it was already well on the way to becoming the greatest textile machinery maker in the world. By the early 1870s it employed seven thousand people. The furnaces of its vast, and rapidly expanding, engineering works in Werneth were using some twenty thousand tons of coal a year. Action had to be taken to ensure continuity of supplies. Leases were obtained of several local collieries - Butterworth Hall, Tunshill, Jubilee, and later Brushes Clough, all in the Milnrow and Shaw areas. But, all of these together would not suffice. Moston alone would be able to satisfy Platt's ever increasing requirements for the foreseeable future.

The company secretary's report of 13th July 1874 gave the total assets of the Moston Colliery as £21,472 3s. 10d.

Coalpit Lane c.1915

Colliery railway line crossing Nuthurst Road c. 1915

Money had to be spent immediately to curb the volume of water incessantly pouring into the mine workings. It seemed the money had been spent to little avail when serious flooding occurred in 1876. Platt Brothers proposed to install more powerful pumps. Their partners refused to invest more money in Moston. So, Platt's took complete control of Moston Colliery on 1st January 1877. It would remain 'Platt's Mine' until 1947. The report to the directors of 12th July 1880 showed that the Moston Colliery was producing 1,100 tons of first grade coal per week. Its assets had reached £96,205 15s. 4½d. The owners confidently expected that coal production would have trebled by the end of 1885. The catastrophe of 1884 put paid to their hopes and ambitions. Phase one of Moston Pit was about to end.

The seams of Moston Colliery were very steep, ranging from 1 in 1.5 to 1 in 2.5. A case in point is the 'Big' or 'Roger' seam, which ran up under White Moss. From a depth of some 370 yards near shaft number two it rises over a distance of 500 yards to a mere 120 yards below the surface at a point two hundred yards west of the Gardeners Arms. It was at this point on Sunday morning, 9th November 1884, that water cascaded into the 'rise' workings of the Roger mine about 200 feet below ground. Miners ran for their lives to number two pit bottom to make their escape. Some were unable to make the ascent at number two. These fled past the pit ponies in their stalls, made their way along the higher 'Colonel' tunnel, and reached number one pit bottom and safety. There were no casualties. Even the ponies were rescued unharmed later that day.

For over forty years it was thought that the flooding had been caused by breaking into the Alkrington Colliery workings. Then, in the late 1920s a geological survey revealed the true cause. The men tunnelling up to the 'rise' had pierced an uncharted preglacial channel at the base of the surface drift. Through a fissure in the rock floor of this underground river five million gallons of water per day poured into the pit. Mather & Platt Ltd installed two 32 inch bucket pumps with a stroke of 10 feet and a capacity of four million gallons per day in number two shaft, and pumps in number one shaft. The pumping operations lasted for over two months without success. On 26th November 1884 the water level in number two shaft rose by 22 feet in one day. By 12th December the water had risen above the point where it first entered the mine under White Moss. The decision was made by the board of Platt Brothers to abandon the colliery, and to sink shafts three and four to the south of number one.

Four hundred men and boys were thrown out of work by the flooding of the pit. The consequences for these were tragic. Not only had they lost their jobs; but they were prevented from working in any other mine. In those days the collier had to purchase all the tools for his work, such as picks, spades, hammers, wedges, powder, tallies, lamps and oil. In the hurried exodus from the old colliery all the tools had been left behind. Without the tools of their trade no colliery owner would employ them. The area bounded by St Mary's Road, Tymm Street, Ferranti's and Worthington Street, was known as Welsh Square. In it there were 27 houses inhabited by Welsh miners and their families. Without work or unemployment benefit, within two weeks of the pit accident they had to sell their furniture to buy food. One witness found several families dying of hunger. The members of the families were seated on bricks, with flagstones being used for tables.

Platt Brothers gave their former employees some financial assistance, but it was inadequate. A Moston Pit Distress Fund was established. Several local bodies, including the Failsworth Industrial Society, made contributions. Mr J. Holgate, of Rose Villas, St Mary's Road Moston, supplied the miners and their families with soup, bread and potatoes. Mr Joseph Ball, a steeplejack, of Oldham, bought and distributed among the miners a cartload of picks, spades and hammers. Eventually fifty men were employed by Mr Radcliffe, manager of Dukinfield Colliery. It was several months, however, before all the miners, many of whom came from Hollinwood and Failsworth, found work.

One day in November 1879 John Ward and Thomas Lancashire decided to take a walk around the boundary of Moston township. As they walked alongside Moston Brook, passing by the end of Mill Lane, Failsworth, they saw a stream flowing down from Moston into the Brook. I shall give Ward's description, and then add a comment: 'Down a gulley in these meadowlands, came joyously leaping a sparkling wholesome stream of excellent water, sufficient in volume to supply a small town. What was its source? The second coal-pit shaft sunk in Moston, the one in what is called the Kop-thorn, was suddenly flooded, and Mather & Platt put down engines to pump it out. Not being able to lower the water, they put down stronger engines; but that was of no use, the inflow was so great. When left to itself it rose to a certain level up the shaft but not higher. This bright water was pumped out of the coalmine, and when the pumping ceased, the clear stream fell down to a small rivulet. They tried for a long time to empty the pit; but it was found to be useless, and finally the effort was abandoned, as also was the whole working. The engines were removed and now there is little left but the tall chimney. Another shaft was sunk to take its place which has answered the purpose for which it was sunk.' (Moston Characters at Work, p. 175).

Writing over thirty years after his strenuous walk, John Ward has confused the pit floodings of 1876 and 1884. The stream he describes was a relic of the earlier flooding. After the sinking of shafts three and four, and throughout the following sixty years, water was pumped out of the old disused mine and into the reservoirs of the new colliery and Moston Mill. The soft water, according to my information, kept boilers and pipes from furring. Other survivors of the old Moston Colliery were the pitch pine headgear of shaft number two, dismantled in 1933, and its chimney which was still being used by Moston Mill in the 1960s. The engine from number two was installed in the winding house of the new shaft number four in 1888.

After the abandonment of the old mine in 1884 work began immediately on two new shafts, to be known as numbers three and four. The site chosen for them was about two hundred yards south of number one. The location of the new pits, which were only about thirty yards apart, is the square of grass bounded by Bradford Court, Moston Court, the last section of Woodstock Road, and Teddington Road alongside the Miners' Club. The sinking of the shafts was completed in 1887. Shaft number three (downcast) was 586 yards deep and six yards in diameter. Shaft number four (upcast) was 205

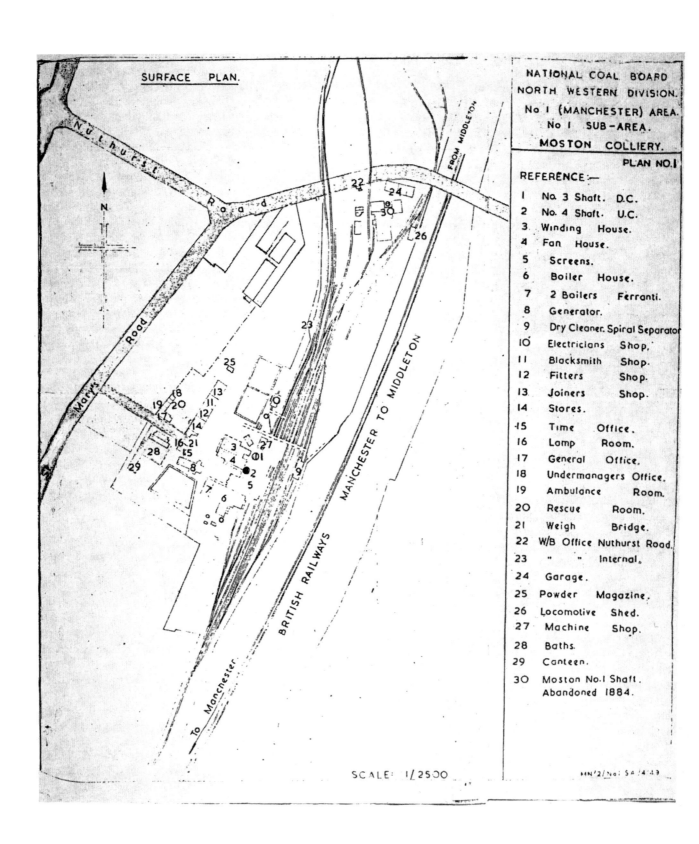

SURFACE PLAN.

NATIONAL COAL BOARD
NORTH WESTERN DIVISION.
No I (MANCHESTER) AREA.
No I SUB-AREA.
MOSTON COLLIERY.

PLAN NO.1

REFERENCE:—

1   No. 3 Shaft. D.C.
2   No. 4 Shaft. U.C.
3   Winding   House.
4   Fan   House.
5   Screens.
6   Boiler   House.
7   2 Boilers   Ferranti.
8   Generator.
9   Dry Cleaner. Spiral Separator
10 Electricians   Shop.
11 Blacksmith   Shop.
12 Fitters   Shop.
13 Joiners   Shop.
14 Stores.
15 Time   Office.
16 Lamp   Room.
17 General   Office.
18 Undermanagers Office.
19 Ambulance   Room.
20 Rescue   Room.
21 Weigh   Bridge.
22 W/B Office Nuthurst Road.
23 "   "   Internal.
24 Garage.
25 Powder   Magazine.
26 Locomotive   Shed.
27 Machine   Shop.
28 Baths.
29 Canteen.
30 Moston No.I Shaft.
    Abandoned 1884.

SCALE: 1/2500

HN'2/No: 54/4:49

56

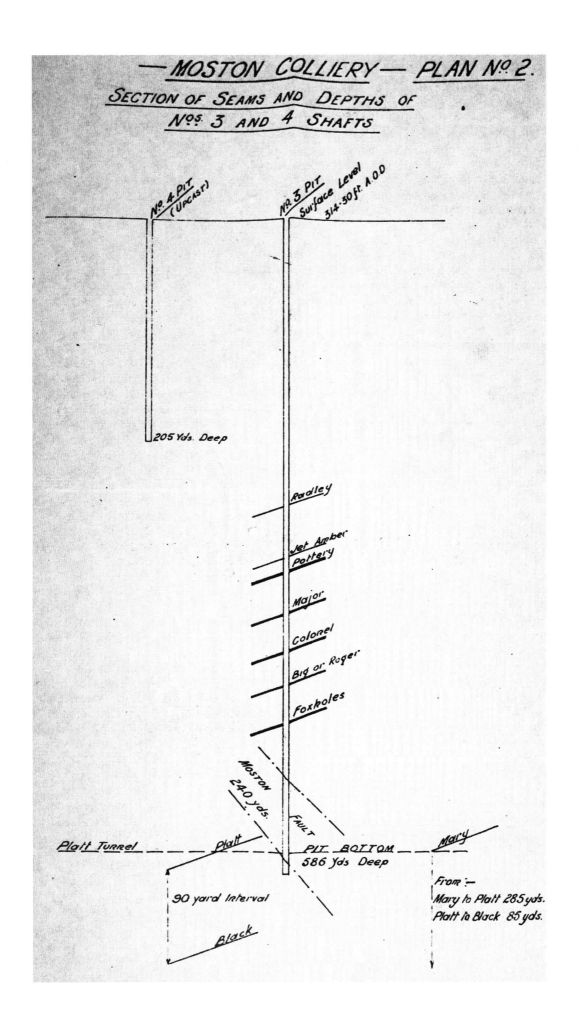

— MOSTON COLLIERY — PLAN Nº 2.

SECTION OF SEAMS AND DEPTHS OF
Nºs. 3 AND 4 SHAFTS

Nº 4 PIT (UPCAST)

Nº 3 PIT Surface Level 314·30 ft. A.O.D

205 Yds. Deep

Radley

Jet Amber
Pottery

Major

Colonel

Big or Roger

Foxholes

MOSTON 240 yds.

FAULT

Platt Turrel

Platt

PIT BOTTOM 586 Yds Deep

Mary

90 yard Interval

From :—
Mary to Platt 285 yds.
Platt to Black 85 yds.

Black

57

yards deep and seven yards in diameter. The engine house for number three pit was constructed with a steel headframe by Heenan & Froude of Newton Heath. The winding house for number four pit was designed and built by Mr A. E. Wolstencroft, of Platt's Hartford Works, who utilised the engine from number two pit. The timber headframe for number four was built in the colliery workshops. A special problem was encountered in sinking shaft number three. The last hundred yards passed through the Moston Fault. Here the strata were crushed. It would be necessary to drive exploratory tunnels to determine the existence of viable seams. By 1888 the new mine was operational.

Moston Colliery was part of the Eastern or Oldham coalfield, which is separated from the main South Lancashire coalfield by the Bradford Fault. There are thirty six seams in the Oldham coalfield. Over twenty of these seams have been worked extensively in the past. Among the hundred or so collieries that have worked in this coalfield the most important were Platt Bros' Moston Colliery Company and the Chambers Colliery Company, the latter group including Ashton Moss, Wood Park and Oak collieries. Seven seams were worked at Moston; nine at Ashton Moss. The Moston coalfield was an isolated one, bounded by Ashton Moss in the southeast, and Bradford Colliery to the southwest. In thinking of Moston Pit the Roger mine immediately comes to mind. It is true that this fine coal was the keystone of mining in the southeastern part of the Oldham Coalfield for many years, having been explored to depths of over 2,000 feet. Certainly, in the Moston district the Roger and its associated seams were worked with great success. But, other types and grades of coal were mined at Moston, satisfying a variety of needs, industrial and domestic. Production exceeded 100,000 tons annually for fifty years.

By driving the Platt and Hardman tunnels between 1896 and 1898, large areas of the Oldham Great and Black mines were opened out on the upthrow side of the Moston Fault. From the beginning good coal was obtained from the Mary mine until its closure early in this century. Rich measures were provided down the years by the Major and Platt seams. In the 1940s the Colonel and Foxholes seams were worked. Among domestic consumers, however, the Pit is best remembered for its 'Moston Best,' the superb Roger coal. In speaking of the Roger seam, the first thing to remark is that it is only mediocre until it reaches Hollinwood. Here it loses its dirty character, and begins to acquire its hard, blueish purity. At Moston the Roger face went from four feet to over six feet with a thin dirt parting. 'Moston Best' has been described to me as 'Roger 6' seam 3% ash.' Many older residents of these parts will recall it. Various coal merchants collected it from the Pit and delivered it to houses in the area. A blue slate colour, it was sold in very large lumps. To break it into smaller pieces for the fire it was necessary to hit it with the grain. Once ignited, this coal would burn for hours, leaving behind a fine residual ash. Of course, not everybody could afford 'Moston Best.' In years of recession it was not uncommon to see men, women and children scavenging for pieces of coal on tips and slag heaps.

Moston Pit was very good for Platt Brothers. Just how good can be seen from these Output figures from 1937 until 1948:-

Year	Saleable Output Tons	Face Cwts.	All Under-ground Cwts.	Under-ground & Surface Cwts.
1937	161,046	50.5	22.9	15.3
1938	163,990	57.2	22.6	16.3
1939	176,881	61.3	23.2	16.6
1940	152,491	54.6	22.0	15.1
1941	140,385	57.9	21.7	15.5
1942	121,632	58.1	20.1	13.9
1943	109,829	50.6	16.7	12.1
1944	111,835	52.1	15.8	11.6
1945	106,254	49.1	16.4	11.6
1946	119,767	51.9	20.1	13.7
1947	131,670	58.0	21.6	15.7
1948	127,055	47.8	20.1	14.7

The highest tonnage wound at Moston Colliery was the 176,881 tons in 1939. Many reasons under the general heading of 'wartime conditions' could be adduced for the decrease in production after that year. Someone who knew it well has said that Moston Colliery was a very old fashioned works, with most of the machinery out of date. For many years Platt Brothers were content to extract the rich seams of Moston Pit, feeling no obligation to reinvest any of the profits. Lack of maintenance and consequent roof falls, coupled with the steepness of the seams, made life unnecessarily difficult for the men below ground. In the stop press of the Manchester Evening News, 6th March 1942, it is recorded that over forty miners employed in the Colonel Mine of the Moston pit of Messrs Platt Brothers (Holdings) Ltd went on strike against conditions. The strike lasted a week; the outcome is unknown. It was more by good luck than good management that there were no fatalities for many years. The luck ran out on 11th March 1940.

Forty three years have passed since the accident at Number 17 Slant. In presenting this account of the event I have no desire to stir the grief of the bereaved; nor, in seeking to find an explanation, do I wish to apportion blame. For my information I have to rely mainly on the version given in the Manchester Evening News of the day. It may seem lurid to some, but the immediacy of the narrative and the reactions of the eyewitnesses have the ring of truth. And the truth about mining is that it is a difficult and dangerous occupation. Here is the newspaper account verbatim:-
Manchester Evening News, Monday 11th March 1940 —

5 KILLED,
MANY HURT IN MANCHESTER PIT CRASH
— TRUCKS CRUSH THEM TO DEATH.

Five men were killed and many injured at Moston Colliery, Manchester, today when seven trucks on which they were riding became derailed. The accident happened on what is known as No. 17 slant - which has a gradient of one in three. It was more than half a mile from the bottom of the shaft. An official list gives the names of the killed as:

James Bennett, of Derbyshire Road, Newton Heath;
Luke Scholes, of Horncastle Road, Moston;

Road enlargement at Moston Colliery

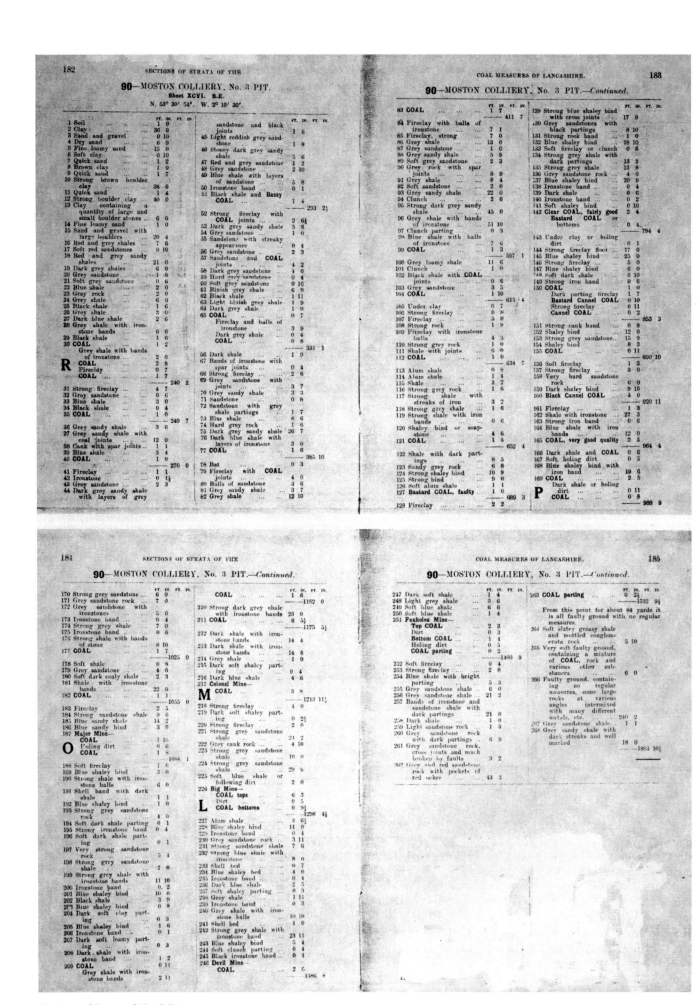

Sections of Strata of No. 3 Pit

Tom Wild, of Elder Grove, Northfield Road, New Moston;

John Espie, of Poplar Street, Middleton Junction;

Ernest Farrington, of Back Hadfield Street, Ancoats.

James Bennett (23), who registered in the last age group, was to have been married in a week. He was the youngest of the dead.

Nine injured were taken to hospital and six treated at the colliery.

Injured and taken to hospital:-

Joseph McCulloch, of St Mary's Road, Moston;
John McManus, of Wanstead Avenue, Chadderton;
James Heywood, of Ruskin Avenue, Chadderton;
George Booth, of Henshaw Lane, Hollinwood;
John P. Williams, of Oldham Road, Failsworth;
Pierce Mellor, of Shooter Street, Newton Heath;
George Wood, of Oldham Road, Failsworth;
Arthur Darlington, of John Harrop Street, Moston;
Joseph Haughton, of Grimshaw Avenue, Failsworth.

Injured and taken home after treatment:

Charles Nixon, of Brampton Street, Newton Heath;
Harold Hartington, of Glebe Street, Chadderton;
Joseph Ashcroft, of Farm Street, Failsworth;
Richard Boardman, of Branston Road, Moston;
Harry King, of Stable Street, Hollinwood; and
William E. Wilde, of William Street, Oldham.

James Tansey, of Kirkstone Road, Moston, was one of two men on the trucks who escaped injury. As he stood outside the ambulance room awaiting news of his injured colleagues he told the Manchester Evening News: "About forty of us were riding on the trucks. The train consisted of seven flat-topped bogies. Almost at the bottom of the slant it suddenly began to gather speed. Instinctively I knew it was not going to stop and, with another man whom I do not know, I took a risk and flung myself off into the road. I went rolling over and over. Clouds of dust arose. I could not see. A second or two later I heard a crash. It was terrible. When I got up, I realised I was not hurt, and in the dim light of the miners' lamps, I saw that men had been crushed against the roof and the sides of the road by the bogies which were all flung into a heap.

Two of the men had their heads smashed against the roof and another had his neck broken by a truck which pinned him against the wall. Men were groaning under the weight of broken wood and metal, and one man who was rescued had a broken leg. To reach him we had to lift away two men who had been killed instantly. I probably owe my life to the instinct which made me jump."

William Chappell, of Frank Street, Failsworth, was waiting at the bottom of the shaft for the train to come back. "We heard the awful noise of the crash though it happened half a mile away," he said. "We grabbed stretchers and rescue tackle and ran as fast as we could down the slant. It was terrible to see the jumbled trucks and men all mixed up together. One of the first men I found was my old pal Tommy Wild. We started work together here 18 years ago. When we got him out poor Tommy was dead. I helped to carry him up the slant. I feel terribly sorry for Farrington. Usually he went to his place at the coalface by walking along the main haulage road. Today, for some reason, he decided to ride on the train. It was the first time he had ever done so and he was killed. Only a few minutes before we had been joking with him

and pretending that after all these years of walking to work he was not entitled to ride."

A full trainload of miners was waiting at the shaft bottom when the accident happened. So many voluntary helpers came forward that there was no need to send for a rescue brigade. Some of the injured men were able to walk and help themselves. Mr Thomas Potts, of Silton Street, Moston, missed his place on the train through waiting for someone else. "A few minutes after I arrived at the accident," he recalled, "Ernest Cartwright came down the slant with a stretcher. He was looking for his brother Jack. We found Jack lying beneath two men who had been killed instantly."

Mr J. Turner, a pit representative of the Lancashire and Cheshire Miners' Federation, who was working in another part of the colliery, was brought to the slant after the accident. His face blackened with coal dust, he stood outside the manager's offices, and said: "When I got there most of the men had been pulled out of the wreckage. Some of the injured had been only slightly hurt, and were able to walk to the pit bottom; but others more badly injured showed the kind of heroism that you always expect from mining men when there has been a smash."

The rescuers went in to fetch the injured without any thought for their own safety. In less than twenty minutes there was not a man left in the wreckage. The colliery, which has elaborate ARP arrangements, has 17 ambulance stations underground. Within a few minutes of the accident happening 80 first aid men were at work. The moment the news of the accident was telephoned to the surface a general ambulance alarm was sent out, and in a few minutes four Manchester police ambulances and ambulances from Oldham and other areas were waiting in the colliery yard to take the injured to Oldham and Manchester hospitals. Every man hurt and killed had to be carried a thousand yards to the shaft, yet everyone was brought to the surface within two hours.

Doctors living nearby were sent for, and soon several buildings at the pithead were being used as ambulance rooms. The accident happened as the day shift was beginning, and judging by the number of miners at the pithead it looks as though the majority of the men not involved in the accident had come up again.

Mr H. Richford, the general manager, said later in the day: "The Company - Platt Bros & Co. (Holdings) - regrets that an accident occurred at Moston Colliery at approximately 6.45 a.m. during the process of lowering men down the incline of one in three, known as No. 17 slant. The grip (a special train designed for riding men underground), for some reason at present unknown, got out of control. The Inspector of Mines, Mr D. Coatsworth, and the representative of the workmen, Mr T. Brown, are at the colliery investigating the cause of the accident." ' Thus far the newspaper report of the event.

Where was slant No. 17? One mining engineer, who had known Moston Pit well, told me it was near the junction of Oldham Road and Broadway. How did the accident occur? It would appear there was an unwritten law which stated that when the men are riding the mantrain should always be in gear. By mistake the clutch was let out, and the train began to free-wheel, just running on the brake. Now, the impetus of a wagon train with forty men aboard is greater than six tubs of coal making the same descent, in this case one in three. The slant was some three hundred yards in length. From the account of James Tansey quoted above it seems that the gears were not disengaged until near the foot of the slope, which would seem to indicate that the operative was trying to bring the train to a gradual halt. If the declutching had happened sooner, the death toll would undoubtedly have been much greater. In the event, the brake band burst on the haulage engine, and the train careered out of control down the brow. No blame attaches to the operator of the train. It was wartime. Inexperienced men were having to do the work of the skilled. In any case the margin of error in such situations is slight. There is no record of any other serious accident in the history of Moston Pit.

One of my informants went to Moston Colliery when the proprietors decided to start a Brass Band. Evidently the band made good progress, winning one or two lower prizes at Belle Vue during the second world war. Perhaps Platt Brothers thought the morale of the work force needed boosting. Before the nationalisation of all coal mines in 1947 plans were made to introduce modern skip winding at Moston, and a start was made by enveloping number four headframe in a tower of concrete, prior to deepening this shaft and working a large tract of land enclosing the Roger mine and others. A new railway siding was intended to deal with the envisaged increase in tonnage. Upon being shown the overall scheme of modernisation, designed to make Moston one of the most automated collieries in the country, the then manager was asked if there was enough coal in the mine to justify the great expense. He replied that the intention was to go for the coal on the Lightbowne side, since there was still a hundred years of work there - plus the fact that it was the highest grade coal in the country. When nationalisation became certain Platt Brothers suspended all proposed improvements to the mine.

The National Coal Board, upon assuming control of the local pits, drilled two tunnels - a large one from Bradford to Ashton Moss, and a smaller one from Ashton Moss to Moston. The decision taken by the NCB in 1950 to close down Moston Colliery provoked a stay-down strike at the pit. It was a dramatic but futile gesture. Here are the newspaper accounts of the event:- Manchester Evening News, Thursday 18th May 1950: 'Denied food and drink by NCB officials until they return to the surface, 170 stay-down strikers at Moston Colliery this afternoon pooled their remaining rations and water. They decided to remain at the pit bottom in protest against the Coal Board closing down the colliery in a fortnight's time. Rations for each man worked out at one sandwich and a cup of tea. At 2 p.m. 50 haulage men, maintenance men, boys, and old miners came to the surface, leaving 170 of their colleagues below - all members of the day shift who went down the pit this morning. Angry women with food and cans of tea demanded to see the manager. 340 of the miners went down at 2 p.m. yesterday with only a bottle of tea and a packet of sandwiches. A Coal Board official said, "The Colliery has been losing £1 per ton of coal produced. We know there is plenty of coal down there; but it can be more easily worked from the other side. Men have been offered jobs elsewhere." '

Manchester Evening News, Friday 19th May 1950: 'NCB Firm: Would cost £200,000 to modernise pit.' 'No Reprieve for Moston: All Miners to go.' 'The 500 miners will be transferred, and only a small percentage of surface and underground workers kept on for a few months to wind it up. The stay-down ended last night. The order to cut supplies of food and water to stay-down strikers came from six members of the North-West Divisional Coal Board.'

Moston Colliery closed on 5th June 1950. In its last full year of production the colliery employed 658 men and produced 121,776 tons of coal, at an average productivity rate of 16.16 cwts per man. Until 1968 Moston served as a ventilation station for Bradford Colliery, from where local seams were worked by means of the tunnel to Ashton Moss. Great controversy surrounded the decision to close Moston Colliery. Moston had all the facilities for modernisation:- acres of storage space; excellent rail communications; lots of room for garaging motor transport; and proximity to a modern highway system. Most of the Moston miners went to work at the recently reconstructed Agecroft Colliery. Millions of pounds were spent on modernising Bradford Colliery, which had few of the advantages of Moston, and in addition was situated in the midst of thousands of dwelling houses. In 1968 Bradford Colliery was closed down. Coal mining in this area had come to an end after some four hundred years. There are, however, two memorials to Moston Colliery - the Miners' Club and the Miners' Estate. The Miners' Club was originally built in 1931 as the Pit Baths. It closed as such in 1950. Then, for some years it served as a Stationery Office. Finally, in 1966 it opened its doors as the Bradford Colliery Miners' Welfare Institute. In 1961 concrete dams were constructed at Numbers 3 and 4 Pit Bottoms, and both shafts were filled in. The whole pit site was cleared for housing development.

Between 1960 and 1964 the NCB built the Miners' Estate on the pit site to house its employees and their families. Most of the tenants were employed at Bradford Colliery. With the closure of Bradford in 1968 many of these men and their dependents left the district to work elsewhere. The result was that a number of houses on the estate were vacant for several months. An item in the Daily Express, 17th June 1969, stated: 'Squatters moved into empty houses on Miners' Estate, owned by the National Coal Board. A spokesman for Manchester Corporation said that the estate would become the property of Manchester Corporation within a matter of months, and then the houses would be filled.' It is difficult now to imagine that on the present sites of the Miners' Estate and St Matthew's Upper School there once stood four pit shafts with their headgear; three huge chimneys; boiler houses, reservoirs, workshops, storerooms; railway sidings with their rolling stock (the 'Robin Hood', an old saddle-tank steam locomotive, painted green and red, regularly crossed Nuthurst Road, hauling wagonloads of coal from the Pit to Moston Mill); and mountainous slag heaps where the Mill Estate now stands. The most poignant recollection of Moston Pit for many local residents was the sight of pit ponies brought to the surface to frolic in the fields.

11

Methodism in Moston

A popular tradition, recounted by John Ward in 'Moston Characters at Work,' describes in dramatic fashion how Methodism came to Moston. In 1819 two devout followers of John Wesley, named Owen and Jacques, set out from Oldham Street Chapel along St George's Road. On arriving at the junction with Moston Lane, they sought divine guidance by the simple device of throwing a walking stick in the air. The direction in which it pointed when it fell to the ground was to be regarded as the divine finger, guiding their missionary steps. The stick pointed up Moston Lane. So, without more ado, the two apostles of revivalism went in that direction, and began to preach to the peasants of Moston, establishing a missionary centre in one of the Birk Houses (small houses near Hough Hall). I like the story of the walking stick; but I must reject it as fanciful. In 1797, only nine years after the aged John Wesley had filled Oldham Street Chapel to overflowing, Dr Jabez Bunting preached his trial sermon in the old Wesleyan meeting room, which stood on the site of the present Harpurhey Baths. In 1801 the Wesleyans were conducting Sunday schools and holding services in cottages in Blackley village. Then, in 1806, the original Blackley Wesleyan chapel was opened for divine service. There was a footpath leading down to Sodom Fields in Lower Crumpsall, a sparsely populated area. In fact, therefore, Messrs Owen and Jacques (even their identities are disputed) had no option but to turn their attention to the conversion of Moston.

In 1821, while still residing in the Birk Houses, the pioneers of Methodism in the township held Charity sermons in Hough Hall barn to mark the second anniversary of their arrival. In 1822 a Sunday school was begun in Smith's Farm at Shackliffe Green. Three years later in 1825 at Street Fold the first Methodist place of worship in Moston was built at a cost of £80. This building was replaced in 1840 by the second Sunday school. Although much voluntary labour was used in the project, the cost still came to £200. In 1835 Dr Warren and his followers seceded from the Wesleyan church. In that same year the Wesleyan Association was formed, and took over the premises at Street Fold. John Wesley had asserted in 1782 that the predominant characteristic of the English nation was ungodliness. Deprived of any church or chapel throughout its history, Moston in those early Methodist years would seem to have epitomised the national vice. The first preachers met with 'much reviling and threatening and vulgarity.' (Ward, Moston Characters at Work, p. 59). As for the families at 'the ginnel' (the area about the junction of Moston Lane and Nuthurst Road, near Barcliffe Avenue), they 'were pretty well steeped in unbelief, from whatever quarter they got it, and it remained with them so long as I knew them.' (ibid. p. 45). But, opposition from without and schism from within were all the same to the staunch followers of John Wesley. Nothing impeded the march of Methodism. In 1857 the Wesleyan Association and Wesleyan Reformers united and formed the United Methodist Free Church.

Shortly afterwards, in 1862, the Methodist society at Street Fold decided to open another school for those people living at the Chadderton end of Moston. A cottage was obtained for the purpose from Mr James Moore, a silk manufacturer of Turnpike Farm. The school took its name from the nearby toll bar, or rather toll chain; hence Chain Bar Methodists. The Sunday school register commenced on 5th October 1862. There were two superintendents, one secretary, and seven teachers for forty nine boys and thirty eight girls. In December 1866 the new chapel at Chain Bar was opened at a cost of approximately £370, 'unfurnished and unbeautified.' This chapel was still standing in 1962, the centenary year. Known as 'the old school,' it was later demolished to make room for the youth centre. In 1882 a local resident gave land for a caretaker's house. James Ryder, the chapel caretaker from 1867 until 1912, had formerly lived in the Chain Bar tollhouse. In 1900, with £177 borrowed from the Moston Burial Society (a Methodist charitable trust), land was purchased for a new church. In early references to Methodism the terms 'church' and 'school' are interchangeable. This was natural enough, since Methodism was a civilising movement, which strove to educate the minds and improve the lot of the illiterate poor, while at the same time imparting the good news of salvation. Among other factors, not the least of which was the charismatic zeal of the founder, it was the way in which Methodism cared for the whole person that appealed to the hitherto despised and neglected working class.

Meanwhile at the Blackley end of Moston there was much activity. In 1872 the United Methodist Free Church was opened in Gill Street, to be followed in 1875 by Gill Street school. In 1877 the Wesleyans opened a preaching room in a cottage at the Moston Lane end of Winston Road. Sixty years of Methodism in Moston were celebrated in 1879 with services held in a large tent, pitched on the site of Moston Lane school. The site selected could not have been more appropriate; it was only about fifty yards from the first missionary centre in the Birk Houses. In 1881 the Wesleyan school-chapel was opened at the corner of Whitman Street and Ashley Lane. The United Methodist Free Church in 1884 reopened the second Street Fold Sunday school as a chapel-school. The expansion continued unabated through the turn of the century. In 1895 the Primitive Methodists had built a temporary chapel on Lightbowne Road. On the same site in 1902 they built the Primitive Methodist church. In 1903 the Wesleyan Methodists opened Moston Wesleyan church on Ashley Lane. An important event occurred in 1907 when the United Methodist Free Church, the Methodist New Connexion and Bible Christians united in forming the United Methodist Church. Then in 1910 the United Methodist church was built at Street Fold. A tragedy occurred in 1913 when Gill Street church was destroyed by fire. The tragedy, however, turned to triumph twelve months later, when the United Methodists built the second Gill Street church.

1932 saw another important stage in the reunion of John Wesley's followers. In that year the Primitive Methodists, United Methodists and Wesleyan Methodists united to form the Methodist Church. In 1952 the Methodist Church built the third Sunday school at Street

Moston Methodist Church

Fold. 1962 saw large scale reorganisation of the Moston Methodist scene. Lightbowne Road Methodist church closed on 1st January. Streetfold Methodist church closed on 1st September for rebuilding. Also on 1st September Gill Street and Ashley Lane Methodist churches closed their doors. On 2nd September Moston Methodist church, as it was now designated, took over the premises on Ashley Lane while work took place on the Streetfold church and school. Finally, on 4th September 1965 the new Moston Methodist church, Street Fold, was opened and dedicated. Four churches came together to form one congregation. The former Lightbowne Road Primitive Methodist church, Ashley Lane Wesleyan Methodist church, Gill Street United Methodist church, and Streetfold United Methodist church, became Moston Methodist church, Moston Lane.

While all these developments were taking place things had not stood still at Chain Bar Methodists. Land had been purchased in 1900 for a new church. The golden jubilee in 1912 was the occasion for a gigantic effort to raise £1,000 for further extension. The First World War brought several projects to a halt. Every effort was made after the cessation of hostilities in 1918 to bring the young men returned from the war into the church community. A member gave money to purchase an army hut from the partly finished aerodrome that was being built behind the chapel. For many years, from 1918 onwards, the hut known as the Institute was the venue for sport and entertainment, linking the social and religious lives of the members. In the post war years church football and cricket clubs flourished. Tennis courts were built at the side of the old school. In the 1920s new housing estates and roads raised the need for more extensive premises for

a graded Sunday school. The efforts of many years were rewarded on 2nd May 1936 when the new church and ancillary buildings were opened at a cost of £5,000. The original chapel built in 1866 was riddled with dry rot. It had been converted into a hall in 1937. During the centenary year 1962 plans were put in hand for a new youth centre. Eventually in 1965 the youth centre was opened. Because of the boggy nature of the terrain the youth centre was built on the foundations of the original Chain Bar chapel. Those foundations were nine feet deep.

New Moston in 1864 was a remote hamlet, orientated to Failsworth rather than Moston. Because of this, Methodism in New Moston looked to Failsworth for its inspiration and many of its officials. In 1864 four men from New Moston attended a leaders' meeting in Bourne Street church, Hollinwood. These men, with another colleague, set about finding a room in which to hold meetings. They obtained a cottage, the end one of a block of four, known as 'Gilded Hollies.' This row of houses was situated in Moston Lane (later called Moston Lane East). The upstairs room was used as a chapel, and the ground floor as a Sunday school. In 1881 the New Moston Primitive Methodist church was opened in Eastwood Road. The church was in the Hollinwood and Bourne Street circuit. The names of some founding fathers have come down to us: William Andrew, William Thompson, George Taylor, George Barton and Robert Clarke. Charles Goddard was Sunday school superintendent for many years until his death in 1923.

Many people sent their children to the Methodists for their early religious education. Along with children from New Moston, a good number of children from the

Failsworth Wesleyan and New Jerusalem churches passed through the New Moston Methodist Sunday school. The church had an excellent social life. For many years there was a successful cricket team. Until 1928 the church had its own amateur orchestra. The Scout troop boasted a fife and drum band. With the amalgamation in 1932 of the Primitive Methodists, Wesleyan Methodists and United Methodists, the church in Eastwood Road became New Moston Methodist church. Bazaars and other fund-raising events paid for the new Sunday school, which was opened in November 1933. Mr A. Heyhurst compiled a history of the church for its seventy fifth anniversary in 1956. The church in Eastwood Road closed as a Methodist place of worship in 1972. Later in the same year it reopened as a Pentecostal church. The church still houses a Sunday school. Sadly the fine Sunday school building was vandalised and damaged by fire in 1981, and had to be demolished.

In 1884 the firm of Moston Malleable Castings, St Mary's Road, was started by Thomas Parkin and Joseph Doughty. Joseph Doughty and his wife Harriet came from Dudley. They were staunch Methodists. Soon after coming to Moston Mrs Doughty and her friend Miss Annie Hopwood began to attend services at Culcheth Lane Methodists, Newton Heath. For a year or two local Methodists held meetings in a cottage adjoining the old Dean Brook Inn. In the 1890s St Mary's Road United Free Methodist school-chapel was built on land adjacent to Moston Malleable Castings' factory. There was a large drive up to the chapel. The Doughty family lived in a house alongside this drive, which was then numbered 56 St Mary's Road. With increased demand for its products

(malleable iron founders were never numerous in the north of England), Moston Malleable urgently needed a larger factory area. It became a limited company in 1913. About the same time the decision was taken to incorporate the chapel building into the factory premises. The last wedding to take place in the old chapel, which still forms part of the factory, was that of the founder's son, Joseph Doughty junior, and Edith Norris. Their son, also Joseph Doughty, was a director of the firm in 1982, working in the factory where his parents had been married in 1913.

A site for a new chapel was available higher up St Mary's Road on the opposite side. The new chapel was opened in 1914. It was in regular use until dry rot brought about its closure and demolition in 1976. St Mary's Road United Methodist church was in the Newton Heath circuit until 1966, when Newton Heath and Harpurhey circuits amalgamated. After 1966 the minister of Moston Methodists had pastoral charge of St Mary's Road Methodist church. The church was situated opposite the present Launderette and Dry Cleaners, and backed onto Johnson's playing fields. The Revd Gordon Chisnall is the present Minister of Moston Methodist church. The Revd Arthur Collin came out of retirement to serve a second term as Minister of Chain Bar Methodist church. He finally resigned in 1983, and was succeeded by the Revd Stephen Williams. The social life of the Methodist churches in Moston continues to flourish. Youth fellowships, Scouts, Girl Guides, Cubs and Brownies cater for young people of different faiths. Chain Bar Boy Scouts Pipe Band raises money for charity, and gives concerts in hostels for the elderly.

Tennis Match at Chain Bar 1921

Chain Bar Methodist Church

12

St Joseph's Cemetery

On Saturday, 13th July 1872, Manchester experienced its most disastrous flood on record. The rainfall of the previous week had been enormous. Then, in two days - the 12th and 13th - the amount of rain that fell equalled the monthly average for July. By mid-morning on the 13th the river Medlock at Clayton Bridge had risen twelve feet above its ordinary level. About 11 a.m. the river burst its banks. The flood waters swept away everything in their path. In Medlock Vale a dyeworks, bridges, railway embankments, cottages and farmsteads were destroyed by the surge of water. By the time the flood had reached the Manchester cemetery, Philips Park, Bradford, it had grown in volume and power. About noon it broke through a stone boundary wall, and rushed with tremendous force across the Catholic section of the graveyard. The torrent washed away headstones and tore coffins out of the ground. The coffins were then dashed to pieces against the weir of an adjoining print works; and the corpses were swept away downstream to Ancoats, London Road and Chorlton-on-Medlock. The number of bodies disturbed was never determined. More than fifty were recovered and reinterred.

By a sad coincidence, as the storm grew in intensity on the morning of 13th July 1872, Dr William Turner, the first bishop of Salford, died peacefully after a short illness. His successor, Bishop Herbert Vaughan, conscious of the anguish caused by the flooding of Philips Park and fear of a repetition, appointed a cemetery board to consider the advisability of purchasing land for a Catholic cemetery. The board met for the first time on 23rd July 1873. The establishment of a diocesan cemetery was a matter of vital concern for the Catholics of Manchester. Until the opening of Philips Park in 1866 they had been dependent upon the good will of non-Catholic clergymen for permission to bury their dead in Protestant graveyards. It has been suggested that, as a result of this necessity, the custom arose of bereaved Catholics taking some earth from the precincts of a Catholic church and throwing it on the coffin, as it was being lowered into the grave. In this manner they consoled themselves that their deceased loved ones had some holy ground in their Protestant graves. The replacement for Philips Park cemetery had to satisfy three requirements: first, it had to be on high ground (no more floodings); secondly, it must be extensive, taking into account the rapid growth of the Catholic population; and thirdly, it should be reasonably close to the city.

Land was available in Moston, which met these requirements and had the added advantage of being to the north of the city, where the greatest concentration of Catholics was to be found. On 20th July 1874 the Salford diocese bought fourteen acres of land adjoining that section of Moston Lane between the Blue Bell Inn and Bacup Brow, known as Bell Lane. It had formerly been Thorpe's Farm, and consisted of the Barn Field, on which stood the barn, stables and other farm buildings; The Great Field, the Little Meadow, the Long Field, and the Further Field. The total area was fourteen acres. The area of the cemetery would eventually be doubled by the purchase, on 13th August 1896, of another fourteen acre tract of land to the southeast. This would be let out for farming purposes until it should be needed for burial ground.

Bishop Vaughan lost no time in having a small mortuary chapel built, with a broad drive up to it from Moston Lane. The cemetery was consecrated on 1st August 1875. Under the chapel altar were placed relics of Saints Urban, Lucidian and Prospera, early Roman martyrs, brought from Venice by Bishop Vaughan. The original sanctuary and altar are still there today; but the body of the chapel had to be demolished in 1979. The present structure was erected in 1981. In his pastoral letter, commemorating the consecration of the cemetery, Bishop Vaughan had this to say: 'A cemetery, like a church, in order to be solemnly consecrated to God must be the absolute freehold of the Church. Otherwise, it may be blessed as a place of interment, but cannot be consecrated. The Catholics of Manchester and Salford now possess a cemetery of their own, in which their mortal remains may rest after death in ground solemnly consecrated to Almighty God. It is appropriately dedicated to the great patriarch, St Joseph, under his title of Patron of a Happy Death.'

As soon as the land in Moston had been acquired, Bishop Vaughan was pursuing another cherished ambition: to have a Religious Order of men in residence at the cemetery. These devout men would supervise the obsequies, maintain the graves, and pray for the souls of the departed. With the influx of thousands of Irish Catholics into Manchester, the Bishop of Salford was fortunate to have dedicated priests from the Continent to tend his impoverished flock, mostly refugees from the Irish Potato Famine. Dutch, Belgian, German, French, Irish and Italian priests worked heroically, along with a few English priests, to bring spiritual and material comfort to the starving, downtrodden Catholics, floundering in the maelstrom of misery that was Manchester in the 1870s. One of the German priests (exiles from Bismark's persecution of the Catholic Church) was Father Saffenrueter, parish priest of St James's church, Pendleton, who was a native of Aachen. Father Saffenrueter told Bishop Vaughan about the Alexian Brothers of Aachen, a great Religious Congregation that for over five hundred years had cared for the destitute sick and mentally ill; nursed the dying, ensuring that they received the last rites of the Church; and then laid out the dead, gave them Christian burial, and tended their graves.

At Father Saffenrueter's suggestion, Bishop Vaughan went to Aachen to see for himself the model Alexian Brothers' cemetery, and to consult Pater Clement Wallrath, the Rector General of the Congregation, about the possibility of establishing an Alexian House in Moston. The Bishop's request met with a favourable response from Pater Clement, a man under intense pressure from the Prussian authorities. Up until 1874 the Alexian Brothers, as a nursing Order, had been exempted from the punitive measures taken against other Catholic Religious Orders, such as exclusion from teaching in public schools or downright expulsion from the German Reich (the Jesuits, Redemptorists, Vincentians and Holy

St Joseph's Cemetery, Moston, c. 1965

Ghost Fathers had already been expelled). But, in 1874 the Alexian Brothers were viciously attacked by Hinschius, the chief theorist of the Kulturkampf. The stage was set for an all-out attack on the Brothers. Against this background the General Council of the Order endorsed Pater Clement's views and acceded to Bishop Vaughan's request.

In June 1875 the first three Alexians arrived in Manchester. Brothers Peter Verheyen, Cyril Kranepohl and Gerard Teubensel were accommodated in the dilapidated farmhouse in the Barn field. This was to be home to a small group of Alexian Brothers up till 1893, when it was condemned, and Mr Oswald C. Hill was instructed to prepare plans for a suitable residence. The fine new building, adjoining the chapel (built in 1875), housed four Brothers, a spacious board room, and the registrar's office. The Brothers vacated this building in 1967. It was demolished some eighteen months later.

In his pastoral letter of 1st August 1875, commemorating the consecration of the cemetery, Bishop Vaughan introduced the Alexian Brothers and their work:-

'For the benefit, therefore, of the dying and of the deceased, and to stir up the faith and the charity of the living towards the departed, an Order or Religious Congregation of Brothers has been founded in the Church, whose duty it is to nurse the sick, to lay out the dead, to bury them, and to pray for them.

A branch of this Order has been established at St Joseph's Cemetery. The Brothers will cheerfully perform these religious acts of charity, as far as they may be able, for the Catholics who call for their services, they will take charge of the cemetery, and above all will daily offer up public prayers in the chapel, especially for those who sleep within the precincts of St Joseph's Cemetery. A chaplain has also been appointed, and the adorable sacrifice of the Mass will be offered during the week at the Privileged Altar in the Cemetery Chapel over the remains of the holy martyrs.'

From the outset the Brothers performed their tasks with great fervour and devotion. Wentworth (History & Annals of Blackley, p. 210) writes: 'Nearly all the duties are performed by the Brothers. Public prayers are said by the Brothers every weekday at 5 a.m.; 2 p.m.; and 6½ p.m.; and on Sundays at 4 p.m. and 9 p.m.; for the repose of those buried in the cemetery.' The three (later, four) Brothers were responsible for the maintenance of the grounds, and had to be in attendance at all funeral services in the chapel. For performing its many duties the Alexian community was paid £1 a week by the Cemetery Board. In addition the Brothers could accept alms. I have been told that for a fee of five shillings a year, in recent times, the Brothers would maintain a grave in perfect order.

In 1876 Bishop Vaughan decided that Moston Cemetery should have a clergy vault. Permission was obtained from the appropriate authorities for the removal of Bishop Turner's remains from Weaste cemetery. On 12th August 1876 the body of the first Bishop of Salford was reburied in the clergy vault. The remains of other notable ecclesiastics and Religious were subsequently reinterred in the consecrated soil of St Joseph's Cemetery. In August 1909 the remains of the great missionary priest of Manchester, Father Rowland

Broomhead, were brought to Moston from Granby Row. Father Broomhead had built St Mary's, Mulberry Street, and St Augustine's, Granby Row. When he had been appointed priest-in-charge of St Chad's, Rook Street, in 1778, the mission included Bolton, Rochdale, Trafford, Stockport, Glossop and Macclesfield. In this huge area there were only some 600 Catholics. Fifteen years after his death, which occurred in 1820, one parish alone, St Patrick's, Livesey Street, contained 30,000 Catholics.

Nikolaus Pevsner, the architectural historian, found the Campo Santo of St Joseph's cemetery an interesting building, but did not say why. The 'Holy Field' of Moston is modelled on the famous fourteenth century cemetery of Pisa, with its shiploads of soil from the holy places of Palestine deposited in an enclosure surrounded by colonnades, decorated with frescoes by noted artists of the day. While no comparison can be made between the humble Campo of Moston and the Pisan masterpiece, a similar spirit of reverence inspired both monuments.

Bishop John Bilsborrow, third Bishop of Salford (1892-1903) and Bishop Henry Vincent Marshall, sixth Bishop of Salford and a modern crusader for Catholic schools (1939-1955), are among those buried in the Campo Santo. The famous and the obscure; rich and poor; Clergy, Religious, Laity; men, women, children; English, Irish, Italian, Polish, Ukrainian, Lithuanian, every nationality; in their hundreds of thousands their bodies rest in the soil of Moston. Throughout the world among Catholics the name Moston evokes the memory of loved ones buried in St Joseph's Cemetery, and elicits a prayer for the repose of their souls.

There have been only three Sextons in the past seventy years: John Flannery, John Lavin, James Croarkin. For many years the Hall family of Moston was associated with Sunday Benediction in the Cemetery chapel. A member of this family, Fr James Hall, was responsible for building the new church of the Immaculate Conception (St Mary's), Failsworth, in 1964.

13

The Alexian Brothers' Nursing Home

By a singular coincidence, about the time that Ralph of Moston was residing in the original tún or settlement on the site of Moston Hall (c.1200) the foundations were being laid in Germany of the great Alexian Brotherhood, whose Nursing Home nearly seven centuries later would stand close to the Hall. The origins of the Alexian Order lie in the lay movements, which sprang up in the Rhineland and Low Countries during the eleventh and twelfth centuries as a reaction to the laxity and worldliness of the clergy. In Europe during the thirteenth century there was a spectacular growth in the number and size of towns and villages. People drifted in from the countryside to the new centres of population, many to end up homeless and destitute. In addition, veterans of the Crusades returned after years of absence to find their former homes had disappeared in the changing landscape. These old soldiers wandered about, homeless, hungry, often crippled and ill. Apart from occasional relief afforded by the monasteries, nothing was done for these casualties of war and changing society.

It was left to lay men and women, many of high standing, to give up wealth and privilege in order to form themselves into communal religious groups, mendicants, dedicated to serving the poor - feeding, nursing, and eventually burying them. They took as their model the early Christian community as it is described in the Acts of the Apostles: 'The faithful all lived together and owned everything in common; they sold their goods and possessions and shared out the proceeds among themselves according to what each one needed.' (Acts 2: 44,45). The various names by which they were known are suggestive of their life style:- Begarden (the German verb beggan means to beg or pray); Lollarden, as they were known in Antwerp (Lollard is Middle Dutch, meaning 'mumbler'; hence, one who mumbles prayers. The Oxford English Dictionary says of the word Lollard, 'The name was originally applied c.1300 to the members of a branch of the Cellite or Alexian fraternity (also called lollerbroeders) who devoted themselves especially to the care of the sick and the providing of funeral rites for the poor.'; Cellebroeder (Brothers of the monastic cell, or grave Brothers).

One of the most evocative titles was that of the Aachen Brotherhood, Brot-Begarden or Bread-Beggars, whose cry of 'Brot durch Gott' (Bread for the sake of God) beautifully conveys the notion of serving Christ in the least of his little ones. The Beghards, as these groups became known generically (the female groups were called Beguines), were humble practical people, not concerned to chronicle their work. They were often suspected of heresy, and suffered much persecution by Church authorities. Still they persevered without bitterness in their self-appointed task of serving Christ in his poor. Their patience would be rewarded. A pestilence unprecedented in the history of mankind would gloriously vindicate the Beghards or Cellites, or Alexians as they came to be called.

In the first epidemic of bubonic plague, xenopsylla cheopis, to visit Europe (1347-1350) some twenty million people died. Generally referred to as the Black Death, or in Germany simply the Jungfrau, the deadly disease reached Cologne in 1349, and proceeded to wreak havoc. There were recurrences of the plague in 1357-1362, 1370-1376, and 1380-1383. During these visitations of the Jungfrau, the Angel of Death, there was utter chaos Medical knowledge was non-existent; fear and superstition abounded. The crises brought out the best and the worst elements in men and women. Crime increased. There were savage pogroms of the Jews, who were blamed for economic ills. The Black Death, however, also brought about the end of slavery in Europe, because the chronic shortage of manpower enabled the labourer to offer his services for wages. From our point of view the greatest change brought about by the Jungfrau was in the status of the Cellites or Alexians. The courage and selflessness of the Brothers gained them the esteem of civic and ecclesiastical authorities. Many towns invited the Brothers to establish cloisters, and granted them licences as burial guilds with exclusive rights for the preparation and burial of the dead. Of the fifty four Cellite houses that existed on the eve of the Reformation, the vast majority was founded after the Black Death. In 1472 the Holy See, in three bulls from Pope Sixtus IV, established the Cellites as a Religious Order under the patronage of St Augustine and St Alexius. Some Cellite houses were already affiliated to the Augustinian Order, whose Rule they adopted.

St Alexius (or Alexis), called 'the Man of God', gave his name to the new Order. An almost contemporary account says that there died in hospital in Edessa, Mesopotamia, c.430 a nameless man who had lived by begging, sharing the alms he received with other poor people. After his death it was discovered that he was the son of a Roman patrician, and that he had left behind a life of luxury to live in poverty in Syria. There are other later and more extravagant accounts of his life in Greek and Latin. The legend of St Alexius had wide-spread popularity in the later middle ages. In the eleventh century he was made the subject of a long epic poem. About 1350 he was chosen as patron saint of the nursing society of Cellites, who were from then onwards also known as the Alexian Brothers.

From their origins in the middle ages the Brothers, with their principal centres at Cologne, Aachen, Liege and Antwerp, catered for the 'outsiders,' vagabonds, lepers, plague victims. In many towns they became the official morticians and pallbearers. Besides caring for the terminally ill, the Alexian Brothers can be considered as pioneers of social visiting and home nursing; also they were leaders in the field of psychiatric nursing, establishing mental hospitals and experimenting with new therapies. The sharpness of perception into mental illness shown by early directives issued to Brothers caring for neurotic and psychotic patients shows remarkable insight and enlightenment at a time when such sick people were shunned and feared. The Alexian Brothers' ministry was always directed to serving Christ in the most lowly and despised of his human brothers. Persecution was no stranger to the Alexians, whether by Church authorities, the Bismark regime, or Hitler's Nazis. They have never sought publicity, and consequently are little known even by Catholics outside the communities where they work.

In April 1875 Bishop Vaughan of Salford wrote to the rector-general of the Alexian Brothers, Pater Clement Wallrath, requesting the establishment of an Alexian house in Manchester. The burial ministry of the Alexians was not the bishop's only concern. He writes: 'We have two needs. The greater and more urgent need would be the establishment of an asylum for the mentally ill, especially for the middle and lower classes. We have none of this type in the whole of England. Every effort that experienced Brothers would make to supply this lack, would certainly receive the approval of the Bishops of England. . . . . The other need is one of Religious, who by their presence, their Rule, their accomplishments and piety would further devotion for the dead and would arouse respect for the memory of the deceased. . . . . It means much to me to have the assistance of a Brotherhood to care properly for the services in the first Catholic cemetery in the large city of Manchester.'

The dynamic and far-sighted Bishop was dealing with a man of similar stature and vision in Pater Clement, who had worked with Pater Dominic Brock, Reformer and Founder of the modern Alexian Congregation, helping him to draw up the new constitution in 1856 (it was revised in 1870). Clement Wallrath sent the Brothers to the United States of America, establishing the first Alexian houses in Chicago, Ill. (1866) and St Louis, Mo. (1869). By acceding to Bishop Vaughan's request for Brothers Pater Clement ensured that Moston became only the third Alexian house ever to be founded outside the continent of Europe.

In June 1875 the first three Alexian Brothers arrived in Moston and were accommodated in the tumble-down Thorpe's farmhouse. The three Brothers were Peter Verheyen, the first rector, Cyrillus Kranepohl, and Gerhard Teubensel. Inured to austerity, the Brothers yet had to lead a very lonely existence. Whereas in the United States the Brothers had large communities of German Catholics to support them in making the transition from one culture to another; here in Moston they were isolated from their fellow Catholics. Moston was off the beaten track. The local people were doubly suspicious of the Alexian Brothers - because they were Catholic Religious and foreigners. A few words about two of these courageous men. Peter Verheyen had been novice master in Aachen; had served with other Alexians as a battlefield nurse during the Danish War (Prussia and Austria v Denmark); and for

three years (1871-1874) had been rector of the Alexian house in St Louis, Mo. Sadly this great Brother had to leave the Order sometime before September 1877. Shortly afterwards he died a tragic, lonely death. But, nothing can detract from his years of selfless service to God and the poor. Brother Cyrillus Kranepohl served as the second English provincial from 1885 until 1891, years of great difficulty and slow progress.

It was the Brothers' intention from the beginning to open a private hospital for the mentally sick. With this in view in late 1878 Brother Celestine Mohnen, Brother Peter's replacement, sought permission from the General Council to purchase the present house in St Mary's Road, Moston. Writing to Brother Pius Welter, the first provincial, he describes the house, which had been built in 1869 for Thomas Hill, a wealthy manufacturer: 'It is situated on an elevation, looks like a castle, surrounded by grounds and a vegetable garden. Moreover a fish pond and hot house are on the grounds . . . The house has twenty rooms and there is another house to the side of it which could serve for the isolation of the very sick. I venture to say dear Brother Provincial that if our Pater were here and saw this house, he would buy it at once.' Authorisation was received on 6th February 1879 to negotiate a suitable price for the property. Eventually, with Father Saffenrueter acting as agent, the house and property were purchased on 10th April 1879 for £1,630. Five Brothers, two newly arrived from Aachen, took up residence in the first Alexian Nursing Home in England. Known at first as Mariaheim (Mary's Home), later as St Mary's Home, the ownership was in the secular names of the five Brothers, since a foreign Religious Order could not own property in England.

The hardships and struggles of the Brothers to make ends meet - they relied primarily upon begging for funds - would occupy a book. Refused government permission to open a private mental hospital, the Brothers took in poor sick and elderly men. Brother Eusebius Klütermann (later to succeed Brother Cyrillus as provincial) struggled manfully to pay the bills for the fifty patients in residence by 1889. With the admission of the first English and Irish postulants a new chapter opened in the annals of the

The Alexian Brothers' Nursing Home, Moston

Moston community. A notable influence in the affairs of the English province was the sometime Rector at Moston Cemetery and St Mary's Home, Brother Camillus McGill. A force for modernisation, Brother Camillus kept St Mary's Home from closure and then built it up into a modern nursing institute.

Perhaps his greatest achievement was the establishment of Mount St Columb's Nursing Home between Warrenpoint and Rostrevor in Northern Ireland. Through this house, directed by another charismatic figure Brother Columcille McGuinness, a steady flow of Irish postulants would come into the English province, many serving in St Mary's Home, Moston. During the 1950s and 1960s St Mary's Nursing Home, along with other Alexian Houses, evolved from a hospice giving custodial care to a modern hospital unit. Many of the young Brothers had been studying nursing at York General Hospital since 1944. The presence of a good number of professional nurses within the Congregation enabled the Alexian Nursing Homes at Twyford Abbey, St Mary's, Moston, and Mount St Columb's, Warrenpoint, N.I., gradually to be absorbed into the National Health System.

Down through the years the Alexian Brothers have carried out district nursing in the Moston area. They have also done private nursing in the homes of patients. St Mary's Home at present houses eighty four patients. There are currently nine Brothers on the staff, all of whom play an active part in the running of the Nursing Home. Some of the Brothers are S.R.N. trained, some Psychiatric trained, one is a S.E.N, one is cook, one is in charge of the laundry. Untrained Brothers assist on the wards. Trained nurses and ancillary workers help to maintain a high standard of efficiency in the Home. All the Brothers were originally German. They are now English or Irish, though many studied in Germany. The fine old house purchased in 1879, enlarged and refurbished, is still in use. In 1964 a hospital section was built to care for thirty two National Health patients in two wards. Many of these patients are cared for to give their relatives a rest, as well as being admitted for terminal care. Twenty six patients are in Part 3 accommodation, that is they are maintained by various local authorities' social service departments. The remainder of the patients are paid for privately. There are two private wards. The rest of the private accommodation is in shared rooms (2 beds) or single rooms. St Mary's Nursing Home is registered with the Area Health Authority, and is open to inspection by the Authority biannually.

A special apostolate of the Alexian Brothers is the care of sick and retired priests. There are usually about six priests in residence. The Home has its own Catholic chaplain. Clergy of other denominations make regular pastoral visits to patients of their persuasions. An innovation is the Day Care Centre, which caters for ten patients daily. These are local men and women who are lonely in their homes. The Brothers' van provides transport for them. For forty two years Dr Peter J. Geraghty, a greatly loved and respected general practitioner in Moston, has served the Home as a skilled physician and most loyal friend of the Brothers. During most of its hundred and four years existence an average of seventeen Brothers has worked in the Home, until a dramatic expansion of the Alexian Order into Ghana, Nigeria and the Philippines, dictated a reduction in the number of Brothers in Moston. A brief catalogue of the Brothers' activities in eight countries makes impressive reading. They work in surgical hospitals, psychiatric hospitals, nursing homes, clinics, rest homes, hostels for drug addicts and alcoholics. Their Health Centres in Third World countries specialise in the treatment of tropical diseases, including leprosy. The Brothers run child welfare and outpatients' clinics, in addition to domiciliary visiting. The routine work of their Bush Clinics includes treating snake bites, scorpion stings, tropical ulcers, wounds and lacerations.

Although less spectacular, the work of the Brothers in St Mary's Home, Moston, has been characterised by the Alexian virtues of humble, unassuming devotion to the sick, and the observance of the Holy Rule with its vows of poverty, chastity and obedience. Of the many Brothers who have worked in Moston twenty five are buried in St Joseph's Cemetery, which was tended by the Brothers with loving care for some ninety years. I append a list of the Superiors of the Alexian Brothers' Home from its foundation as Mariaheim to the elegant and well equipped St Mary's of today. Through this list of the Superiors I wish to pay tribute to all the Brothers who have served in Moston during the past one hundred years. The Alexian Brothers have earned the admiration and affection of Catholics and Protestants alike. St Mary's Nursing Home is an important part of the Manchester area hospital system. Much has been achieved against great odds by men dedicated to the ideals of the Gospel. The Brothers down the years worked at their tasks with quiet, self-effacing persistence; their vocation was to serve those sick in mind or body: to God belonged the glory.

Superiors of the Alexian Brothers' Nursing Home, Moston

1879-1882 Celestine Mohnen;
1882-1886 Bonaventure Thelen;
1886-1888 Cyrillus Kranepohl;
1888-1894 Eusebius Klütermann;
1894-1901 Gerhard Teubensel;
1901-1904 Thaddaus Otten;
1904-1910 Anthony Marcelle;
1910-1919 Camillus McGill;
1919-1920 Edward Sanders;
1920-1925 Willibald Morbach;
1925-1927 Vincent Brewer;
1927-1931 Gilbert Holmes;
1931-1933 Camillus McGill;
1933-1936 Benignus Kennedy;
1936-1937 Basil McVeigh;
1937-1943 Celestine Diggins;
1943-1949 Benignus Kennedy;
1949-1951 Cormac O'Reilly;
1951-1952 Ambrose Coyne;
1952-1954 Cormac O'Reilly;
1954-1955 Maurus O'Sullivan;
1955-1960 Joachim O'Riordan;
1960-1963 Edmund Kelly;
1963-1967 Dominic Walsh;
1967-1973 Anthony Ferri;
1973-1982 Montfort Eames;
1982-   Gerald Fitzgerald.

14

The Anglican Church in Moston

Moston was from time immemorial a part of the ancient parish of Manchester, the northern boundary of the township being coterminous with the common boundary of that parish and the old parishes of Prestwich and Oldham. In the graveyard of the Manchester Collegiate Church there was a section called 'Moston Hill.' Various members of the Moston gentry had pews in the Collegiate Church (later the Cathedral), and were eventually buried in its vaults. The hamlet of Moston paid tithes to the parish church of Manchester. In 1565 and 1590 there were disputes in the Duchy of Lancaster Court concerning the tithes of Moston and Blackley. When the chapel of All Saints, Newton, was rebuilt in 1814 the cost of the rebuilding was met by a rate levied by the churchwardens on all the rateable property in Newton, Failsworth, Moston and Droylsden. Moston had the right of electing one of its inhabitants every third year as a warden of Newton chapel. The linking of the tithes of Moston and Blackley in the sixteenth century seems to indicate that part of the township belonged to St Peter's, Blackley.

When Christ Church, Harpurhey, was built in 1838 it was intended to serve an ecclesiastical district comprising Harpurhey, Moston, and part of Collyhurst. In 1844 a Church of England school was built on the high ground of Moston, near the boundary with Nuthurst. The cost of the school, £285, was borne jointly by the National Society and the Committee of Council. The site, including a small field adjoining, was given by Samuel Taylor esquire. The building was used as Sunday and Day school. By 1853 there were sixty Sunday scholars and forty five Day scholars on roll. Another Church Sunday and Day school was opened in 1844 in an old barn behind Lightbowne Hall. John Ward says this Sunday school was in a cottage on Kenyon Lane, and the Church of England gave relief in kind to the poor people, who made application. (Ward, Moston Characters at Work, p. 104).

On 6th October 1869 St Mary's church, Moston, was consecrated by James Prince-Lee, first Bishop of Manchester. Built alongside the school on land donated by Samuel Taylor, St Mary's was the last and certainly not the most imposing church to be consecrated by Bishop Prince-Lee in his distinguished period of office. But, the importance of the new church for the people of Moston cannot be overstated. It is the Mother church of Anglicans in Moston. While the church was being built the first Rector, Revd John Goodwin, held services in the little parish school. The second Rector of St Mary's, Revd Thomas Wolstencroft, established the first St Mary's rectory in Lightbowne Hall. Little is known of these pioneering Anglican priests. It was the third Rector of Moston, the far-sighted and energetic Revd John Appleyard, who initiated the missionary enterprises that would lead to the establishment of three daughter churches.

Soon after taking up office in May 1899 Rector Appleyard turned his attention to the Lightbowne area of his parish. The expansion of the Lancashire and Yorkshire Railway Carriage Works in nearby Newton Heath, together with the annexation of Moston by the City of Manchester in 1890, brought about a large increase in the population of this locality. The Rector began to hold services in the old barn behind Lightbowne Hall, and assumed control of the Sunday school. His insistence on conformity to the Prayer Book and Catechism in the Sunday school and his High Church manner of conducting worship alienated some evangelical members of the congregation. After remonstrating with the Rector a group of erstwhile parishioners of St Mary's left the barn to form the Lightbowne Evangelical Church, independent of the Church of England.

Rector Appleyard had an iron building erected near the Lightbowne Hall rectory. This was opened in December 1900 as St Luke's mission church. The congregation continued to grow, notwithstanding the secession of the evangelicals. During the ten years that Revd John Appleyard was Rector of Moston he was ably assisted by other priests and stipendiary lay readers. Two more mission churches were founded - St Michael's at Streetfold in 1904 (on the site now occupied by St Dunstan's church) and St Chad's, New Moston, in 1907. A member of the congregation, recalling these years, has written: 'There were three missions and the parish church, and we were encouraged to help each other; and with the Rector to lead us spiritually and socially we did. Spiritually there were the Communicants' Guild, Quiet Afternoons, Missionary Meetings and regular meetings at each church in turn. Socially there was something for everybody, a Women's Guild, Churchmen's Society, Church Lads' Brigade, Girls' Guild, Musical Society and Amateur Dramatics. We had talented singers among us, also good entertainers. And, when needed, there were men willing to undertake repairs.'

The congregation at St Luke's was soon the largest of the four in the parish of Moston. It was necessary to provide a permanent church. A Building Committee was appointed by the Rector, and Mr E. Lingen Barker was engaged as architect. The new church was to be cruciform in shape, with aisles and shallow transepts off the nave, a side chapel and organ chamber on either side of the chancel, a baptistry at the west end separated from the nave by an arcade of three arches, and a tower and spire at the northwest corner over the main entrance. In the event the tower and spire were never built, owing to lack of money. From 1906 to 1910 everybody was involved in working for the new church and the mission at New Moston. There were many schemes for raising money, and each section of the congregation had a special part to play. Even when the tower and spire were omitted, and a grant of £2,500 had been received from the Bishop's new churches fund, there was great difficulty in raising the remaining £1,218.

There were no wealthy people in the area. The population was almost entirely working class, the majority being employed by the Lancashire and Yorkshire Railway Company. In May 1908 the Building Committee decided that the barn in which St Luke's had originated should be demolished and 'that labourers at $5^1/2$d an hour be employed, with working foremen at 6d.' It will be remembered that the old barn had served for years as Day as well as Sunday school. A former parishioner of St Luke's, now in his eighty eighth year, recalls attending the Day school in the barn. It was an all-age school. The pupils paid a penny or twopence a week for tuition. St Luke's Day school was closed about 1902, when the scholars transferred to a small corrugated iron school on Jackson Street (now Joyce Street) near the junction with Dean Lane. This little school closed when Lily Lane school opened in 1904. The children went in procession to Lily Lane for the ceremonial opening.

In November 1908 the foundation stone of St Luke's church was laid. The building was ready for inspection in July 1910, the same month in which John Appleyard left Moston to become Rector of St John's, Cheetham. Various groups made presentations to the new church. The Communicants of the four churches in the parish of Moston gave a silver chalice and paten. The younger children gave the font costing £11; while the older children gave the oak pulpit. The screen between the Lady chapel and the chancel was made by some of the men. A brass cross had been bought by the Girls' Guild in 1904. It was this cross which became a sign of contradiction in the troubled times to come. The Revd Harry Ogden writes: 'Like the Ark of the Covenant, this brass cross shared the wanderings of the congregation - it was used in the iron mission church for six years, for a brief period it was on the altar of the new church, for fourteen years it went into exile with most of the congregation, and returned home with them in 1924. It was stolen from the church in 1970.'

As soon as St Luke's church was completed the diocesan authorities decided to create a new parish of Lightbowne. This decision prompted the leaders of the Lightbowne Evangelical Church to approach the Bishop of Manchester, Dr Knox. They promised to return to the Church of England on condition that a Low Church clergyman was appointed first Rector of St Luke's. The Bishop was in agreement with the suggestion; and accordingly the Revd R. Clews was appointed Rector. A foretaste of things to come was given on All Saints' Day 1910, the day of the consecration of the new church. Bishop Knox removed the brass cross from the altar. After the consecration somebody replaced the cross on the altar. The Revd Clews removed it. But it was soon back again, affixed to the altar with strong glue. This time the Rector used a crowbar to remove the cross. This was the signal for disruption of the services in St Luke's, with young devotees of the High Church party waving small wooden crosses at the Rector as he preached, and the Rector making forays into the congregation to snatch at the crosses. Orangemen were imported from Collyhurst to lend moral support to the Rector. A pamphlet, signed 'A Resident of Lightbowne', was distributed to non-churchgoers in the parish. Its language was emotive:

'During the last five months a section of the congregation which previously attended the Mission Church, where extreme Ritualism was taught and disseminated, have tried their utmost to make it impossible for others to worship in the new church in peace and quietness, unless the Rector adopted the mummery of Ritualism. These Ritualists tell us that the glorious Reformation, which gave us liberty of religious thought, is the black spot in the history of England. They say that the Reformation, for which the martyrs Cranmer, Ridley and Latimer were burnt at the stake,

St Mary's Church, Moston

was a curse, a sham, and a fraud. If you believe that Protestantism, for which our ancestors fought and bled, has the making of the salvation of England, then rally round us and vote for the names below as People's Warden and Sidesmen.' On 1st June 1911 the Building Committee of St Luke's, composed of 'Ritualists', was asked by Bishop Knox to 'give some pledge for the good conduct of the services, so that the same may be restored to law and order.' The Building Committee refused to accept responsibility for the disruption of worship.

The High Church party was shocked at the disgraceful scenes in church. Its adherents decided to leave St Luke's and continue as a separate congregation within the Church of England. They rented an upstairs room of Wild's Works (on the site of the present Dean Mount Garage). Here for three years they conducted Prayer Book services and a flourishing Sunday school. Shortly afterwards the members of the Lightbowne Evangelical Church withdrew from St Luke's, and continued as a separate church, while claiming to belong to the Church of England.

The 'Ritualists', worshipping in Wild's Works, had a few influential friends in the diocese, who wished to regularise their position in the Church of England. With the encouragement and assistance of Canon Peter Green and others an accommodation was reached. A mission church was erected on Kenyon Lane, a quarter of a mile from St Luke's, but just within the boundary of St John's parish. The foundation stone was laid by Canon Peter Green. On 28th February 1915 the church was dedicated as St Elizabeth's in the presence of four hundred people. During the next nine years St Elizabeth's flourished. The congregation had no priest of its own. There was a monthly Eucharist. On other Sundays members went to St John's for Holy Communion. Lay readers conducted Mattins and Evensong each Sunday. During the period 1915 to 1923 Easter Communicants at St Elizabeth's grew from eighty five to a hundred and sixteen; while down the Lane at St Luke's they dropped from eighty six to twenty two. 1924, however, was to see a healing of the breach.

The appointment of a High Church Rector of St Luke's and the restoration of the full liturgy convinced the exiles at St Elizabeth's that it was time to return home. On 3rd February the last Sunday services were held at St Elizabeth's. The following Sunday in St Luke's church the two congregations became one. Many improvements were made in the church building. The altar from St Elizabeth's was placed in the south transept, and on it stood the once controversial brass cross. The new Rector, the Revd William Gower-Jones, was also on occasion choirmaster. At one time St Luke's had a mixed choir of sixty two members with an extensive repertoire of religious music.

St Elizabeth's was sold and became the Liberal Club. A new parish hall was built behind the church and rectory. This became the centre for church organisations, including several flourishing football and cricket teams. The dance floor was said to be the best in north Manchester; and it was well used. Fr Gower-Jones left St Luke's in 1931, being succeeded by Fr Hubert Hiller, another Anglo-Catholic. Fr Hiller built upon the traditions of St Luke's, celebrating the full liturgy of the Anglican Church, maintaining the high standard of choral music, and further embellishing the church. With the departure of Fr Hiller in 1936 the Revd J. Duffill became fourth Rector. He was a Low Churchman and did not waste time in eliminating (his own word) Catholic practices. During his two years as Rector congregations dwindled alarmingly.

In 1938 the patrons appointed Fr F. H. Petherham, Precentor of the Cathedral, Rector of St Luke's. At the annual meeting in 1939 Mr Raw, the secretary, reported that 'A marked improvement has taken place in the life of the church, deep spiritual teaching is being given, and all Saints' days are again recognised, with the Eucharist as the chief service of the day.' The outbreak of World War Two disrupted church life. Children were evacuated; men and women joined the forces or were directed to war work. The church railings were taken to help the war effort. The parochial hall was requisitioned for use by a barrage balloon company; and the old iron mission became a Home Guard post. Fr Kenneth Gates, who succeeded Fr Petherham in 1942, maintained the High Church tradition. The Rector kept in touch with members of the congregation on war service, and published news of them regularly in the magazine.

After the war renovations and improvements were carried out in the church. Fr Eric Weir was Rector from 1952 until 1956. He introduced Midnight Mass at Christmas, the Veneration of the Cross on Good Friday, and the use of the Paschal Candle at Eastertide. As a result of his work among the children, one has become a nun, and another a priest. The next Rector, the Revd W. A. Wood, although partially blind, carried out the duties of parish priest energetically between 1956 and 1961. In December 1961 Fr Harry Ogden became Rector. Fr Ogden will be remembered by many parishioners with gratitude and affection. He introduced perpetual reservation of the Blessed Sacrament, and made the liturgy of Holy Week the focal point of the church's year. The whole interior of the church was cleaned and new furnishings were acquired.

A new rectory was built in 1963 to replace the old Lightbowne Hall, which had to be demolished. In 1968 volunteers renovated the parish hall. A licensed bar and lounge with games room were introduced at one end. St Luke's licensed club was a rarity in the Church of England at that time. It has proved to be a great asset to the church, socially, financially and pastorally. This account of St Luke's parish is largely based on Fr Ogden's 'History of St Luke, Lightbowne.' The Anglo-Catholic tradition of St Luke's has been continued and enhanced by Fr Alan Park, Rector from 1969 until 1982, and the present Rector, Fr Arthur Lewis. In October 1970 the sixtieth anniversary of the consecration of the church was observed by a fortnight of special services and social functions. Work was then begun on an extensive reconstruction of the interior of the parish hall and men's club, which together form one of the best social centres in the Moston area.

The parish of St Mary, Moston, in the early years of this century was mainly rural. Even between the most populated areas of Lightbowne and Streetfold there were large open spaces; while west of Streetfold meadows and cornfields reached out to the Clough; and fields - with the occasional farmhouse, duckpond, or cluster of cottages - spread northwest to White Moss, and northeast to the parish church, St Mary's Road and the pit. From this point a rough track known as Coalpit Lane, formerly a private colliery road, led through the pit and more fields to the hamlet of New Moston. We now turn our attention to this easterly corner of the parish, bounded by Chadderton and Failsworth.

The freehold estate laid out by Elijah Dixon and his friends of the Bridgewater Land Company in the 1850s had not spread far. Its links were with Failsworth rather than Manchester. Housing development was slow but steady (some 125 houses in 1900 increasing to 250 in 1912), thus enabling the assimilation of newcomers and the preservation of a homely, village atmosphere. Despite its proximity to the busy township of Failsworth, New Moston remained a somewhat isolated community. The Rochdale Canal and the valley of Moston Brook (the old Morris Clough) contained the small pocket of population, ensuring its separate identity, and preventing any encroachment from Failsworth. The Canal provided a few jobs; but the textile mills of Failsworth provided most of the employment. The slump in the cotton trade in the 1890s meant hardship for most people. But, the impact of the slump on the New Moston community was cushioned to a certain extent by the opening of the Ferranti factory in Hollinwood in 1897. Many New Mostonians joined the workforce of seven hundred, employed in the manufacture of generating plant, transformers, switchgear and meters.

In 1881 the Primitive Methodists opened their chapel in Jones Street (now Eastwood Road). In 1895 the Failsworth Co-operative Society department store in Eastwood Road was opened. Over the store, which catered for most of the needs of the community, were upstairs rooms for meetings and socials. Then, in 1901 came the New Moston Board School on Moston Lane (East). A largely self-sufficient New Moston community had emerged. In one respect, however, New Moston was sadly lacking. The Anglicans had a long walk to church at St Mary's along Coalpit Lane, an unpaved road rutted by the iron wheels of colliery carts and virtually impassable in wet weather. Church of England parents were understandably worried about their children having to walk to Sunday school along this lonely and sometimes dangerous road. In 1905 the problem was aired in the correspondence columns of the Manchester Evening Chronicle. Several meetings were held to rally support for a Church of England place of worship in New Moston. As a result, a piece of land was rented on Moston Lane opposite Eastwood Road, with a view to erecting such a building.

In 1907 a group of men met the Rector, Revd John Appleyard, at Vine House, the home of Mr W. W. Ingham, to discuss the possibility of forming a Sunday school or mission church. A circular, describing the project and appealing for funds, was delivered to all the residents of New Moston. The cost of a temporary building was £400. Men and women went from house to house, asking for one shilling per week to build the 'Tin Tabernacle.' By the end of 1907 £107 6s. 6d. had been raised in this manner. The following year, by means of socials, concerts and the first Old English cricket match, the sum of £80 was added to the fund. An interest-free loan was obtained; and the land previously rented was purchased from Lancashire's farm. On 23rd November the Bishop of Manchester, Dr Knox, dedicated St Chad's

mission church.

In the early days services were conducted by Mr Clegg, a lay reader. After a while the services were taken by the Revd W. Williams and Mr Howard of St Michael's, Streetfold. The church building was also the social centre; and after the Saturday night social everybody lent a hand in the task of preparing the church for Holy Communion, held at 8.00 a.m. on Sunday. There was a beautiful little chancel behind the partition and a harmonium for the services. A piano, when needed, was borrowed from a member of the church, who lived on the opposite side of Moston Lane. The church was lit by gas, and heated by a coke stove in the centre. There was a small kitchen, so small that the gas boiler used to boil water for social events was outside the church. In 1911 Dr A. C. Keene was inducted as fourth Rector of Moston, and the Revd W. Williams was appointed to a living outside Manchester. Mr J. J. Robinson, a lay reader, was appointed to take the services. He was later ordained and became the first curate at St Chad's.

Due to the growth in membership of the church and Sunday school, it was necessary to build a wing onto the church. This wing, clergy vestry and choir robing room, was built in 1910. A further extension was added in 1919. Known as the Institute, this room was used for Sunday school and as a clubroom for the older members of the church. During World War One all funds raised were diverted from the building fund to the Red Cross. After the war a great effort was made for the building fund, and the enormous sum of £2,000 was raised as a war memorial. In 1921 Dr Keene left Moston for health reasons. He was succeeded in July of that year by the Revd J. E. Wareham. Rector Wareham would remain at St Mary's for nearly thirty years. In 1923 the Revd J. J. Robinson, who had served St Chad's as lay reader and curate, was inducted as vicar of All Saints, Farnworth. He was succeeded as curate at St Chad's by the Revd W. P. Bullock. A primary Sunday school was started in 1924. Seating accommodation was inadequate, and structural alterations were made to the west end of the chapel to accommodate the growing congregation. A kitchen was also installed. In 1927 the original gas lamps were replaced by electric lighting at a cost of £60.

At last in early 1931 the foundation stone of the new St Chad's church was laid by the Bishop of Manchester, Dr G. Warman. The church was consecrated on 11th July 1931. Actually, only two thirds of the present church had been completed in time for the consecration. A false back wall was put in to allow for the remaining third portion to be added. This last stage of the building was completed in 1933. On 17th December 1931, by order of the King in Council, St Chad's became a legally constituted parish. The first Rector, the Revd W. Poyser Bullock, was inducted in February 1932. He was to hold this office until his death in 1955. In September of that year the Revd H. P. W. Day was inducted as second Rector. By this time the parish had grown enormously. Prior to the First World War New Moston was very compact. Although from 1890 a part of Manchester, it was in fact an overspill from Failsworth. It was easier to take a tramcar or train from Failsworth to Manchester than to walk the mile or so along the Lane to Moston Station at Broad Lane Bridge. Between the village of New Moston and the Lancashire and Yorkshire railway line, lay the Failsworth Golf

St Mary's School: Scholars at drill 1906

Course, which boasted the longest hole in Manchester. A resident of New Moston writes: 'The tee was behind Moston Station and the hole alongside the old school (New Moston Board School), and at 600 yards plus ranked as a par 6. Part of the course was in Newton Heath, most of it was in New Moston, and none of it was in Failsworth.'

During the formative years of the mission traditions were established, which would flourish for many years, in some instances up until the present. A great annual social occasion, and important fund-raising event, was the annual Old English cricket match, played on Schofield's field. Together with the cricket match, in which for many years the Rector was a participant, there were gala stalls, concert parties, Rose Queen procession, and many more enjoyable activities. Money for the church building fund was also raised by two-day sales of work. A strong social life was always a feature of St Chad's parish. An Operatic and Dramatic Society, formed in the early years by Mr W. Smith, led a healthy existence until well after World War II. The Brownie Pack, started in 1924, has had an unbroken continuity to date. The Scouts were in existence long before that, but the troop had to be disbanded during the Second World War. The Whitsun procession of witness is a zealously maintained feature of parish life.

St Chad's mission church owed its existence to the men and women who cared deeply about their children's religious upbringing and wanted a Sunday school in New Moston. That concern for the spiritual wellbeing of the young has been the first priority in St Chad's parish throughout its history. In 1955 there were five hundred children in the Sunday school, one hundred and ninety six

of them on the Primary register. Something had to be done if all these children were to be accommodated in comfort. In June 1957 a new church hall was built alongside the mission church (known as the old school). In 1962 the Revd H. P. W. Day left St Chad's, and was succeeded as Rector by the Revd D. A. Willoughby. A memorable event took place in 1971 when the new Sunday school and Parish Centre was built on the site of the mission church.

The old church had been built in 1908 with a guaranteed life of fifteen years. It had stood proudly for sixty three years. On 23rd February the new building was opened by the Bishop of Manchester, the Rt Revd Patrick Campbell Roger. In 1972 the Revd J. D. Hayward replaced the Revd D. A. Willoughby as Rector. Revd Hayward stayed until 1977, when the present Rector, the Revd Gordon G. Roxby, took over the care of St Chad's. In 1981 special celebrations took place to mark the fiftieth anniversary of the parish. A short history of the church and parish was written by a lifelong member, Edith Buxton. I have relied heavily upon her work for this account. Eleven members of St Chad's church and Sunday school have been ordained to the sacred ministry of the Church. They are: the Revd Kenneth P. Bullock; the Revd Harold Weston Buxton; the Revd Douglas Fletcher; the Revd Donald Gray; the Revd John F. Hearder; the Revd Lawrence Wraith; the Revd Norman Peet; the Revd John Eckersley Smith; the Revd William Smith; the Revd Geoffrey White; the Revd Duncan Whitworth.

The histories of St Luke's mission and St Chad's mission are integral parts of the history of the mother church. Situated in the central area of Moston, facing the

St John's Church, Ashley Lane

fields, with the colliery at its back, St Mary's witnessed many changes in the Moston scene. The opening of Johnson's Wireworks in 1910 led to the extending of St Mary's Road and a growth of population in the vicinity. The parish, however, remained a rural one until the Lightbowne estate was built in the 1920s. The rectory had been Lightbowne Hall. After St Luke's became a parish a new rectory was built in the fields opposite the church. This is now the North Manchester Music Centre. The fifth Rector of St Mary's, the Revd J. E. Wareham (1921-1950), saw the establishment of St Chad's parish in 1931. In 1951 after his retirement a bell and plaque were bought in his memory.

On Sunday, 5th October 1969, the Bishop of Manchester, Dr W. D. L. Greer, conducted a special service to celebrate the church's centenary. By then the parish had been built up considerably. The opening of the Ferranti Radio Works in the former Johnson's Wireworks led to a diminution in the population of St Mary's Road. Houses were demolished in 1935 to make way for the first extension on the Newton Heath side of the existing factory. In 1936 some of the old Welsh Square houses were pulled down. A large air raid shelter complex was built on the site at the outbreak of the Second World War. It is now the main car park. In 1919 Sir Edward Tootal Broadhurst gave land to Manchester Corporation for playing fields and a small park. The Corporation entered into a covenant with Sir Edward not to build houses on this land (the present Broadhurst Fields and Broadhurst Park). In fact, an estate of prefab houses (Yardley Avenue, Thornham Crescent) stood on Lightbowne Road, opposite St Joseph's cemetery, from 1946 until

1967. The transformation of St Mary's parish from rural to suburban began with the construction of the new Lightbowne Road in 1922.

The Housing Act of 1919 had given Manchester City Council limited power to build houses to let. A second Act of 1923 extended this power. But it was the third Housing Act of 1924 that was to change the face of Moston and New Moston. Under this Act 1,226 houses were built between Moston Lane and Nuthurst Road, many of them in St Mary's parish. Between 1960 and 1964 the National Coal Board built the Miners' Estate on the site of Moston pit. In April 1966 building commenced on the Mill Estate with the first four houses on Blandford Drive. The transformation of the parish was completed by the Poco Estate on the old Failsworth Golf Course, begun in the early 1970s. On the occasion of the church centenary (1969) the Rector of the daughter church of St Luke, Lightbowne, presented to St Mary's a horse-mounting stone, a relic of Lightbowne Hall. The Hall had served as rectory for St Mary's and then St Luke's. In 1971 St Mary's primary school was built on St Mary's Road. It replaced the old school, built in 1844 and demolished after the opening of the new school. The new rectory was built in 1972 on the site of the old school. The present Rector is the Revd John Low.

When Christ Church, Harpurhey, was opened in 1838 it was intended to serve Harpurhey, Moston and part of Collyhurst. In the last quarter of the nineteenth century the area about Ashley Lane (formerly Brass Knob Street) began to be built up. The pace of development was stepped up in 1890 when Moston became a suburb of Manchester. There was great need of an Anglican church for the numerous members of the Church of England in this the most densely populated part of Moston. Eventually the diocesan authorities recognised this need. On 24th March 1909 the beautiful church of St John, Ashley Lane, was consecrated by the Bishop of Manchester, Dr E. A. Knox. A fine rectory was built at the same time. Almost the entire cost of these buildings was defrayed by a generous benefactor, Mr John Railton. The architect was R. Bassnett Preston. From time to time valuable gifts were made to the church. With a grant from the Carnegie Trust a fine organ was installed.

From the beginning a small corrugated iron hut served as a Sunday school. It was very inadequate; so a fund was started to build a permanent Sunday school. The First World War delayed progress in this direction. In 1923 a great effort was made to raise money, resulting in the bazaar of 1924 which realised £769. A penny to shilling per week scheme brought in about £300 in one year. Substantial outside help was also given. At last in 1927 the Bishop of Manchester, Dr W. Temple, laid the foundation stone and opened the new Sunday school. It was worth waiting and working for. A brick building in keeping with the church, it contained a large hall, classrooms and kitchen. Upstairs was a clubroom for the men of the parish, which was always well supported.

The total cost of the school was £7,112, of which £3,278 had been raised before the building was erected. A great bazaar was held in October 1928, which yielded £1,000. In addition to Sunday school classes, every kind of social event was held in the hall: pantomimes, concerts, dances (there was an excellent dance floor), whist drives, sales of work, meetings of the various parish societies. The

Whitsun procession of witness around the parish boundary was a feature of church life throughout the years. To date there have been eight Rectors: the Revd W. Holden, who was also Rural Dean; the Revd A. L. Robinson, who served the parish for twenty three years; the Revd C. H. G. Davey; the Revd E. D. Ratledge; the Revd A. W. R. Hughes; the Revd J. McDonald; the Revd D. Yates; the Revd R. Evans. On Sunday, 22nd July 1917, in the presence of over five hundred scouts, parishioners and friends, a memorial service was held for Norman Victor Holden, the Rector's eldest son, who had been killed on active service. A memorial tablet in the chancel was unveiled by Mr J. L. Paton, High Master of Manchester Grammar School, and Mr Allen, Scoutmaster of the 31st Manchester Troop. It reads as follows:

In affectionate remembrance of
Lieut. Norman Victor Holden, B.A., Cantab,
(Eldest son of the Rev. W. Holden, M.A., Cantab,
First Rector of this parish and Rural Dean of Cheetham),
Who died of wounds on the Gallipoli Peninsula.
4th June 1915,
Age 25,
And is buried in the Military Cemetery at Cape Helles.
He was for some years Hon. Organising Secretary of the
Boy Scouts' Association for Manchester and District, and
also an Assistant Master at the Manchester Grammar
School.
Faithful unto Death.
This Tablet was given by the Officers and Scouts of
North Central Division and Friends.

St Luke's Church, Lightbowne

St Chad's Church, New Moston

From 1915 until 1924 St John's had St Elizabeth's mission church, Kenyon Lane, within the parish. We have dealt with St Elizabeth's in connection with St Luke's, Lightbowne. At present St John's is awaiting a replacement for the Revd R. Evans, who has just left to take up a new appointment. The Ashley Lane district has seen much housing clearance and population movement in recent years. There is now a licensed club in the upper storey of the Sunday school building. It helps to defray the running expenses of the church and to promote the social life of the parish.

The Lightbowne Evangelical Church, Kenyon Lane, was formed in the early years of this century by former members of St Luke's, Lightbowne, as a reaction to the High Church practices in the then mission church. After St Luke's became a parish church in 1910 the evangelicals returned to the fold. Later, however, they left to resume worship in their own chapel. Mr Hayward was president for a number of years. Many Mostonians attended service in the 'Evan', as it was commonly called. There was a flourishing youth section; Sunday schools; Boys' and Girls' Brigades, the latter having its own fife and drum band. The members of the Lightbowne Evangelical Church follow the Protestant tradition of the Anglican Church, but do not accept its episcopal structure. The Church's method of government owes more to the Free Church tradition than that of the Church of England. Only in recent years has there been a paid minister to conduct services. The Revd Arthur Fryer was minister at Kenyon Lane for five years until his departure for Teddington in July 1980. Then there was a gap of almost three years until the induction of the present minister, the Revd Tom Cooper, in June 1983.

15

Industry in Moston

The factories of Moston, with three exceptions, were located near the perimeter of the township. In an earlier section we surveyed the first three industrial concerns: the wadding mill, built in 1714 near the border with Harpurhey; the first Moston Mill, built before 1820; and the Dean Brook Dyeworks, dating back before 1848; the last two impinging upon Newton Heath. In 1884 Moston Malleable Castings' factory, previously mentioned in connection with the Doughty family, was built close to Newton Heath; while Chain Bar Mill, now a component of the Harbour Lane Group, using the most advanced machinery for knitting and weaving all types of cleaning cloths, began its hundred years' existence as a cottage industry on its present site near Chadderton. The three exceptions to the rule of peripheral industry were Johnson's Wireworks, whose factory was subsequently acquired and extended by Ferranti's; the Moston Brick and Building Company; and the recently closed Moston Mill, now used as an electrical warehouse.

In the main, however, Moston has depended upon industries outside its boundaries: Levenstein's Chemical Works (later absorbed into I.C.I., Blackley); C.W.S. Biscuit Works, Lower Crumpsall; Small and Parkes Ltd (now Don International), Lower Crumpsall; Mather and Platt Ltd, Newton Heath; British Rail (first as the Lancashire & Yorkshire Railway; later as the L.M.S.), Newton Heath; Ferranti's, Hollinwood; A. V. Roe (later Hawker Siddeley Aviation; now British Aerospace), Chadderton. With the introduction on 7th March 1904 of a tram service between Lightbowne Dean Lane and Thorp Road Oldham Road, local people were able to travel into Oldham or Manchester to work. The through service by tram from Lightbowne to Piccadilly, commenced on 2nd October 1905, unquestionably brought about an increase in the population of Moston.

Nevertheless, the opening of the wireworks of Johnson, Clapham and Morris about 1910 must be regarded as a historical landmark. For the first time there were jobs for men and women within easy walking distance. Even though the factory was in the somewhat isolated district of St Mary's Road and employed many Newton Heath people, it was accessible through Jackson Street (Joyce Street) or across the fields from the built-up part of Moston. Nearly two hundred men and women were employed in all kinds of wire drawing. Among the wide variety of products were fireguards, machine guards, window guards, all kinds of baskets, pea covers, spark arresters for locomotives travelling through North American forests, elements for miners' lamps. The founder of the company, Sir Richard Lindsay Johnson, had a playing field laid out on the opposite side of St Mary's Road. Football and cricket are still played on Johnson's field. The recession of the early thirties, together with stiff competition from firms with more up-to-date plant, brought about the closure of Johnson's Wireworks in 1933. In December 1934 the entire freehold works were purchased by Ferranti Ltd of Hollinwood.

Born in Liverpool in 1864, Sebastian Ziani de Ferranti formed the company which bears his name in London in 1882. His object was to manufacture the alternator invented independently by himself and Sir William Thomson. Subsequently he designed and built the world's first high voltage alternating current power station at Deptford. This interest in electrical generation and supply soon led to the manufacture of alternators, meters, transformers, fuzes and switchgear. In 1897 the company moved to Hollinwood, which is still the headquarters. Dr Ferranti is generally acknowledged to have been the most inventive electrical engineer of his time. The company became interested in radio when the founder applied his experience of transformer design to improving the low frequency inter-valve transformer of early valve receiving sets. By 1924 a wide range of radio components was in production. In October 1934 a Board decision was taken to expand the radio side of the business, then at Stalybridge. A month later Ferranti Ltd purchased from Richard Johnson, Clapham and Morris for the sum of £14,500 a freehold factory in Moston, area 30,250 square yards or thereabouts

The new Radio Works, Moston, was officially opened on Wednesday, 29th May, 1935. Before the opening a new extension had been built on the Newton Heath side. £1,000 was spent on a coal siding. In June 1936 a fire, which probably started among the radio components, completely destroyed a timber section of the factory facing onto the railway. This was promptly rebuilt in brick. Ferranti was one of the first manufacturers of T.V. sets. On 26th August 1936 the first television broadcast was made from Alexandra Palace. At the time there were only two hundred T.V. sets in the country, most of them within twenty miles of the transmitter. Between the first regular broadcast on 2nd November 1936 and the final television transmission on 1st September 1939 the number of T.V. sets had grown to 20,000, many of them manufactured by Ferranti, Moston.

In January 1937 work commenced on an extension for fuze production. This extension, 85,185 square feet in area, was completed by the end of 1937. Production began in February 1938. At this time products manufactured in Moston included radio, T.V., fuzes, Military Defence equipment, Instruments, Gyroscopes, Telecommunications equipment, Amusement machines. In June 1943 the Admiralty Signals Establishment extension was completed. The need for this building arose out of the company's involvement in the production of munitions, which brought it into new fields: radar, cathode-ray tubes, fire-control equipment, and navigational aids.

In 1951 an epoch-making event took place in Ferranti's Moston factory. In July of that year at Manchester University the Ferranti Mark I Digital Computer was inaugurated. With the Mark I, made in Moston, Ferranti became the first company in the world to introduce a digital computer to the commercial market. In a true sense the computer age can be said to have started in Moston. Ferranti was moving away from radio and T.V. Eventually, these interests were sold to Ecko, which continued to manufacture radiograms and T.V. sets under the Ferranti name into the late 1950s. At Moston the emphasis was shifting to instrumentation for civil and military use. On 30th August 1977 a new factory was sited in the old Belfast Roof area. This houses the production facility for the Weapons Equipment Department. The workforce at Moston was at one time about nine hundred. With increased automation it dipped to below four hundred. Recent contracts with British Telecom for computers will mean two hundred and fifty new jobs in Moston.

The former Radio Works is now Ferranti Instrumentation. It is an important part of the Ferranti company, which employs 18,000 people in more than forty factories in the U.K., and has subsidiary companies in the U.S.A., West Germany, Belgium, Australia and Ireland. The following products are made by Ferranti Instrumentation, Moston: Clip-on instruments, Ammeters, Volt ammeter, Wattmeters, Closed circuit television systems, Cameras, Camera control and switching units, Environmental housing, Monitors, Motion detectors, Pan and tilt heads, Time and date generators, Video recorders, Current transformers, Disturbance recorders, Electronic summators, Energy management systems, Maximum demand alarm relays, Maximum demand monitors, Automatic load controllers, Meter test sets, Three-phase meter test sets, Single-phase desk-type meter test sets, Single-phase Type R meter test sets, Microprocessor applications, Plastic mouldings, Post Office subscriber call charge meter, Summation metering, Precision and commercial grade Polyphase meters, Impulse operated meters, PULSVA electronic kVA meter, Electronic summators, Electronic printometer, Metering information data acquisition systems, Transmitting meters, transducers, Viscometers, Ferranti-Shirley cone and plate viscometers, Portable co-axial cylinder viscometer. I am indebted to the staff of Ferranti Archives, Hollinwood, for most of this information. Some other large commercial enterprises might well imitate this splendid service to the researcher.

According to Miss Mary Taylor's census of Moston, taken in 1841, there were five bricksetters in the township. The 1848 Plan of Moston, based on the Ordnance Survey of that year, shows a 'Brick Hole' on Kenyon Lane in the area between the present Lily Lane school and Tulketh Street. The outline of the brick works can be seen on the Ordnance Survey of 1893; and it is identified as such on the Ordnance Survey of 1908. In a photograph of the works, taken in 1909, there is a sign, 'The Moston Brick Co. Ltd. Public Mortar Mill.' On the Ordnance Survey of 1932 the brick works extend from Kenyon Lane to Ashley Lane. Almost opposite the Adelphi cinema on Kenyon Lane (for years this section of road was Dean Lane) stands 'Norman House.' It is now a shop called 'Flower Corner.' Here, in the first decade of this century, lived Mr C. Charlesworth, the owner of the Moston Brick Company. He is remembered as a kindly man and a considerate employer, who drove the first Daimler car in Moston. It would seem, however, that he was not a good businessman. The brick produced at Kenyon Lane was of an inferior quality, and could only be sold at an uneconomic price. The result was that in 1907 Mr Charlesworth was compelled by circumstances to take Mr John Bullivant into partnership. In the same year the two men established the Moston Brick and Building Company Ltd.

John Bullivant was one of three sons of W. R. Bullivant. Towards the end of the nineteenth century

The Moston Brick Company's Yard in Kenyon Lane 1909

Moston Mill

there was in Moston a firm of building contractors, W. R. Bullivant Sons Ltd. It was a substantial concern, with offices and extensive works (joinery, masonry, etc.) on the site of the present Moston Market (formerly the Moston Imperial Palace cinema). John Bullivant lived in a beautiful house, built by his company, on Rochdale Road, Blackley. This house is now the convent of the Daughters of the Cross. The firm of W. R. Bullivant Sons Ltd handled many large contracts, including the building of Stuart Street power station, Miles Platting. But, even in its heyday there was evidence of incompetence that would lead to downfall. The crash came in 1908, when the Union Bank of Manchester (later absorbed into Barclays) appointed a Receiver to handle the company's affairs. W. R. Bullivant Sons Ltd was compulsorily wound up between 1908 and 1910.

John Bullivant had left his father's company in 1907 just as it had begun to go downhill. He had gone into partnership with Mr C. Charlesworth, whose brick making business was also in decline. The new company's prospects were none too bright. In 1912 Mr Charlesworth emigrated to Australia with his family. John Bullivant carried on as yard foreman until 1916, when conscription of the workforce caused the works to close down. The brick works, whose offices were in Tulketh Street, stood empty until the end of the war in 1918. They presented a forlorn spectacle: a group of dilapidated timber buildings; adults taking away anything they wanted; children playing all over them. This sad state of affairs continued until soon after the war when John Bullivant formed a partnership with Ralph Platt Barker, an excellent brick maker. Shortly afterwards in early 1920 Bullivant and

Barker were joined by Patrick Edward (Ted) Murphy, and the modern Moston Brick and Building Company Limited came into being.

It might be well to pause for a moment to consider these three men, under whom 'Moston Brick' was to become one of Manchester's most successful business enterprises. John Bullivant was a sort of public relations officer, rather than a practical man. Ralph Platt Barker brought expertise and business acumen to the brick making, introducing modern plant and techniques. It was Ted Murphy, however, who was to be the inspiration and driving force of the Moston Brick and Building Company. A joiner by trade, Ted Murphy had been general site foreman and supervisor on the Stuart Street electrical project in 1902 when he was twenty seven years of age. John Bullivant had been in charge of the contract. Over the years they kept in touch, and as soon as the opportunity presented itself John Bullivant approached him with the offer of a partnership. One of their first contracts in 1921 was the Moston Imperial Palace cinema on the site of the old Bullivant's yard. In the early years the M.I.P. not only showed silent films, but also staged wrestling matches and the occasional variety act.

The early 1920s were a period of appalling economic depression. There was a chronic shortage of money to finance projects, and profits were minimal due to cutthroat pricing by competitors. Generally speaking, however, the development of the construction side of the company was slow but steady. The brick making operation was becoming more streamlined. Many people will remember the brick works on Kenyon Lane. The clay pit reached a depth of some fifty feet at its lowest part. It

An aerial view of Ferranti's Moston Factory c. 1973

was terraced at five levels. A narrow gauge railway track led from the works down to the bottom of the pit. Originally the clay was obtained by manual digging. The small railway tubs or bogies, when filled with clay, were drawn by horses out of the pit and into the mixing shed.

Mr Barker introduced a high degree of automation into the process. A machine digger cut the clay, which was then loaded into the bogies. These were then attached to a continuous chain, wound around capstans at different levels. An engine then hauled the truckloads of clay upwards to the sheds. In the mixing process shale was added to the clay, then the two were mixed with water. The clay and shale composition was then forced into a dye, which was the same section as a brick. It emerged as a continuous strip. At regular intervals a wire cutting machine descended upon it and cut it into brick shapes, ten at a time. These were then pushed onto bogies and carried by rail into the drying shed. After superfluous moisture had been removed they were fed into the kiln. The bricks were handled into the kiln, and also taken out by hand. The fuel for the kilns was pulverised coal from Moston pit. This was introduced into the kilns and in between the bricks as a continuous fire. In the intense and constant heat of the kiln the clay and shale fused. It took about seven days to bake and cool off the bricks. An enormous amount of coal was used, but it was very inexpensive. Shale, likewise, was got cheaply from Moston and Hollinwood pits.

The quality of the bricks made by Mr Barker led to increasing demand from other contractors. During the First World War the horse transport had been supplemented by a 'Sentinel' steam wagon. A fleet of these colossal vehicles was eventually operating in and out of Kenyon Lane. The noisy Sentinels, with their solid rubber tyres, often pulled a trailer. They were in time superseded by a fleet of petrol lorries. Several types of brick were made at Kenyon Lane: commons, used for inner walls; common facing bricks; rustic commons; multicoloured rustics. The Moston Brick commons were considered by many experts to be the best of their kind in Manchester. The first rustic bricks were produced by the Moston Brick Company. In the case of the multicoloured rustics, red, blue and cherry colours were obtained by blowing iron filings onto the bricks in the kiln. All the bricks, except the commons used for inner walls, were loaded and unloaded by hand to avoid damage. Moston clay was recognised as an excellent material for making bricks. There was another clay pit in Kenyon Lane, also owned by Moston Brick, which was reached by a tunnel under Lily Lane. The clay pit on St Mary's Road and that alongside Moston Brook at the back of the present Rishworth Drive provided material for brick works outside Moston. The Moston Brick Company used its own bricks in many of its construction works, as we shall have occasion to mention. Up until the Second World War Moston common bricks were sold for fifty shillings a thousand, delivered free within a fifteen mile radius.

The construction side of the company slowly got under way about 1922. The Housing Acts of 1919, 1923 and 1924, enabled Manchester Corporation to build thousands of houses to let. By the provisions of these Acts the Government put out a subsidy on such municipal development. This gave Moston Brick a wonderful opportunity for expansion, which it was not slow to take. During the 1920s and 30s the company built hundreds of Corporation houses in Newton Heath, Burnage and Salford, along with much private house building. In Moston it built the Shackliffe Road estate on the site of Jones' Farm. There was also some private housing in New Moston. But, it is for its large-scale building operations that the Moston Brick and Building Company will be mainly remembered. The following list of Moston Brick building contracts is by no means exhaustive.

Harpurhey High School for Girls, with room for four hundred and fifty pupils, was opened in 1926. The same year saw the opening of St Patrick's Infant Boys' School, Collyhurst, and the Public Wash House in Kenyon Lane. In 1928 came the 'Ideal' Billiard Hall at the foot of Sankey Brow on Moston Lane. 1929 was the busiest year to date. In that year the original St Clare's church (now the social club), Blackley, was opened. It was built entirely of Moston Brick rustics. Also, in 1929, work was started on two impressive buildings: the new Manchester Grammar School at Birch-in-Rusholme; and Sunlight House in Quay Street, Manchester's first high-rise office building. In 1931 the Manchester Grammar School removed from its old site in Long Millgate to the spacious new building in Rusholme, designed by Dr Worthington and built by Moston Brick. Also in 1931 Moston Brick completed Our Lady of Grace church, Prestwich, on a difficult site above the Pendleton fault.

The list of buildings completed in 1932 includes St Clare's Junior School, Blackley, (faced with Moston Brick rustics); Beech Mount Maternity Home; Broadway

Baths; the Bishop Henshaw extension to St Bede's College, Whalley Range. 1933 was the year of Corpus Christi church, Hollinwood; Pickup's Mineral Works, Lightbowne Road; Wardley Catholic cemetery and chapel.

The most significant event of 1933, however, was the completion of Sunlight House. For the Russian born architect, Joseph Sunlight, it was a triumph tinged with disappointment. He had seen his original design for sixteen storeys reduced to fourteen by the Town Hall Planning Department because of the right to light. Even so it would remain Manchester's highest building for nearly thirty years. A magnificent structure, faced with Portland stone, it included among many innovative features the famous Herriot's galleried swimming pool in the basement. For Moston Brick, the principal contractors, the satisfaction of erecting this great edifice was marred by a running feud with Joseph Sunlight over payment. This culminated in a legal hearing, held in the Midland Hotel during January 1934. Moston Brick's share of the contract was worth at least £63,000. Joseph Sunlight died in 1978. In 1979 the administrator of the property, Mrs Edith Marshall, turned down an offer of £5m for Sunlight House. In January 1983 Manchester's first skyscraper, Sunlight House, was sold for an undisclosed figure to Fairclough Construction, which soon embarked on an ambitious programme of modernisation of the fifty year old office block.

In the late 1920s Ted Murphy brought his son James into the company. In most of the large contracts Ted Murphy acted as clerk of works. His son James, a master builder, later became a director of the company, carrying

The world's first Digital Computer in commercial use, made in Moston

on his father's tradition of craftsmanship and integrity. A cousin, Michael Murphy, and his son Thomas (two of many first-class tradesmen, who came to be associated with Moston Brick) joined the firm. Tommy Murphy often acted as surveyor and site foreman. The Murphys of Moston Brick must not be confused with the firm of Elijah Murphy, contractors, also of Kenyon Lane, which built the present Gardeners Arms Hotel (the old Gardeners Arms was on Glossop Terrace, Broad Lane, the present Hollinwood Avenue). About 1929 Mr Barker's son, another Ralph Platt Barker, joined the company. Ralph Platt senior, however, foresaw brick making in Moston coming to an end. Consequently, after a few years the father set up his son in a new brick making plant, Lathom Brick Company Ltd, near Appley Bridge, Wigan. Ted Murphy died on 11th September 1935, aged sixty years, and was buried by his friend Bishop Thomas Henshaw of Salford, in the plot he (Ted) had chosen within Wardley cemetery. His mantle passed to his son James, ably assisted by cousin Tommy. In that same year John Bullivant brought his youngest son, Alfred David Reid Bullivant, into the company as a director.

Throughout the 1930s the company continued to flourish. Some three hundred men were employed in construction work and about sixty in brick making. In 1935 St Anne's church, Cook Street, Oldham, was opened. In the same year Moston Brick started work on St Patrick's church, Livesey Street, Collyhurst. It took eighteen months to build this huge church. Harold Greenhalgh, the architect, went to Rome to study various church ceilings. St Patrick's is mostly built in Moston Brick rustics, except for the front which is in Accrington sand-faced bricks. The church was completed in 1936. Also in 1936 St Margaret Mary's Parish Hall, New Moston, was built. It served as Mass centre for the parish until the church was opened in 1957. 1936 saw the completion of Kennet House flats, Smedley, and two schools: Christ the King Junior School, Newton Heath (later demolished because of subsidence); and St Hugh of Lincoln Junior School, Lostock. There was more school building in 1937 (St Catherine's Junior School, Didsbury) and in 1938 (St Margaret Mary's Junior School, New Moston).

In 1938 the company built the new sanctuary of Corpus Christi Basilica, Miles Platting. The architect of the extension was Leon Lamy, a nephew of Dr Lamy, abbot of Tongerloo in Belgium. The architect presented to the church the fine crucifix, which is suspended over the entrance to the sanctuary. During the 1930s Moston Brick built two cinemas: the Adelphi, Kenyon Lane, on the site of an old cinema that dated back to the early days of silent movies; and the Heaton Park cinema, Prestwich. There was also some private house building in Prestwich. 1939 saw the completion of two prestige apartment blocks: Appleby Lodge, Rusholme, for many years the residence of Sir John and Lady Barbirolli; and Lansdowne House, Didsbury. The Presentation Convent, New Moston, was completed in 1940. During the war building activity was severely curtailed. Soon after the war the company built St Thomas of Canterbury Secondary School, Higher Broughton.

In 1947, after much disagreement with John Bullivant, James Murphy resigned his directorship and left the company. His cousin Tommy Murphy went with him. For the next twenty five years they worked for Greenhalgh and Williams, architects. After the departure of the Murphys the company lost money steadily, and was only saved from bankruptcy by venturing into speculative house building. About 1950 the clay at Kenyon Lane had been exhausted. Bringing clay from elsewhere proved to be expensive, and the brick making petered out. According to the minutes of the Annual General Meeting of 13th December 1962 the Registered Office was still at Tulketh Street. By July 1972 it had been moved to Chadderton Park Estate, Chadderton. Between these dates Mrs Florence Starkey, who had served the company as director and secretary for many years, reached retirement age and resigned her offices. In 1973 it was decided to wind up the company. Mr T. G. Webb was appointed as Liquidator in that year. It was late in 1975 when all the affairs of the Moston Brick and Building Company were finally settled. The Tulketh Street Industrial Estate now stands on the site of Moston Brick's yard.

In 1910 the new Moston Mill was built on a site next to the disused shaft number two of Moston Pit, in the area once known as the Copthorn. It was originally intended to become a double mill. Consequently, the engine for the first half of the building (the second half was never built) was equipped with the crankshaft and flywheel needed to achieve full power, when it should be required. A concrete bed was provided for the other half of the engine. The outer end of the crankshaft ran upon this additional bed. The flywheel, nineteen feet in diameter, had the sixty rope grooves that would have been required to deliver full power for the two mills. Since this engine was in constant use from 1910 until 1958, except for an interval of six years from 1939 until 1945, it may be of interest to give a brief description. Built in 1909 by Carels Brothers of Ghent in Belgium, with their works number 875, the engine was constructed with cylinders 30 and 53 in. bore by 3 ft 11$\frac{1}{2}$ in. stroke. It developed 1,200 hp at 90 rpm, superheated steam being provided by Tetlow boilers. Coal was brought to the mill by colliery train across Nuthurst Road from Moston Pit. Water for the boilers was pumped out of the flooded shaft number one near Nuthurst railway bridge. In 1958 electric drives were installed, and the old engine was scrapped. The mill was lit by gas until the 1950s. The tall chimney of shaft number two of Moston Pit served the mill until 1961.

Moston Mill was a cotton spinning mill until the outbreak of World War Two. After being closed for the duration of the war production switched to the spinning of rayon, a textile fibre made from wood pulp or other forms of cellulose. Acquisition by Courtaulds meant another switch in production, this time to courtelle, a patented synthetic acrylic fibre resembling wool. Two generations of local people worked at Moston Mill. After the Second World War many immigrant workers were employed. There was round-the-clock working until the late 1970s when the decline in the textile industry eventually overtook Moston Mill. Production ceased in November 1980. The mill now serves as a warehouse for electrical goods.

16

The Catholic Parishes

In the early years of this century there was a rapid increase in the Catholic population of Moston. St Joseph's cemetery chapel became too small to accommodate the numbers attending Masses on Sundays and Holydays. Therefore, on 1st February 1912 the Bishop of Salford, Dr L. C. Casartelli, appointed Fr James M. Routledge first Rector of the new parish of St Dunstan, Moston. Fr Routledge, well known as a preacher with the Catholic Rescue and Protection Society, came from St Edmund's, Miles Platting, to start the new mission. On 11th February 1912 Dean Bradley of St Edmund's introduced him to his parishioners in the cemetery chapel, which was to serve as parish Mass centre until a temporary church was erected. The new parish priest took up residence at 10 Bluestone Road, his home for the next twenty six years. On 4th June 1913 Fr Routledge obtained land for a church and school at the corner of Bluestone Road and Fold Street. An iron church was purchased from Canon Rothwell of English Martyrs, Urmston. Two bays were added to the original structure, increasing the accommodation to three hundred and fifty. On 9th November 1913 Bishop Casartelli opened and blessed the church.

In his address the Bishop saw a propitious omen in the fact that the little church was opened on the feast of St John Lateran in Rome, the first Christian church to be built after the peace of Constantine. Many parishioners remember Fr Routledge and the 'tin church.' One of them gives this description of the founder of St Dunstan's: 'a character in his own right . . . . He was a thin, shabby but elegant man, who always wore a top hat and carried an umbrella.' Since he was to remain in Moston for nearly thirty four years and is responsible for the magnificent church and presbytery at the Ben Brierley, Fr Routledge has a unique place in the affections of St Dunstan's parishioners. The iron church, which had been in use in Liverpool and Urmston, was furnished in pine wood throughout and had its own particular smell. It was heated by an old boiler and rusty water pipes, the latter emitting puffs of steam from their ill fitting joints.

During the first twelve years of the parish's existence all social events, such as dances and fancy dress balls, were held in the Conservative club opposite the Adelphi cinema. Later they would be held in the school. On 29th September 1923 the foundation stone of the new school was laid by Monsignor Provost O'Kelly, the Vicar General of the Salford diocese, in the unavoidable absence of Bishop Casartelli. The new school, built at an estimated cost of £5,685, was formally opened by Monsignor O'Kelly on 4th February 1924. When eventually, on 22nd June 1924, Bishop Casartelli made his first visitation of the parish and confirmed one hundred and fifty five children and adults, he expressed his delight with the new school. The debt on the school, which finally reached £7,000, was paid off in 1930. An extension to the school in November 1933 enabled it to accommodate four hundred and forty children. This building was in continual use, first as an all-age school, then as a primary school, and lastly as an infant school, up until four years ago. It was demolished in 1980.

On 13th October 1932 Fr James Murphy was appointed first curate of St Dunstan's. A prominent site for a new church and presbytery had been acquired at Streetfold, where St Michael's mission church had once stood. In 1935 the first sod was dug for the new church foundations. The little ceremony was performed by Mr Thomas Igoe, a native of County Roscommon and at ninety two the oldest parishioner. On 30th May 1936 the foundation stone of the church was blessed and laid by Bishop Thomas Henshaw. In September 1936 Fr R. Carey was appointed second curate to Fr Routledge, who had reached the age of seventy three. The new presbytery was ready in November 1936. 1937 saw a double silver jubilee - of the parish, and of Fr Routledge as its parish priest.

The old man's dream came true on 30th May 1937 when the new church of St Dunstan, for which he had laboured so long, was opened with great solemnity. Three Bishops were present, representing England, Ireland and Wales: Dr Henshaw of Salford; Dr Patrick Morrisroe of Achonry; and Dr Michael McGrath of Menevia. The church, designed by Reynolds and Scott, is an imposing building, which bears eloquent testimony to the determination and generosity of St Dunstan's loyal parishioners. Fr Routledge, the man of vision, died on 30th November 1945. He was succeeded as parish priest on 2nd February 1946 by Fr J. V. Murphy. Although Fr Murphy spent only a few years at St Dunstan's, he saw the church freed from debt and consecrated on 23rd August 1950 by Bishop Henry Vincent Marshall. Sadly Fr Murphy died on 26th September 1950. Fr L. H. Maxwell was parish priest from September 1950 until 18th November 1954, when he moved to St Mary's, Burnley.

The population of St Dunstan's parish grew steadily through the years. After the new parish of St Margaret Mary's, New Moston, was formed on 8th December 1935 from St Dunstan's and St Mary's, Failsworth, the population remained at over 4,000. Sunday Mass attendances averaged about 2,400. Every sodality flourished. St Dunstan's was one of the first churches in the Salford diocese to have the novena to Our Lady of Perpetual Succour. The people's piety was nourished by the procession of the Blessed Sacrament and open air Benediction after Forty Hours' Exposition; the May procession and Crowning of our Lady; and the Trinity Sunday procession of witness. St Dunstan's always had a good social life, with activities for all age groups being held in the school on Bluestone Road. On 25th November 1954 Fr T. Falkner became the fourth parish priest of St Dunstan's. A man of immense energy and enthusiasm, Fr Falkner will be remembered for his pastoral care of the parish and the material improvements he brought about. It is an easier task to catalogue the latter.

In 1955 the whole exterior of the church and presbytery was pointed. A new parish hall, at the corner of Kenyon Lane and Bluestone Road, was opened in June 1957 by Bishop George Andrew Beck. The value of this amenity has been proved many times over. The parishioners showed their appreciation by paying for the hall (complete cost, £20,000) in under three years. One particular social and cultural activity in St Dunstan's parish is deserving of special mention. In October 1954 members of the parish choir held a meeting to discuss the possibility of staging music and drama presentations. Fr Falkner, upon his arrival in November, gave the nascent society his blessing and support. St Dunstan's Amateur Operatic and Dramatic Society gave its first production, 'The Mikado,' in the school on Bluestone Road during April 1955. Since then the Society has averaged three productions a year, and at present is as vigorous as ever. Hundreds of members have given generously of their time and talent. Of the original sixty five members five are still actively engaged in productions: John and Rita Goggins, Ged Farrell, Evelyne and Dan Farrelly. After the first production in the school the Society hired the Blackley Institute until 1957, when it made its home in the new parish hall. During its twenty nine years' existence St Dunstan's A.O.D.S. has given a great deal of pleasure to audiences and received much critical acclaim.

On 28th July 1957 Thomas F. Manley, a member of the parish, was ordained to the sacred priesthood in St Dunstan's church by Bishop Beck. Fr Manley is the present parish priest of St Edmund's, Miles Platting. Improvements were made in the church. In 1960 a new organ was installed at a cost of £3,400. The entire church was decorated in 1961, special attention being given to the sanctuary. Mr E. Blackwell and Mr R. Lupton drew up designs for the sanctuary in mosaic and marble. The work was started in January and completed in August 1961. Fr Falkner's greatest satisfaction was to see the completion of spacious modern schools, catering for the needs of St Dunstan's children. In 1963 came St Anthony's, Beverley Street (now St Matthew's Lower School), serving St Dunstan's and Mount Carmel; and St Gerard's, Nuthurst Road (now St Matthew's Upper School), serving St Dunstan's and four other parishes. The new Junior School, Edale Avenue, was opened in two phases, each of four classrooms - phase one in 1964, phase two in 1968.

On 20th May 1967 two members of the parish, Michael Lavin and David Lupton, were ordained to the priesthood in the Metropolitan Cathedral of Christ the King, Liverpool, by the Apostolic Delegate Archbishop Cardinale. Fr Lavin and Fr Lupton, both priests of the Salford diocese, were among seventeen priests ordained in a special ceremony, which was the climax of a week of celebrations in connection with the consecration of the

St Dunstan's Church. Moston

Cathedral. In 1967 Fr Falkner persuaded the Salford diocesan trustees to purchase land and houses in Platt Street and Teddington Road with a view to erecting a temporary church on part of the site, and at a later date a presbytery and permanent church on the remaining part. On 2nd April 1968 the new chapel of ease to St Dunstan's, dedicated to St John Vianney, was blessed and opened by Bishop Thomas Holland. Fr Falkner left St Dunstan's on 24th September 1968. He was succeeded by Fr F. Tetlow, who stayed until 5th October 1977.

In October 1977 the present parish priest, Canon James Christie, came to St Dunstan's from St Veronica's, Helmshore. A year after his arrival Fr Christie was appointed Rural Dean of St Patrick's deanery, a post he was forced to relinquish through ill health in 1982. Shortly after his resignation Fr Christie was honoured by being appointed a Canon of Lourdes. A priest in the mould of Fr Falkner, Canon Christie has been a tireless worker, completely devoted to his people and parish. In 1981 extensive improvements were made to the interior of the church. The whole interior was painted, a new baptistry was introduced, and the sanctuary was re-ordered. Improved lighting enhances the alterations. Canon Christie has also extended the public address system, and installed the loop auxiliary system to assist the wearers of hearing aids. A beautiful new Infant School was opened in 1979. From September 1983 this building will also accommodate a nursery class. St Dunstan's parish has been served by nineteen curates. Parishioners remember with gratitude and affection Fr J. Murphy, Fr R. Carey, Fr P. Henchy, Fr T. Corry, Fr T. Sheils, Fr F. Higgins, Fr F. Kilfoyle, Fr F. Duggan, Fr D. O'Mahony, Fr G. O'Donoghue, Fr J. Kennelly, Fr P. Dillon, Fr W. Jones, Fr M. Timothy, Fr E. A. Denneny, Fr H. E. Fullen, Fr P. J. Burke. The present curates of St Dunstan's are Fr M. Saunders and Fr B. Wilson.

New Moston remained a somewhat isolated village, with small-scale but select housing development, until after the First World War. Then, Manchester Corporation drew up plans to house a vast number of people from the slum areas of the city. In 1920 the Medical Officer of Health estimated that Manchester needed 20,017 new houses within the next three years to cope with the demand arising from population growth, demolition of unfit houses and new development. Ultimately, he calculated, 52,191 new houses would be needed. In 1921 it was estimated that there were 150,000 persons living in slum property. Three Acts of Parliament (1919, 1923 and 1924) gave Manchester Corporation powers to build huge overspill housing estates. Under the Act of 1924 the first Lightbowne estate (1,226 houses) was built. New roads had been made beforehand. In 1922 we have the new Lightbowne Road, Victoria Avenue (East), Broadway, and Hollinwood Avenue (part of this was the former Broad Lane-Moston Lane). Corporation housing development continued up until 1930. By this time it extended from Moston Lane to the present Nuthurst Park. The early 1930s saw a corresponding growth of private housing in New Moston and Chadderton.

Many of the new tenants were Catholics. They were far removed from a Catholic church, the nearest being St Dunstan's or St Mary's, Failsworth. Only the latter could be reached by public transport. The number 80 bus service (Chorlton Hardy Lane to Moston Nuthurst Road), which commenced on 28th March 1938, was extended to the Fourways, Charlestown Road, on 24th March 1939. Broadway was intended to provide a fast tram link between Chadderton and Failsworth; but no trams ever ran along Broadway. By the time that the Corporation housing had reached Broadway the tram was giving way to the bus. On 9th December 1929 Manchester Corporation Transport Department took over the Tognarelli bus route from Chadderton to Lower Mosley Street via Broadway. It was against this background that the Salford diocesan authorities decided to form a new parish, serving the needs of the Catholic community in part of Moston, the whole of New Moston, and the adjacent portion of Chadderton.

On 26th March 1935 the Salford diocese purchased three acres of land in New Moston with the intention of establishing a mission church. The cost of the land was £2,300. On 15th October 1935 Bishop Henshaw appointed Fr George Richardson to start the mission under the patronage of St Margaret Mary Alacoque. Fr George Richardson came to New Moston from Haigh near Wigan, where for a short time he had been the parish priest of Our Lady of the Immaculate Conception. Soon after his appointment Fr Richardson began to visit known Catholics in the area, and gradually came to know many of his parishioners. He travelled each day from the family home in Whalley Range; but after 2nd November 1935 he stayed every weekend at the Gardeners Arms Hotel. Meetings of parishioners were held in the Gardeners Arms. Soon after his arrival in the district Fr Richardson met Mr William Bostock, a former parishioner of Corpus Christi, Miles Platting, who was the resident manager of Broadway Baths. Through the good offices of Mr Bostock permission was obtained to use the Baths for the celebration of Mass on Sundays between 9.00 a.m. and 12.00 noon, at a weekly rent of twenty five shillings.

During the winter months one of the swimming pools was covered with sprung flooring for dancing. On 10th November 1935 at 9.00 a.m. Mass was offered in the Baths for the first time. The attendance was 350. The following Sunday saw such a large increase in numbers that a second Mass at 11.00 a.m. was introduced on Sunday 24th November. After the dancers left the building on Saturday night volunteers from the parish set up the altar and put out the chairs for the Holy Sacrifice. The midnight Mass of Christmas 1935 started only fifteen minutes after the end of a Christmas Eve dance. It was impossible to have reservation of the Blessed Sacrament in the Baths; so there could be no Benediction. On 21st November 1935 permission was granted by the diocesan Finance Board for the erection of a brick building in Mirlees Road (later St Margaret's Road). This was to serve as a temporary church, and at a later date as a school hall. The architect was Harold Greenhalgh, and the contractors were the Moston Brick and Building Company. Building commenced in January 1936. On 6th December 1935 Fr Richardson took up residence at number 259 Moston Lane East, which was rented at £50 a year. The front bedroom was converted into a chapel for daily Mass. The Blessed Sacrament was reserved in this domestic chapel.

Bishop Henshaw laid the foundation stone of the church hall on 14th February 1936. This was a joyful event for the large crowd of parishioners. But a serious problem would arise at the end of March, when the wooden cover was taken off the pool in Broadway Baths and swimming took over from dancing. The church hall was incomplete; so a room was rented in Briggs Club (now the Conservative Club) on Hollinwood Avenue. The premises were dirty and smelly, necessitating a vigorous spring-cleaning by parishioners. Nothing, however, could be done about the size of the room. Three Masses were needed to accommodate all the people. The chairs were so close together that the congregation was forced to sit through most of the Mass, only standing at the Consecration. This state of affairs lasted for eight weeks from Palm Sunday, 5th April, until Whit Sunday, 31st May 1936, when it was possible to have Mass in the church hall. Even though the hall was unfinished and littered with building materials, it was spacious enough to allow the people to kneel. Two Masses (at 9.00 a.m. and 11.00 a.m.) were now sufficient. The temporary altar that had served in the Baths and the Conservative Club continued to be used. The Blessed Sacrament was reserved in the Priest's House. Since the workmen were still busy about the hall, daily Mass was offered at 259 Moston Lane East.

Sunday, 5th July 1936, was a landmark in the history of the young parish. At last the hall was ready for the erection of the altar and tabernacle. The altar, a gift from Bishop Henshaw, was from the Bishop's private chapel at Wardley Hall. The attendances on that day were as follows: 278 at 9.00 a.m. Mass; 297 at 11.00 a.m. Mass; and 190 at the first ever Benediction in the evening. In May 1936 two acres of land, lying mainly in Chadderton, were purchased for a new school. The Presentation nuns, Livesey Street, agreed to take one portion for a convent in connection with the new mission. On 25th September 1937 Fr Gerard Prescott was appointed curate to assist Fr Richardson. In the same month the contract was signed for the new school. The contractors were Moston Brick: their quotation £7,419. From 26th September onwards it was necessary to have three Masses each Sunday.

The new school opened in August 1938 with two hundred pupils. Sister Margaret was the headmistress. Her assistants were Sister Teresa, Mr Joseph Wielding, Miss Ella Murray, Miss Mary McElin and Miss Anne Ward. Fr Richardson moved into the new presbytery on St Margaret's Road in October 1938. It now became necessary to have four Masses in the hall because of the growing congregation. On 22nd October 1938 Monsignor H. V. Marshall, Vicar General of the Salford diocese, blessed the school and erected the crucifix. The ceremony had been delayed because of the death of Bishop Henshaw. The following day four Presentation nuns took up residence in a rented house on North Crescent. On 7th May 1939 there took place the first Procession and Crowning of Our Lady. By now the parish had a Men's Blessed Sacrament Confraternity, Union of Catholic Mothers, Children of Mary, and Guild of St Agnes. All the sodalities and a large number of other parishioners took part in the Corpus Christi Procession and Benediction in June 1939.

The outbreak of World War Two on 3rd September 1939 would bring disruption to the school. Most of the schoolchildren and teachers were evacuated to Rishton and Clayton-le-Moors. But, as the 'phoney war' dragged on they began to drift back home; and by the end of the year only thirty seven children were left in Rishton with Sister Margaret, Miss Ward and Miss McElin. On 24th January 1940 the new parish of St John Bosco, Blackley, was formed from St Margaret Mary's and Mount Carmel. Bishop Marshall confirmed one hundred and fifty three children on 12th October 1940. Fr Richardson's Silver Jubilee on 30th January 1941 was marked by a generous testimonial from the parishioners. On 28th November 1941 Fr Prescott joined the Royal Air Force. He was succeeded by Fr John Corbett. Fr Corbett left to join the Army on 5th January 1942. On 13th January his replacement, Fr Terence Cotton, took up his duties in the parish. The proximity of the school to A. V. Roe, Chadderton, brought many air raids, alarms and interruptions of the curriculum. On Sunday, 18th January 1942, a special Mass at 12.25 p.m. was introduced for the workers of A. V. Roe. There were two hundred in the congregation. During 1942 Scouts and Cubs were started.

In June 1943 Sister Margaret resigned from the headship of the school, which had been an all-age one since April 1940. Sister Teresa was the new headmistress. Sister Francis became the deputy head. On 5th October 1944 Fr Cotton became an Army chaplain. His place was taken by Fr John Henderson. Bishop Marshall made a visitation of the parish on 28th January 1945, and confirmed one hundred and sixty seven children and adults. Among the adults were twenty three Armenian members of the armed forces from Warrington. In November 1945 Fr Henderson moved to St Peter's, Mill Hill, Blackburn. He was replaced by Fr Corbett, who returned to the parish partially paralysed from wounds received in the Normandy landings. The first annual procession of witness around the parish took place on 3rd June 1951. On the occasion of the parish visitation of 14th February 1954 Bishop Marshall confirmed two hundred and eighty five children and adults.

One of Bishop Marshall's last public engagements was the laying of the foundation stone of St Margaret Mary's church on 16th August 1954. The new church was blessed and opened by Bishop Beck on 16th March 1957. It was a day of rejoicing and thanksgiving to God for Fr Richardson and his loyal, hard-working parishioners. Geoffrey Williams was the architect of the church, which was built at a cost of £25,436 by James Hartley & Sons. On 6th March 1958 Fr Vincent Sweeney took the place of Fr Corbett, who became parish priest of Sacred Heart, Gorton. Fr Francis Frost came as second curate in August 1958. In October work commenced on a new marble floor for the sanctuary. On 10th November 1960 - twenty five years to the day since the first Mass in Broadway Baths - Bishop Beck consecrated the church. Three hundred and fifty four schoolchildren were confirmed by Bishop Beck on 12th February 1961.

Fr George Richardson, the founder of the parish, died in the Alexian Brothers' Nursing Home on 2nd May 1964. Fr Sweeney acted as administrator of the parish until the appointment of Fr Herbert Power as parish priest on 27th November 1964. While Fr Richardson was in hospital Fr John Williams had come as second curate. The tragic deaths occurred on 6th May 1965 of Fr Herbert Power, Canon Peter Taylor and Canon George Motler. The aeroplane taking them on holiday to Tenerife crashed and burst into flames while landing in fog on the island. On the feast of Corpus Christi, 17th June 1965, Fr Thomas Campbell came from St Vincent's, Openshaw, to

St Margaret Mary's Church, New Moston

become parish priest. Bishop Holland confirmed three hundred and thirty children and adults on 26th June 1966. In September 1966 Fr Williams joined the staff of St Bede's College. He was replaced by Fr Terence Greenwood. In March 1967 a new pipe organ was installed in the church as a memorial to Fr Richardson. Extensions were added to the presbytery, which was also renovated, in 1967.

Dr Ramsey, the Bishop of Hulme, preached at an ecumenical service in St Margaret Mary's hall on 25th January 1968. In December 1968 the church bell was converted to electrical operation. The new parish hall was blessed and opened by Bishop Geoffrey Burke on 10th July 1970. A grand carnival dance marked this happy occasion. In January 1972 the parish of St John Vianney, Moston, was formed out of St Dunstan's, St Margaret Mary's and St Mary's, Failsworth. Two joyful events took place in 1973. On 7th April William Green, a former member of the teaching staff of St Margaret Mary's, was ordained to the priesthood by Bishop Holland. The Mass of ordination and Fr Green's first Mass at 11.00 a.m. the following day were celebrated in St Margaret Mary's church. On 2nd June David Ryder, a native of St Margaret Mary's parish, was ordained priest by Bishop Holland in the King's Hall, Belle Vue. The next day Fr Ryder celebrated his first Mass in St Margaret Mary's church. In October 1974 Fr Greenwood was succeeded by Fr Michael Watson. The sanctuary of the church was reordered by Alberti Lupton in 1975. Bishop Holland confirmed over two hundred schoolchildren on 7th March 1976. The Right Reverend Patrick Campbell Roger, Bishop of Manchester, was the preacher at an ecumenical

service in St Margaret Mary's in January 1977. Early in 1977 Fr Watson was appointed to St Patrick's, Walton-le-Dale. His successor was Fr Thomas Keeley, who is still curate at St Margaret Mary's. On 3rd June 1977 Fr Campbell died in Baguley Hospital. Fr Gerard Fearon, previously parish priest of St Mary's, Blackburn, became parish priest of St Margaret Mary's on 19th July 1977. In 1980 Sister Francis retired from the headship of St Margaret Mary's school. She had served the school for twenty seven years, having been headmistress since 1959. Sister Alphonsus succeeded her as headmistress.

Many people remember the pioneer days of St Margaret Mary's parish: Fr Richardson's wry slogan, 'sixpence per worker per week - perhaps'; St Margaret's Road ankle deep in mud, and brides having to be carried in and out of church; the hectic activity in the school hall, which was in rapid succession church, classrooms, ballroom, theatre, and the venue for all parish events. The success of St Margaret Mary's parish, with its many flourishing societies and well supported social events, is indicative of the loyalty and enthusiasm of its members. Mention must be made of the Amateur Dramatic Society, which has staged many highly enjoyable productions. No account of St Margaret Mary's parish would be complete without specific reference to the Presentation Sisters. The excellence of the school and the music and ceremonial of the church owe much to the Sisters. Their involvement in and commitment to the parish have been wholehearted and generous.

The religious congregation of the Presentation of the Blessed Virgin Mary was founded by Honora 'Nano' Nagle in the city of Cork about 1777. Actually, the name

Nano chose for her society was Sisters of the Charitable Instruction of the Sacred Heart of Jesus. This title clearly denotes the foundress's main object: the education of the poor, deprived Catholics of Ireland. Since the love of Our Lord for His poor, which animated the Sisters, knows no bounds, the congregation spread rapidly to other countries. Today it is found throughout Ireland, England, Australia, the United States, Canada, India, Pakistan, New Zealand, the Philippines, Zimbabwe. In 1836 three Presentation Sisters came from Clonmel, County Tipperary, to make a foundation at St Patrick's, Livesey Street, Manchester. They had been invited by Fr Hearne, the parish priest, who had the cure of some thirty thousand souls living in the most awful poverty and ignorance. Mr Patrick Lavery, a native of County Cavan and a retired silk manufacturer, had bequeathed £2,000 for the establishment of a Presentation convent in Manchester. Mother Magdalen Sargent, Sister Francis Mulcahy and Sister Baptist Murphy took possession of the convent built out of the legacy.

On 2nd February 1836 the Sisters opened the first Catholic girls' school in Manchester. The Sisters shared the hardships of the Catholic population. They experienced desperate poverty, being cold and hungry. In addition, they were subjected to bitter anti-Catholic and anti-Irish discrimination. On 30th March 1837 Sister Francis Mulcahy died, a victim of the harsh conditions. Father Dominic Barberi, who received John Henry Newman into the Catholic Church, described the convent in Livesey Street as a scene of holy misery rather than holy poverty. The daily routine was one of unremitting labour. After day school there were evening classes for the factory children. In 1845 the Sisters opened St Brigid's Orphanage with twenty girls. Eventually forty children were in residence. The orphanage closed in 1890, when the orphans were transferred to the Daughters of the Cross at Moston House. Despite the many difficulties, the work of the Sisters progressed. The convent had to be enlarged several times. Large schools replaced the tiny one opened in 1836. God blessed the Presentation community in Livesey Street with spectacular and lasting results. Vocations abounded. Daughter houses were founded in Audenshaw and New Moston. Many thousands of men and women are indebted to the Presentation Sisters for their education and the consolidation of their faith.

In March 1936 Fr George Richardson, Rector of the newly opened parish of St Margaret Mary, New Moston, visited the Presentation convent in Livesey Street. The object of his visit was to obtain Sisters for his school, which he hoped to build in the near future. Reverend Mother acceded to his request. It was decided to build a Presentation convent in New Moston. The Sisters purchased one acre of land from Fr Richardson for this purpose. Harold Greenhalgh would be the architect of the new convent. The Moston Brick and Building Company was engaged to build it. The entire cost of the convent was borne by the Sisters. When digging out the foundations of the convent the contractors came across concrete and barbed wire from the First World War German prisoner of war camp, which had occupied a great part of Chadderton and a small area of New Moston. Even when the convent was built, it was deprived of its garden. A. V. Roe requisitioned the

ground for war work. Two large concrete slabs still mark the sites of the gantries. On 22nd August 1938 St Margaret Mary's Junior School opened, with Sister Margaret as headmistress and Sister Teresa as an assistant. There were four lay teachers. For two months the Sisters travelled from Livesey Street every day by bus, until they were able to rent a house in North Crescent. Four Sisters moved into 'Sunshine Villa' on 22nd October 1938. Mother Austin Thompson was appointed first Superioress. A Presentation nun for sixty years, Mother Austin was the sister of Francis Thompson, poet, essayist, and the author of a fine biography of St Ignatius Loyola. The Thompson Room in the library of Boston College University, Massachusetts, has versions of his mystical poem 'The Hound of Heaven' in seventy languages, including Hebrew and Chinese. The other Sisters who lived in North Crescent were Sister de Sales Flood, Sister Margaret Tarrant and Sister Teresa Higgins.

We have already alluded to the difficulties experienced by the Sisters and lay staff in the early years of the war. During the evacuation the staff returned in pairs to take up tutorial work with the children who had come home to Manchester. By March 1940 all the staff and children had returned. As a result of wartime conditions St Margaret Mary's school re-opened in April 1940 as an all-age school. In January 1940 the Sisters moved into their newly built convent in St Margaret's Road. The convent was blessed and formally opened by Bishop Marshall on 27th February 1940. On 1st November 1960 Bishop Beck blessed and offered the first Mass in the new convent chapel. The sanctuary of the convent chapel is dominated by a large hand carved crucifix, donated by the then Archbishop of Birmingham the Right Reverend George Patrick Dwyer, whose sister Mother Monica Dwyer is a member of the Livesey Street community. Owing to an increase in the number of Sisters in St Patrick's and the need for more accommodation, Reverend Mother arranged for an extension to the convent at St Margaret Mary's. Plans were drawn up for a workroom, boiler house, cloakroom and bedroom on the ground floor; and four small bedrooms and a bathroom on the first floor. The extension was opened and blessed by Monsignor R. Earley on 28th April 1964.

By 1943 the school population had increased so rapidly that most of the classes contained more than fifty pupils. There was a class in the newly built school dining room, and two classes in the hall. The use of the school hall as church, classroom and parish social centre, placed a great strain upon parishioners and school staff. In 1945 a prefabricated classroom was erected in the playground. This and the new canteen were designed as temporary measures, with a 'life' of ten years. In the event, the classroom was in use for nearly thirty years, and the canteen is still in use. In 1949 two new classrooms were completed at the railway end of the school. An additional open-plan Infant block was added in 1973. In 1963, with the re-organisation of secondary education, St Margaret Mary's ceased to be an all-age school and became once more a Primary school. The school now houses a playgroup and a Mother and Toddler group. Hopefully, in the near future a nursery class will commence.

The academic and musical attainments of St Margaret Mary's school owe much to the influence of the Presentation Sisters and the team spirit they have been able to engender among the staff. In addition to their school work, the Sisters have had charge of the sacristy, a church choir, training altar servers, Children of Mary, Agnesians. They have played a very active part in all kinds of social and fund-raising events - Sales of Work, Garden Parties, Sports Days, Fancy Dress Balls, etc. The greatest contribution of the Presentation Sisters to the parish, however, must be the religious spirit that characterises St Margaret Mary's school. There follows a list of Presentation Sisters who have served in St Margaret Mary's parish:- Mother Austin Thompson, Sister de Sales Flood, Sister Margaret Tarrant, Sister Teresa Higgins, Sister Francis Thompson, Sister Anthony Sanderson, Sister Dominic Walsh, Sister Ignatius Hughes, Sister Angela Corcoran, Sister Carmel Aylward, Sister Gertrude Hughes, Sister Gabriel Horan, Sister Agnes Body, Sister Joseph Hughes, Sister Gerard Eatough, Sister Bernard Severn, Sister Gemma O'Flaherty, Sister Philomena Jordan, Sister Alphonsus Mills, Sister Bernadette Nolan, Sister Aloysius Moloney, Sister Pius Cox, Sister Angela Cronin, Sister Rita Lee, Sister Magdalene O'Dwyer, Sister John Shaw, Sister Ursula Mulcahy, Sister Veronica Bates. Sister Pauline Fahy, formerly of Matlock, became Superior in 1983.

When the National Coal Board started to build the Miners' Estate in 1960, it became clear that considerable housing development was imminent in the area of Nuthurst Road. The Miners' Estate was completed in 1964. Two years later the Mill Estate was commenced. The Poco Estate on the former Failsworth golf course belongs to the 1970s. Fr Falkner, the parish priest of St Dunstan's, was aware of the difficulties experienced by his parishioners living near St Mary's Road. A chapel of ease to serve the Catholics in the area was mooted in 1960. Fr Falkner's idea was to build some sort of temporary church in the grounds of the Alexian Brothers' Nursing Home. The idea came to nothing. Later, in 1966, Fr Falkner planned to erect a prefabricated chapel in the grounds of St Gerard's School (now St Matthew's Upper School). Again, nothing materialised. Eventually, in 1967, Fr Falkner persuaded the Salford diocese to purchase land and houses in Platt Street (later Poynter Street). The present wooden church hall, designed by Desmond Williams, was blessed and opened by Bishop Holland on 2nd April 1968. The new chapel of ease to St Dunstan's was dedicated to St John Vianney, a 19th century French saint. From 1968 to 1972 the chapel was served by the clergy of St Dunstan's. There were two Masses each Sunday at 9.30 a.m. and 6.30 p.m. The Blessed Sacrament was not reserved in the chapel.

In January 1972 Bishop Holland decided that St John Vianney's should become a parish in its own right. Fr Michael Timothy, one of the assistant priests at St Dunstan's, was appointed to take charge of the new mission. Agreement was reached between the Salford diocese and Manchester Corporation on a site for a new presbytery, to be available in 1973/4 when old property in Platt Street was to be demolished. It was hoped that a site for a permanent church would be acquired when the land was cleared between Platt Street and Teddington Road (the former John Harrap Street) near Nuthurst Road. Fr Timothy's first task, however, was to find somewhere to live. On 1st February 1972 he moved into number 54 Moston Court, Woodstock Road, which was rented at £28.56 per month. The boundaries were drawn up by Dean Glynn, after consultation with the parish priests of St Dunstan's, St Margaret Mary's and St Mary's, Failsworth, from which the new parish was to be formed. Bishop Holland approved the boundaries on 20th April 1972.

The first parish meeting, called by Fr Timothy, was held on 15th February in the church hall. One hundred and sixty parishioners were present. Times of Masses and other services were decided; planned giving was adopted; and the foundations of the social life of the parish were laid. Bishop Holland carried out a brief visitation of the parish on 26th March 1972. During April and May 1972 a high wire fence was erected around the forecourt of the church. About the same time the church was painted inside and outside by men of the parish. At the second parish meeting, held on 19th September 1972, Mr Joseph McMurray, F.C.A., a member of the parish, was appointed by Fr Timothy to audit the parish accounts. A successful Autumn Fair in October and a Christmas Dance in December raised between them £734. In January 1973 the diocesan finance board approved the building of a presbytery. The St Vincent de Paul Society and the Marian Association were established during February 1973. Twenty children received their First Holy Communion in April 1973. A variety of social and fund-raising events, held between Spring 1972 and the end of 1973, enabled Fr Timothy to deposit £10,000 with the diocese. In April 1974 nineteen children received First Holy Communion. In June of that year the first Blessed Sacrament procession was held. The procession made its way from St John Vianney's to the Alexian Brothers' Home. Benediction was given in the grounds of the Home. A set of Stations of the Cross was erected in the church hall during June 1974. The cost of the Stations (£451) was borne by a parishioner.

On 23rd June 1974 a Donkey Derby was held in the grounds of St Gerard' School, yielding a profit of £650. In September 1974 the old houses in Platt Street were pulled down. Work commenced on digging the foundations of the presbytery on 28th November 1974. On 11th February 1975 Fr Timothy moved into his new home. The first estimate for the presbytery in January 1973 was £13,000. Twelve months later the cost was £25,800. On 19th April 1975 twenty nine children received their First Holy Communion. Afterwards they were treated to breakfast in St Gerard's School. A Car Draw and Dance in April 1975 brought in £1,300. The Car Draw (subsequently replaced by the £1,000 Draw) and the Donkey Derby were to become regular events in the parish's social calendar. Along with the Autumn Fair and several sponsored swims, they would bring in many hundreds of pounds for church funds. Most of the furniture in the church and presbytery had been donated by other churches, which no longer had need of it. In 1974 a pipe organ was given to St John Vianney's by the trustees of St George's Presbyterian church, Moston Lane, which was forced by financial difficulties to close in that year.

St George's stood at the top of Sankey Brow, at the entrance to Moston from Blackley. It was originally built to serve the needs of the Presbyterians of Harpurhey and Blackley. The Victoria History of Lancashire, Volume Four, treats of it under the heading of Harpurhey. The church was built in 1882. The mission hall, known

St John Vianney's Church Hall, Moston

originally as Moston St George's, was built in 1902. St George's at one time boasted a full congregation and thriving societies. Upon the closure of St George's some of its members transferred their allegiance to the Methodist Church in Moston. The organ, which was as old as the church, was eventually replaced in October 1981 by a modern electronic instrument. An expert gave its age as a hundred; it sounded it. A feature introduced in the early days of the parish was the Senior Citizens' Christmas Party, organised by the S.V.P. On 20th December 1975 forty handicapped children were entertained to a Christmas party.

Bishop Burke made the first formal visitation of the parish on 14th March 1976, when he confirmed one hundred and thirty four children. The parish mission in June 1976 closed with a Blessed Sacrament procession to the Alexian Brothers' Home and open air Benediction. In December 1976 the first Christmas pantomime was staged in the church hall. A letter to Fr Timothy from Bishop Holland, dated 9th December 1976, conveyed heartiest congratulations to pastor and people for their tremendous achievement in clearing off the parish debt. The final cost of the presbytery, including interest paid to the diocese, was £27,535. The parish was £465 in credit. A great deal of hard work had gone into raising all this money in such a short space of time. St John Vianney's has been blessed with loyal and energetic parish workers. At a meeting held in April 1978 many of the parents of children being prepared for Holy Communion expressed the wish that their children be allowed to receive First Holy Communion with their classmates in St Dunstan's and St Margaret Mary's. After consultation with the Bishop, Fr

Timothy agreed to the request. A short time afterwards he concelebrated First Holy Communion Mass in both the neighbouring churches. On 4th September 1978 Fr Timothy received a telephone call from Bishop Holland, appointing him parish priest of St John Bosco's, Blackley. Fr Timothy left St John Vianney's on 20th September. On the same day his successor Fr Brian Seale arrived from St John's, Burnley, where he had been curate for sixteen years, to take charge of the parish.

One of Fr Seale's first aims was to forge a link between the parish and the schoolchildren. St John Vianney's, of course, has no school. With the gracious consent of Dean Christie and Fr Fearon, and the kind cooperation of Sister Francis, Mr Denis Conroy and Mrs Vera Bowcock, the respective head teachers, Fr Seale was enabled to make regular pastoral visits to St Margaret Mary's and St Dunstan's schools. Twelve months later, through the chaplain Fr Saunders, he was able to pay frequent visits to the children of St Matthew's school. At a Coffee and Sherry Evening in mid-December 1978 a cheque for £630 and an illuminated address were presented to Fr Timothy by St John Vianney's parishioners, in recognition of his work in establishing the parish.

The pantomime, held on five nights after Christmas 1978, provides an insight into the enthusiasm of St John Vianney's parish workers. During the week of the pantomime, which was held in the church hall, there were three Requiem Masses. The major part of the stage had to be taken down and rebuilt on each occasion. It was all done without a grumble. With Fr Seale's permission, the Union of Catholic Mothers started a fund to send handicapped children to Lourdes. A children's Mass at

11.30 a.m. on the first Sunday of the month was commenced. A lot of work had to be done to the presbytery, which had been badly built. Many alterations were made to the church, in the interests of security and liturgical propriety. In 1979, thanks to the £1,000 Draw, the Donkey Derby and other fund-raising events, it was possible to pay for necessary repairs, some desirable improvements, and also to deposit £7,000 with the diocese towards a new church.

A census of the parish during August and September 1979 was only moderately successful. The enumerators encountered several difficulties: the modernisation of the Lightbowne Estate and temporary re-housing of many tenants; people away on holiday; and Catholics who refused to fill in the census form because they wanted nothing to do with St John Vianney's. A renewal of the planned giving brought about a substantial increase in the offertory collection. A number of useful recommendations came out of the Easter People discussions held in Autumn 1979 and Spring 1980. For a time during Fr Timothy's period as parish priest there had been a flourishing Tuesday Club for handicapped children. But, this had been wound up. Fr Seale decided to take up two recommendations of the Easter People and combine them.

This was the origin of St John Vianney's May procession and crowning of Our Lady by the handicapped, first held in 1980. Handicapped children and adults from all over Manchester take part in the service, which is followed by a tea party for the participants and their families. Thanks to the generosity of North Manchester Circle 168 of the Catenian Association, in future we shall be able to provide transport for the handicapped living at a distance. Fr Seale completed his first visitation of the parish in late 1980. During 1980 a new sloping roof was superimposed upon the vandalised flat roof at the front of the church hall. The work was carried out by voluntary labour, using cost price materials. 1980 closed with a Christmas Fair, a Bonanza Night with £1,000 Draw, and the annual Senior Citizens' party.

On 1st February 1981 Bishop Holland made a visitation of the parish. In order to accommodate one hundred and forty seven candidates for Confirmation, with their individual sponsors, it was necessary to use St Matthew's school hall. Numerous preparations were made: steps to the centre of the stage and special kneeler were made; improvements were made to the stage and house lights; an electronic organ was borrowed, and used with sound reinforcement. About six hundred people attended the Mass of Confirmation. Everybody was thrilled with the church-like atmosphere in the school hall. Fr Philip Doherty, O.F.M. Conv., preached a week's mission in April 1981. During 1980 and 1981 a high fence was erected at the back of the church. This eliminated several nuisances. A concrete wall around the presbytery garden meant a degree of privacy and security. Wherever possible hedges of conifers and quick thorn have been planted, and small gardens laid out. The Donkey Derby, held on 27th August 1981, netted a record £2,400. A splendid Cabaret Dance was held in St Matthew's school hall on 30th October 1981. Two days previously the new Mother and Toddler group held its first meeting. The Christmas pantomime played to packed houses on four nights in 1981. A highly enjoyable Bonanza Night was held just before Christmas.

Our hearts were filled with sorrow during Christmas 1981 as we thought of the imposition of martial law and the suppression of Solidarity in Poland. Two collections raised £320 for aid to the Polish people. 1982 saw the tenth anniversary of the foundation of St John Vianney's parish. Celebrations were held to mark the first decade of the parish. On 17th February Fr Timothy and Fr Seale concelebrated a Mass of thanksgiving. Fr Timothy preached an excellent sermon, which was greeted with applause. St John Vianney's Brownie Pack met for the first time on 19th January 1982. Sister Pauline of the Presentation Convent, Livesey Street, and two young ladies from the parish were in charge. No praise can be too high for the 'owls.' The Pack has been a great success. A memorable Decade Cabaret Dance was held in St Matthew's school hall on 16th April 1982.

The crowning glory of 1982 was the visit of our Holy Father, Pope John Paul II, to Britain. It was also St John Vianney's finest hour. Spiritual and material preparation for the visit occupied the early months of the year. On Monday, 31st May 1982, over six hundred members of St John Vianney's parish were in Heaton Park for the Papal Mass. Five hundred and thirty one, led by the parish priest, had walked all the way, and camped out in the park overnight. Others served as stewards, medics, and members of the choir. Most had to walk home.

Sancta sancte tractanda sunt, holy things should be treated in a holy manner, is an adage of Catholic theology. Fr Seale has refurbished or replaced all the sacred vessels, church ornaments and utensils. The Donkey Derby, held on 22nd August 1982, was only salvaged from the weather by an adroit switch to an indoor venue. Bishop Burke confirmed fifty children and adults in our church hall on 14th October 1982. The Bonanza and £1,000 Draw brought the first decade of St John Vianney's parish to a close. During 1983 several informative and uplifting meetings were held with Chain Bar Methodists, as part of a twinning project, under the auspices of the New Moston Churches United Action Group. The social life of the parish got under way in 1983 with a £1,000 Draw and the most ambitious and successful Cabaret Dance so far.

The future of the parish lies with the young people. In spite of the difficulties involved in having only one room for worship and social life, a youth tournament was held on six Saturdays during the decade year. The casts of the Christmas pantomimes are almost entirely composed of children. The Mother and Toddler group and the Brownie Pack are most important for a parish without a school. Three parish football teams - Under 12s, Under 13s, and All-age - have brought many trophies and great credit to the young parish. In order to comply with the stringent safety regulations attached to the granting of a licence for music and dancing, a massive rewiring operation was carried out in the church hall between November 1982 and June 1983. Afterwards the whole interior of the building was cleaned by volunteers. Much renovation work has been carried out to the church premises. In 1982, to celebrate the decade, Fr Seale announced his intention of writing a history of the parish. The project got out of hand: the result is this book.

17

The Progress of Education

In 1689 the sum of £20 was bequeathed by Elizabeth Chetham for the promotion of religious education among poor children in Moston and Newton 'until they can read the English Bible, and no longer.' As late as 1854 the money was still in the hands of trustees. Such was the pace of education in Moston over many years. There was no place of learning in the township until 1819, when the pioneers of Methodism established their school in the Birk Houses near Hough Hall. Soon afterwards other Methodist schools were set up in Smith's farm at Shackliffe Green (1822), and Streetfold (1825). John Ward (Moston Characters at Work, p. 47) says that prior to 1840 the children in the Blackley Workhouse, which stood on Sankey Brow, were sent to Blackley National School. So, perhaps some of the Moston children living nearby also attended this school.

In 1844 the Church of England opened two day schools: St Mary's, on the site of the present rectory; and another one in an old barn behind Lightbowne Hall. The latter school was for a short time attached to St Luke's mission church. It closed in 1902, when the pupils transferred to a corrugated iron school on Jackson Street (now Joyce Street). This in turn was closed when Lily Lane school opened. The School Board was responsible for Moston Lane school (1899) and Lily Lane school (1904). In between these dates the School Board built New Moston school on Moston Lane (East) in 1901. All three schools operated for many years as all-age establishments. After 1871 the Catholic children of Moston were able to attend Mount Carmel school in Shepherd Street, Blackley. The better off (Catholic and Protestant) could send their daughters to the boarding school, opened by the Daughters of the Cross at Moston House in 1892, and transferred to Blackley Park in 1910.

The Simpson Memorial institute, opened in 1888, was a giant step forward in the educational and cultural life of Moston. It is named after a local man, William Simpson, who could in no way be described as a philanthropist. He started his working life as a handloom silk weaver in a cottage at Streetfold. His employers, Taylors of Newton Heath, gave him the post of cutlooker, in which he proved a strict taskmaster, rejecting any 'cuts' (pieces of silk) for the slightest imperfection. Thus, he was highly unpopular with the handloom weavers, some of whom walked from as far afield as Bowlee to Newton Heath, carrying their bobbins of silk, often to be paid below their expectations by William Simpson. A single-minded application to making money meant that long before his death in 1866 at the age of seventy one he had amassed some £32,000.

By his will a daughter, Mrs Alice Fay, as sole legatee was to receive £1,000 per annum from interest on investments. Should the interest fall short of this amount, it was to be made up from the capital. After her father's death Mrs Fay bought a house in Fallowfield. She was a careful spender and a shrewd investor. John Ward, the author of two books on Moston, was one of the executors of William Simpson's will. The Ward brothers (John, James and Robert), who were related to Mrs Fay, tried to persuade her to endow a public building in Moston. It was Robert Ward who finally convinced her; though his idea for Public Baths was rejected. A clergyman spoke to Mrs Fay of the need for a church; he was wasting his time. John Ward argued in favour of a building which would serve the needs of the whole community, not just a section. The patron, for her part, left it to the discretion of the Ward brothers to determine what form the building should take. She appointed the three brothers trustees, together with a second generation of Wards, George and John. The selection of a committee was left to the trustees, as also was the choice of a name for the building. The decision had been reached by the trustees that the purpose of the building should be educational; hence the title 'Simpson Memorial Schools'.

It was laid down in the deeds that neither politics nor religious doctrine should be taught in the institute; the object being that such controversial subjects should not be allowed to divide the community. The trustees and the committee selected a young architect, Joseph Sankey, and after a few conferences they left him to plan the project. The builders were to be R. Neild and Sons, a reputable firm of contractors. Dr Ward of Owens College laid the first stone. Simpson Memorial was formally opened on 5th May 1888 by Professor Boyd Dawkins. A few words about the architect of the 'Simpson' may be in order at this point. Joseph Gibbons Sankey, a son of John Sankey of Blackley and Southport, was born in Salford. Soon after qualifying as an architect he decided to take a degree in Natural Science at Cambridge. It was after going up to Cambridge that he was commissioned to design the Simpson Memorial. Excited by the challenge, he took two terms' leave of absence from his academic studies. Writing to a friend after completing the Simpson Memorial, he said that he had 'measured, abstracted, and billed the whole job twice over,' and was rewarded by seeing it 'work out' and 'settle up' most satisfactorily. Joseph Sankey, M.A., F.R.I.B.A., died on 1st December 1898 at the age of thirty eight.

The library of the Simpson Memorial was furnished with open shelves; that is, the readers could select their own books. It was, in fact, the first library in Manchester to employ the open shelf system. For the first ten years of its existence the Simpson Memorial library was managed on a voluntary basis. But, on 5th February 1898, at the request of the trustees, it was taken over by Manchester Corporation Libraries Committee. There were about eight hundred volumes in the library at that time. In July 1935 the Lord Mayor of Manchester opened an extension of the library, made possible by the transfer to the Libraries Committee of another room, formerly a gymnasium. The ground floor is now wholly occupied by the library. In the early part of 1981 the library was remodelled, giving it a new and attractive appearance. Then, on 9th July 1981 an arson attack ruined the adult library. The damage caused by the fire bomb was so great that it took ten months to bring the building back to normal. During the period of restoration the Adults' and Children's libraries were crammed into one room. Eventually restoration work was completed, and the library was fully opened on Thursday 13th May 1982.

A bonus of the fire incident has been the acquisition of a complete stock of new books. At present the library houses over five thousand books of fiction, and over three thousand books in non-fiction. The reference section has been enlarged and its scope extended. The Children's library contains thousands of volumes. Anyone who works with children - teachers, playleaders, nursery nurses - may borrow large numbers of books for long periods. A picture borrowing service is operated at a moderate charge.

Writing in 1904, B.A. Redfern ('A Manchester Suburb') had this to say: 'There stands, however, just on the fringe of the district and in a somewhat obscure position, a building of most tasteful design of which we are proud, of which any community might well be proud. It is known as the "Simpson Memorial", and its beneficent founder granted certain rights and privileges to the people of Moston . . . .' Redfern then went on to criticise the natives for not availing themselves of its amenities. He could not have foreseen the Simpson Memorial of the present. At the end of 1981 an extension was built. It contains a lift to take disabled people to the upper part of the building, where many forms of cultural and recreational activity may be enjoyed, and a host of societies meets - including the North Manchester Operatic Society and the local Community Association.

In October 1919 Manchester City Council instructed the Education Committee to provide the maximum number of secondary school places for those children who might benefit from such opportunities. One of the new secondary schools which came into existence in the early 1920s, as a result of this policy, was Harpurhey High School for Girls, which was at first housed in premises in Beech Mount, Harpurhey. These soon proved too small;

so, in 1926 the school moved into new buildings in Church Lane, Moston. A change of name for the school was considered inadvisable; hence the anomaly of a Harpurhey school situated in Moston. The new buildings, with room for four hundred and fifty girls, had been constructed by the Moston Brick and Building Company on the site of Moston House. For some forty years Harpurhey High School for Girls enjoyed a high academic reputation. After fifteen years as a comprehensive school it ceased to exist in 1982, when the Margaret Ashton Sixth Form College was established in its premises. It is too early to evaluate the new college.

On 20th September 1926 North Manchester High School for Boys opened in the Beech Mount premises vacated by Harpurhey High School for Girls. There were one hundred and twenty six boys on roll and five members of staff. The headmaster was James Crawford Burnett, B.Sc. 'J.C.B.' was the right sort of man to get the school off to a good start. An outstanding educationalist, he was a strict disciplinarian who yet exuded warmth and friendship to staff and pupils alike. Of the five original members of the staff two remained at the school for the whole of their teaching careers. They were T.A. Crossley, B.A., who was the English master, and H. Hardman, B.Sc., who taught Chemistry, later becoming deputy head. They retired respectively in 1961 and 1962. In 1930 E. Robinson, M.A., joined the staff to teach French. He too spent his teaching life at the school, retiring as deputy head in 1967. J.K. Elliot, later Manchester's Chief Education Officer, taught at the school in the early days; as also did Mr Rathbone, who later worked at the Education Office in Manchester. D. Kirkpatrick, a

The Simpson Memorial, showing extension

member of the original staff, left in 1947 to become head of Ducie Central School, Manchester.

By September 1930 there were five hundred and two boys on roll and twenty four masters. The buildings in Beech Mount were completely inadequate; so the school moved to new accommodation at Chain Bar, Moston, the present Upper School. Here it had its own playing fields, properly equipped gymnasium, library, art room, and a large school hall. North Manchester Grammar School for Boys was formally opened on 19th June 1931 by the Right Honourable J.R. Clynes, M.P., Secretary of State for Home Affairs. The boys came from districts on the north side of the city, such as Miles Platting, Cheetham Hill, Harpurhey, Blackley, Moston and New Moston. They had to pass an entrance examination, which was later termed the 'eleven plus'.

The first phase of the school's history ended in July 1948, when Mr Burnett retired. During these twenty two years the school had been firmly established in the life of the city. It strove for high academic attainment, and boys were encouraged to make the most of their opportunities. Of the first set of boys entered for the Northern Universities school certificate examination forty six out of fifty one passed, twenty seven of them gaining matriculation. In 1932 ten of these boys took the higher school certificate examination, one obtaining a state scholarship on his results, while several gained distinctions. The state scholar also won an open scholarship to Trinity College, Cambridge, the first of many to be won in later years. From the early forms in the school there came eventually two university professors, a headmaster, a high executive of an important port authority, and one of H.M. Inspectors of schools. A few years later another old boy became a world famous leprologist. Others became doctors, dentists, engineers and teachers. Many state scholarships, city and county scholarships, exhibitions and bursaries were obtained in this early phase.

Sport featured prominently in the school curriculum. Soccer, cricket, tennis, athletics, swimming, and later rugby and canoeing, flourished in a healthy atmosphere of inter-house rivalry. The four houses were Hey, Clynes, Dalton and Scott. Some highlights of the year were the staff versus school football match, annual sports day and swimming gala, drama presentation, and concerts given by the school choir and orchestra or distinguished visiting musicians. School camps, hiking holidays and outward bound schools fostered comradeship and enterprise. Dr Penrose, Mus.Bach., composed the music for the school hymn; Mr Crossley wrote the words. Trips to France were inaugurated, and in 1932 there was a cruise from Liverpool to Algiers. The school magazine was first produced in 1931. In 1932 the Old Boys' Association was formed. It was to provide the Northmen with opportunities for sport, drama, and social activities. It gave an annual prize for academic prowess. From 1940 until 1951 the annual Speech Day was held in the Fourways cinema, just across Charlestown Road from the school.

With the outbreak of war in September 1939 half the staff and boys were evacuated to Bakewell; the rest went to Whaley Bridge. The school shared accommodation with local grammar schools, and the boys were billeted in neighbouring homes. By January 1940 so many boys had

Moston Lane School

98

returned to Manchester it was decided that the school should return to Chain Bar and resume its studies there. During the Second World War thirteen masters left for military service, and six hundred and seventy two former students served in the forces. One master and eighty seven old boys were killed. The following distinctions were gained: D.F.C. (4), D.S.C. (2), D.S.M. (3), M.M. (1), D.F.M. (2). After the war a memorial to the dead was erected in the school entrance hall. It consists of a bronze tablet recording the names of those killed. A memorial library was given to the school. While members of the staff were on war service their places were taken by well qualified women teachers. As the men returned the ladies moved to other appointments in the city. In 1947 the school celebrated its twenty first birthday. A dinner was held in the school hall. It was attended by ninety eight past and present members of staff and their wives.

Mr Burnett retired in 1948, having guided the school for twenty two years. His successor was R.M. Sibson, M.A. (Cantab.), a Manchester man, who took up his appointment in September 1948. Mr Sibson, formerly headmaster of Barrow Grammar School for Boys, was a man of vision and determination. During his headship many physical changes took place in the school. More accommodation was arranged for the boys in the fifth and sixth forms. Realising that scientific studies were increasing he had more laboratories constructed for physics, chemistry and biology. The library was extended, and many more volumes were acquired. A metalwork room was established; the geography room was enlarged; and a geology laboratory was set up. To cope with the large number of boys staying to school lunch, a large dining room and kitchens were constructed outside the main building, to which they were connected by a covered way. In 1961 a block of classrooms was added. It was opened by Lord James of Rusholme. The stage was enlarged, and a splendid system of stage lighting was installed.

These changes were essential because of the greatly increased numbers on roll. Mr Sibson had envisaged a large sixth form that would send many more boys to universities, technical colleges, and teacher training colleges. In 1948 there were twenty boys in the sixth form. When he retired in 1965 the sixth form numbered two hundred and ten. In that year sixty one boys left the school for university. The number of boys in the school reached seven hundred and ninety nine. Mr Sibson was convinced that boys on the north side of the city, from Gorton to Cheetham to Blackley, were as capable as any of entry to and success in the older universities of Oxford and Cambridge. He encouraged boys from North Manchester Grammar School to sit for scholarships to these universities. During his headship at least thirty boys gained entrance, and of these eighteen won open scholarships and exhibitions.

Each year sixth form students achieved great success in external examinations, winning city and county scholarships, exhibitions and bursaries. From these came professors, lecturers, architects, solicitors, researchers at various universities, teachers, doctors, dentists, a musician, and a chartered accountant who was top in the final examinations of the Institute of Chartered Accountants. Like his predecessor, Mr Sibson believed in a broad and liberal education, in which sport featured prominently. It was he who introduced rugby to the school. Many school societies flourished. In 1963 the school chess club produced the Lancashire Junior Champion. There were concerts from the school orchestra, and an inter-house music competition. Each Christmas the school had its annual Nine Lessons and Carol Service in St Ann's church, Manchester. For a few years staff and boys still went to harvest camp at Bickerstaffe. Members of the staff took groups of boys to Austria, the U.S.S.R., and the United States. Each year from 1963 a senior boy from the school was chosen to visit Canada as a member of the Rhodes Educational Trust. There were outward bound schools and field trips to study biology and geology.

In 1951 the school held its first speech day in the Free Trade Hall. It continued to be held there until 1966. Parents and friends always gave great support to the school on these special occasions. In April 1965 Mr Sibson retired as headmaster. He had given of his best to the school, and expected no less from everyone else. He cared for everyone in trouble or distress, visiting many a family to offer help and advice. On leaving North Manchester he went out to Zambia to help the development of education in that country. From 1926 to 1965 the school had thrived under two headmasters.

Changes in school organisation were in the offing. Between 1966 and 1982 there were three headmasters and three acting headmasters. Mr E. Robinson was acting head for a term after Mr Sibson left. In September 1966 Mr P. Slater, M.A. (Oxon), came to the school as the new headmaster. It fell to him to carry through the change that was to affect the whole school. North Manchester was to become a comprehensive school. On the campus of North Manchester Grammar School was a secondary modern school of high standing, Moss House. This school was amalgamated with the grammar school to form North Manchester High School for Boys. The task of linking up these two schools was Mr Slater's. He was fortunate in getting great support from Mr T. Heaton, head of Moss House, and fortunate too that he kept the majority of the staff from both schools.

Moss House became the lower school for boys aged eleven to thirteen years; and the grammar school buildings housed upper school, with boys aged fourteen and upwards. In September 1967 the school had 1,250 pupils. At the time of the link-up there were one hundred and twenty girls at Moss House, but by 1969 they had all left. The sixth form had two hundred boys. Many of them entered colleges and universities, including Oxford and Cambridge. Examination results were still above the average in the city. Mr Slater felt that the sixth form needed a place of its own, and plans were drawn up for a sixth form unit. It was not until 1971 that the unit was completed. In April 1970 Mr Slater left to take up the headship of Finham Park Comprehensive School, Coventry. Although Mr Slater stayed for only four years, he accomplished a great amount of work in the successful link-up of the two schools.

From April to December 1970 the acting headmaster was Mr Jennings, at that time the deputy head. Arthur Jennings was a pupil of the school in 1927, when it was at Beech Mount. He was head boy, won the school scholarship, and entered Manchester University. Here he gained a first class honours degree. He was the first old boy to be appointed to the staff, and, apart from war service, he spent the whole of his teaching career at the school. He became head of the geography department, and was appointed deputy head when Mr Robinson retired. For eight months in 1970 he guided the school until a new headmaster was appointed. After his death in January 1980 his family, friends, staff and pupils of the school, contributed to a memorial fund. This will provide Arthur Jennings prizes for academic achievement to many boys in the school. It is a fitting tribute to a man who devoted his life to North Manchester.

Colin Brook, B.A., took up the headship in January 1971. He stayed for five years. It was he who carried through the final stage of the transition from grammar to comprehensive school. By 1973 all those who had entered the school as grammar school pupils had left. Mr Brook created a pastoral and curriculum structure to serve the wide range of abilities now in the school. Examinations continued to be good at O and A levels. The teaching staff numbered sixty seven. In 1972 a Parent-Teacher Association was founded. This organisation has worked very hard for the school. After Mr Brook left for the Cleeve School near Cheltenham, Mr Briggs, then deputy head, took charge for some months until September 1976, when Dr Martin Ford took up the reins. Dr Ford carried on the programme begun by Mr Brook.

Radical changes would soon remove the sixth form. In Manchester it was proposed that secondary schools should cater for children aged eleven to sixteen years, when they took O Level and C.S.E. examinations. Then those who wished to continue their education should move to a sixth form college. It was an unsettling time for staff, pupils and parents. Dr Ford left the school in July 1981 to become head of a sixth form college, and Roger Guest the deputy head took charge of the school for the coming year. The great change was made in September 1982, when North Manchester lost its sixth form. Some of the staff went to Margaret Ashton College in Church Lane; others went to sixth form colleges in the city; many were drafted to secondary schools.

The new headmaster was Mr R. Clough, B.Sc. His staff was composed of thirty of the existing staff and thirty seven from other schools. Throughout the years there has been a wonderful spirit of cooperation between the teaching and ancillary staffs of North Manchester High School for Boys. Much work has been done for charity:- the Red Cross; parcels for the elderly at harvest and Christmas; visits to Booth Hall Hospital to sing carols and distribute books and toys; sponsored walks and swims; helping with holiday play schemes, etc.

Moston and New Moston were served for over sixty years by the three all-age Board schools, Moston Lane, Lily Lane and New Moston. During the First World War Lily Lane was taken over by the authorities as a hospital for the British and Canadian wounded. The Lily Lane staff and pupils shared the facilities of Moston Lane school for the duration of the war. It was an arrangement that brought considerable inconvenience to the teachers and much light relief to the pupils, with regular trips between Moston Lane, St John's, Ashley Lane, St George's church hall, and the two parks (Queen's Park and Boggart Hole Clough). The 1960s saw the separation of primary and senior education, with the school leaving age being extended to fifteen. Moston Lane and Lily Lane

became primary schools.

New secondary schools and primary schools were built. Moston Field Primary school was built to replace a red painted corrugated iron structure that had stood opposite St Joseph's cemetery for some years. New Moston Primary school would be the only County Primary school in that area. With the opening of North Manchester High School for Girls (1960) and Moston Brook High School (1971), New Moston Board School was no longer needed. Since its closure in 1968 it has served as a Trade Works, and is now to be the headquarters of the New Moston Community Association. Broadhurst Primary school was opened in the 1970s to serve the Poco housing estate on the former Failsworth golf course. In 1974 the school leaving age was raised to sixteen. Comprehensive schools were to take the place of grammar schools. In the Catholic sector children over eleven years of age would go to St Gerard's or St Anthony's, unless they opted for private schools such as St Bede's or Chorlton Convent.

St Gerard's Catholic Secondary School, Nuthurst Road, opened on 9th September 1963 with three hundred and ninety six children on roll and seventeen full time members of staff. The headmaster was John B. Goggins. Mr Goggins would remain as head until 1977, and upon the amalgamation of St Gerard's with St Anthony's he would become the head of the resultant St Matthew's High School. The pupils came from Manchester, Failsworth, Chadderton and Oldham, the main feeder primary schools being St Margaret Mary's, St Dunstan's, Christ the King, St John Bosco's, and a large number from St Mary's, Failsworth. The school was blessed and formally opened on 16th October 1963 by the Rt Revd Monsignor Charles L. Egan, Vicar General of the Salford diocese.

The building stands on land originally covered by slag tips from Moston Pit. There was a plan to build private houses on it. Linford Avenue was intended to link Lightbowne Road and Nuthurst Road (a Geographia street map of 1965 has the projected road running right through the site of the school). The land was poorly drained, and this led to severe flooding in the early years of the school. Difficulties occurred when specialised rooms were delayed through contractual disagreements. The combined hall and dining room also caused some problems. Difficulties that would have daunted a lesser man were overcome by the energetic John Goggins, a stern but fair disciplinarian. The school aimed for good academic standards; but early on a happy balance was achieved between study, sport, drama and music. Mr Goggins' interest in sport, coupled with his standing as a F.A. referee, quickly brought results. Several boys won representative honours. Tony Towers, an old boy of the school, played professional football for Manchester City and Sunderland. On four occasions in the 1960s St Gerard's girls were national basketball champions.

A strong musical tradition has grown within the school. Early stage productions included 'Oliver', 'The Wizard of Oz', and 'Oklahoma'. There was an inter-house drama competition. A pastoral care system and pupil guidance programme were established. The rapid emergence of St Gerard's as a Catholic secondary school, offering a broad range of educational opportunity to pupils of mixed ability, with a fine sporting and cultural record, is a great tribute to Mr Goggins and his dedicated staff. In

Lily Lane School

September 1977 St Gerard's merged with St Anthony's secondary school, Blackley, to form a new split-site high school called St Matthew's.

St Anthony's Catholic Secondary School, Blackley, was opened on 25th March 1963. It was intended to cater for all the children aged eleven to fifteen years (then the statutory age), who lived in Mount Carmel, Blackley, parish, and that part of St Dunstan's parish which was within easy reach of the school. The school should have opened in January, but severe winter weather made this impossible. It was blessed and formally opened by the Right Reverend George A. Beck, Bishop of Salford, on the feast of SS. Peter and Paul, 29th June 1963. The new school was staffed by all the teachers then working in Mount Carmel Boys' and Girls' Schools and St Dunstan's Mixed School, who wished to teach at St Anthony's. The site on which the school was built had been for a number of years the home of Manchester North End F.C., a Cheshire County League club. During the Second World War it became allotments as part of the 'Dig for Victory' campaign. The opening of the school was the realisation of a project to which members of the two parishes had contributed since the early 1930s.

With the opening of St Gerard's, however, in the following September there would be an over provision for Catholic secondary education in the Moston and Blackley areas. St Anthony's never reached its full capacity of six hundred pupils. In fact, a relatively small percentage of St Anthony's pupils came from Moston. It attracted boys and girls from Cheetham Hill and Crumpsall, in addition to Blackley. The school had one head teacher from March 1963 until July 1977, the much loved and highly respected

Kevin Madden. Mr Madden had previously been the headmaster of Mount Carmel Boys' School, where he had himself been a pupil. He soon impressed his deeply held Christian ideals upon St Anthony's. A noteworthy feature of the school was the low turnover of staff; nine teachers each exceeded ten years' service. A talented footballer in his day, Mr Madden encouraged active participation in sport. The school produced a number of fine soccer players. Boys represented their city, county and country. Tony Grimshaw, an old boy, played for Manchester United until a broken leg cut short his career.

The school fostered an awareness of contemporary issues. There was a school Christmas party for senior citizens in Blackley, Moston and the neighbouring areas. The lavish meal and entertainment were organised and paid for through the combined efforts of staff and pupils. V.I.P. guests were invited; and tickets for the event (one hundred and twenty were issued each year) were highly prized. A significant number of former pupils of St Anthony's has gone on to higher education, some to university. A sense of fun was always close to the surface in the day-to-day life of the school. To mark the closing of the school in 1977 a dance was held in the Civic Hall, Middleton. Over six hundred people attended the dance. Sadly, some without tickets could not gain admission. The life span of St Anthony's (1963-77) was brief; but the school's influence on staff and students was considerable. Kevin Madden is the present head of St Pius High School, Victoria Park.

St Matthew's Catholic High School opened in September 1977. It was a comprehensive school with boys and girls aged eleven to sixteen. The headmaster was

North Manchester High School for Boys

John Goggins. A few of the teachers had previously taught in St Gerard's and St Anthony's, but the majority came from other schools in the city. St Anthony's became the lower school, housing first, second and third years; St Gerard's was the upper school with fourth and fifth years. The turnover of staff has been small, the main changes being due to promotion (Mr P. Foley to head of St Mark's High School), early retirement (Mr K. Horrocks), and young women teachers leaving to bring up a family. Steadily, over the years, the teaching staff has been strengthened and academic standards have risen. Many pupils go from St Matthew's to one of the city's Catholic sixth form colleges. The school has a good record in helping its leavers to find employment. Pastoral care is a strong feature of St Matthew's. A continuous day was introduced in 1981.

The Catholic ethos of the school is most noticeable in the good behaviour of the boys and girls during school Masses and other religious exercises. Pupils are encouraged to take part in community projects, such as hampers for the housebound at Christmas and sponsored events for the diocesan Rescue Society. The school music and drama department has performed in hospitals and old people's hostels. Links with the feeder parishes have been strengthened by means of school Masses in the respective churches. There have been enjoyable stage productions. The school band, under conductor Norman Green, has played in many venues for charity. It recently won high praise from many quarters for a fine performance in the Free Trade Hall. Sport continues to play a great part in the life of the school. The Home School Association has worked tirelessly to raise money for school funds. A recent Summer Fair, organised by this parent-teacher association, raised £1,300 for the school.

In December 1982 John Goggins took early retirement, thus ending a period of nineteen years as head first of St Gerard's and then of St Matthew's. His successor, Mr Brian McNulty, M.Sc., has already established a rapport with staff and pupils. In September 1983 Mr McNulty introduced a new system of pastoral care based on years instead of houses. No praise can be too high for the chairman of the governors of St Matthew's, Fr John Bergin, J.C.L., parish priest of Mount Carmel, Blackley. Fr Bergin brings great qualities of mind and temperament to this demanding office. The recent death of Bill Doyle, a loyal servant of the school, has saddened all concerned with St Matthew's. It is surely an irony of history that the senior part of St Matthew's Catholic High School stands only three hundred yards from the birthplace of Dr William Chadderton, who tried so hard to suppress the Catholic religion in south Lancashire and Cheshire.

The Moston Centre of the North Manchester College, Ashley Lane, formerly Moston College of Further Education, stands on part of the old clay pit once used by the Moston Brick and Building Company. Moston College was opened in 1961 to replace Newton Heath Technical College, whose premises had become inadequate to accommodate all the courses offered. A school had been established in Newton Heath Town Hall in 1890 to provide evening classes in science and art. This was followed in 1915 by the opening of a school for full-time students to prepare them for entry into various branches of industry. In 1916 students on Apprentice Day Courses at Manchester University transferred to the

Newton Heath school. From this nucleus there developed part-time day release classes in a variety of engineering and scientific studies. By 1929 the Apprentice Day Courses were well established alongside the full-time courses, which had come to include a full-time course in rubber technology.

The 1944 Education Act led to the creation of Newton Heath Secondary Technical School, which was housed in the same building as the college. The term 'Further Education' was introduced. There was a great deal of expansion in Newton Heath College. Enrolments increased; in 1950 the new workshops and laboratories were fully occupied. This continued development brought about the decision of the Education Committee in 1956 to build a new College of Further Education. A suitable site was found in Ashley Lane, and building began in June 1959.

The new College was completed by 1st September 1961, when the first students entered. It is an impressive structure with two main sections: the main teaching accommodation with communal and administration rooms; and the workshop accommodation. The teaching accommodation is placed in a compact five-storey block in the form of a three directional star; the suite of administration rooms and the Assembly Hall are housed in the ground floor, with the various teaching rooms in the upper floors; while the dining room, kitchen and gymnasium are placed in a two-storey block immediately adjoining and at the rear of the main building. The workshop block is at the rear of the two-storey block and is itself mainly two storeys in height. The General Contractors were Messrs John Laing Construction Ltd,

and there were numerous specialist sub-contractors. The total cost of the building, including furnishing, was approximately £482,000.

By 1st March 1962 an enrolment of 43 full-time and 3,500 part-time students had been made. The number of full-time students would eventually reach 500; the part-time students settling down to some 2,500. Newton Heath Technical College had two departments - Engineering, offering courses in Electrical, Mechanical, Motor Vehicle and Workshop Engineering; and Science, offering courses in Physical Sciences, Dental Technology, Plastics and Rubber Technology. The entire Engineering Department was transferred to Moston; but only a part of the Science Department, higher level work in the latter being moved to the John Dalton College of Technology (now part of the Manchester Polytechnic). The official opening of the College was on Friday, 18th May 1962, by the Right Honourable Sir David Eccles, K.C.V.O., M.P., Minister of Education.

In 1968 Moston College took over the Mather and Platt Works School, which had been operating in the factory for nearly a century. The transfer of the School took place in two stages: the Commercial courses moved over in 1968; the Engineering courses in 1969. New courses offered at Moston included Nursing, Commerce, Aeronautical Engineering, and General Education. An aircraft hangar and Youth Centre were included in the original plan of the College, but had to be deferred. They were eventually built in 1969 and 1970 respectively. The Aeronautical Engineering course provided a special service to the British aircraft industry in the area. The Youth Centre has tried, with some success, to answer a

The Moston Centre of North Manchester College

North Manchester High School for Girls

St Matthew's High School, Upper School

vital need in the local community for recreational activities. The smooth transfer of the College from its former premises in Newton Heath to the new buildings at Moston was due in large measure to the able and resourceful organisation of Mr R. Harrison. Mr Harrison was appointed Principal of Newton Heath College in 1956. In 1961 he became the first Principal of Moston College. When he left in 1962 to become Principal of Stockport College of Further Education, he had seen Moston firmly established. His successor was Mr Wild, who had been Head of Engineering. Mr Wild remained as Principal from 1962 to 1967. From 1967 until December 1981 Mr H.L. Hill was Principal.

In 1974 the Abraham Moss Centre opened in Crumpsall, less than two miles from Moston. It offered many overlapping courses. Other factors that would affect the development of Moston College were the decline in industrial training, reorganisation of secondary schools, raising of school-leaving age and consequent development of Sixth Form Colleges, urban development, recession, and restriction of permits between Local Education Authorities in Manchester. Originally the emphasis at Moston was on Engineering and Science. Recently Commerce and Community Care have come to the fore.

Adult Education Courses and a Link Course for Secondary Schools in the locality have been set up. In 1978 Handicapped Students were introduced into the College. In 1981 Moston College became split-site. The Millgate Centre in Corporation Street was opened to provide many and varied short courses for the training of young students, the majority of whom were school-leavers unable to find employment. These courses were funded by the Manpower Services Commission.

The Iran-Iraq war, which is now in its fourth year, has meant a loss of some one hundred full-time students from those countries. The high number of full-time students at present on roll (some five hundred) can be accounted for largely by Manpower Services Commission courses and Youth Training schemes. After the departure of Mr H.L. Hill in December 1981 the vice principal, Mr M.F. Dixon, became acting principal until he too retired in July 1982. In September 1982 Moston College and the Abraham Moss Centre amalgamated to become North Manchester College. The principal of Abraham Moss, Mr R. Mitson, became principal of the new College. The Millgate Centre closed in August 1983. Its courses were transferred to the former Hague Street Primary School and the old Crumpsall Open Air School.

18

Roads and Public Transport

The most familiar feature of early maps of Moston is the outline of Moston Lane. Its configuration scarcely differs from the convoluted road of the present. There it is, meandering between small farmsteads, making its unhurried way from Blackley to Failsworth. It is almost certainly the lane referred to in connection with the land of Thomas le Bouker, which by 1418 had become the property of the Lord of Manchester. It may even be a section of the Roman Street that Whitaker maintained ran through Moston; and later a section of the road by which salt was brought from Cheshire into Lancashire. On the Plan of 1848 sections of Moston Lane were called Clegg's Lane (Street Fold to the Blue Bell Inn), Bell Lane (The Blue Bell Inn to Bacup Brow), and Nunfield Lane (Bacup Brow to Shakerley Green). We observe on the map of 1820 that the section of road corresponding to the present New Moston section of Hollinwood Avenue, and Moston Lane East to Broadway, was called Broad Lane. The Plan of 1848 has the railway bridge at Moston Station as Broad Lane Bridge. It would continue to be known as Broad Lane until about 1920, when it became Moston Lane. Fifteen years later a part of it was widened, linked to a new road, and called Hollinwood Avenue. The original Gardeners Arms Inn stood on Broad Lane at the end of Glossop Terrace, near the present Moston Travel.

Kenyon Lane is probably the oldest road in Moston. The remains of a Roman pathway were uncovered there at the end of the nineteenth century. In a deed of 1455 it is called Saltersgate. According to Canon Raines, all the roads called Salter Gate or Salter Edge, etc., lead in direct lines to the Cheshire Salt works. The map of 1820 shows an extended Kenyon Lane, stretching to Monsall. In 1890 this straight portion was re-named Lightbowne Road. About the same time Kenyon Lane suffered a further abridgment, when the section from Lightbowne Road to Bluestone Road became the prolongation of Dean Lane. This phase of the Lane's existence is recalled by the short street between Kenyon Lane and Bluestone Road, called Deanway.

Two narrow lanes entered Moston from Newton Heath, one leading to Lightbowne Hall, the other going by Moston Hall to Shackerley Green. Both may be seen on the map of 1820. The first became Dean Lane, the second for part of its course followed the route of St Mary's Road. After the railway was built (about 1837) each lane was given its own narrow archway under the line. The Dean Lane arch was bricked up after the new railway bridge was built over St Mary's Road (this must have been some time prior to May 1925, when the Rochdale Road to Moston Cemetery bus service was extended via St Mary's Road to Brookdale Park; the single deck bus would never have negotiated the old archway). Referring to Dean Lane, John Ward wrote: 'At Dean Brook there used to be a wooden foot bridge, and all vehicular traffic, as well as cattle, had to ford the stream.' (Moston Characters at Work, p. 169).

The year 1922 may be considered a watershed in the history of road building in Manchester. Prior to that year

The Ben Brierley area c. 1928

The No. 24 Tram at Moston Cemetery 1914-1918

the situation in Moston was as follows. The section of Lightbowne Road between Dean Lane and Sulby Street was called Amyas Street. It was adopted by Manchester Corporation in 1911. Moston Lane was paved with granite sets as far as St Joseph's Cemetery; from there onwards it was paved with the larger Yorkshire sets. Nuthurst Road, from Moston Lane to Nuthurst Bridge, was also Yorkshire sets. After Nuthurst Bridge it was a dirt track. With the commencement of large Corporation housing estates in 1920 there arose the need for new roads and additional public transport services. New concrete technology would make for cheaper and speedier construction of straight, broad highways, such as the new Lightbowne Road, Victoria Avenue (East), Broadway and Hollinwood Avenue. In the case of the eastern section of Victoria Avenue, however, progress was not straightforward. It was built during the bad winter of 1921-22, when the severe frost caused the concrete blocks to lift. The fact that the new road was built on moss did not help matters.

There were government grants to city councils which undertook unemployed relief work. Many of the men who built the new roads had been without work since the First World War. In a Corporation directive to the foremen supervising the widening and paving of Nuthurst Road (1925), they are admonished to obtain the utmost effort from the workmen, but to allow a period of time for adjustment to those who have been unemployed. In the same document there is an agreement between the Corporation and Platt Brothers for the colliery railway line to continue to cross Nuthurst Road. As a rule, a new road must be maintained by the Corporation for twelve

months before it is adopted. Victoria Avenue, from Rochdale Road to Moston Lane, was adopted in 1923. It only became Victoria Avenue East in 1932. Lightbowne Road, from Sulby Street to Moston Lane (now Hollinwood Avenue), was constructed in 1922. The section from Nuthurst Road to Moston Lane was adopted in 1924; that from Sulby Street to Nuthurst Road in 1925. Broadway, from Moston Lane (East) to the Failsworth boundary, was adopted in 1925. Moston Lane, from the junction with Lightbowne Road to Owler Lane, became the Manchester section of Hollinwood Avenue in 1935. In 1926 the newly widened and paved Nuthurst Road replaced the old Coalpit Lane, which a local newspaper had suggested was the worst road in Manchester. The roads had come; the houses would soon follow.

We now turn our attention to the provision of public transport in Moston and New Moston from 1904 onwards. I am indebted to Mr Ray Dunning for all the information that follows. Ray is a Mostonian who has an unrivalled knowledge of Manchester passenger services. He has been kind enough to place at my disposal some of the fruits of his research; for which I cannot be sufficiently grateful. The treatment of tram, trolley and bus services will be under six headings: Moston and Stevenson Square; Conran Street and Denton; Lightbowne and Middleton Junction; White Moss and Chorlton Hardy Lane; Brookdale Park and Weaste; Broadway New Moston.

MOSTON AND STEVENSON SQUARE

This service commenced as Lightbowne Dean Lane (now

Making the new Lightbowne Road 1922

Kenyon Lane) and Thorp Road Oldham Road on 7th March 1904. It was run by one open top, single truck, double deck tramcar, which was affectionately known as 'The Moston Ambulance'. The adult fare was a halfpenny from terminus to terminus. Many complaints were made by passengers of having to change cars again at Thorp Road Oldham Road in order to catch other cars into Town, and of having to pay again even if they were only going a couple of stops down Oldham Road. Deputations met the General Manager of Manchester Corporation Tramways, Mr McElroy, and they insisted that a through service of tramcars should run between Lightbowne terminus and Piccadilly. Mr McElroy reluctantly agreed, stating that 'it would be interesting to see how the experiment worked.' The Lightbowne service was extended to Piccadilly on 2nd October 1905. The halfpenny fare was abolished on this route. This provoked an outcry from the Lightbowne residents, who were satisfied with the through running to Town of the trams, but thought that the halfpenny fare should remain. Many men employed in the Carriage Shop on Thorp Road went home for their breakfast and dinner; but, with the fare now being a penny, they would have to walk home for their meals or bring sandwiches. The service was extended to Moston Ben Brierley Hotel and Piccadilly on 9th May 1910. On 4th August 1910 the Town terminus for this route became Stevenson Square. It was extended to Moston Cemetery on 20th February 1913.

In the peak period additional trams ran from the Ben Brierley to Stevenson Square. The 24A service developed out of this practice. An occasional car turned at the former Lightbowne terminus. Later, as service numbers were allocated to the tram routes from the year 1914, the Lightbowne car used the white blank; the Ben Brierley car used 24A; and the Cemetery car used 24. On Monday, 8th March 1937, the 22 tram route (Newton Heath and Chorlton) became the 22 Moston Cemetery and Chorlton. The 24 service Moston and Stevenson Square became a part-day service only. Twelve cars operated the 22 service to Moston Cemetery - six from Queens Road Depot; four from Princess Road Depot; two from Hyde Road Depot. Prior to this there were five service cars on the 24 Moston Cemetery and Stevenson Square route.

On Monday, 28th March 1938, the tram service was converted to the 80 bus service, Moston Nuthurst Road and Chorlton Hardy Lane. Some trams still ran in the peak hours between Moston and Town along with the buses, and they continued to do so up to and including Saturday, 5th November 1938. Just prior to this date the Chief Constable of Manchester, Mr Maxwell, requested that each route should consist of one form of transport only, either all buses or all trams. Later, on 24th March 1939, the 80 bus route was extended to Charlestown Road near the Fourways cinema. Elaine Avenue was used for reversing purposes. Eventually, the 80 bus would run from the Gardeners Arms to Hardy Lane; but that would be sixteen years hence. On 14th July 1941 the 80 bus service was curtailed to Piccadilly and Hardy Lane. It was worked by Queens Road and Princess Road Depots.

The Moston area was worked by trolley buses from Rochdale Road Depot. The first trolley bus service to Moston in 1941 was the number 37 Stevenson Square to

Nuthurst Road. Buses operated a service from Nuthurst Road to Chain Bar in rush hours. On 2nd August 1941 the trolley bus service was extended to the Gardeners Arms and re-numbered thus:- 36 Stevenson Square to Gardeners Arms; 36X Stevenson Square to Nuthurst Road; 37 Stevenson Square to Ben Brierley. On 23rd August 1943 the service was extended to A.V. Roe for certain journeys. On 12th July 1948 services were re-numbered 36 to 31, 37 to 31X. On 31st August 1953 the 31 was re-numbered to 211, and the 31X to 211X. The last trolley bus in service on this route was on 7th August 1955. This service was converted back to the 80 bus service Moston Gardeners Arms and Chorlton Hardy Lane on 8th August 1955.

Before the Second World War letter boxes on trams and buses were used on a particular journey in the evenings on most routes. The service number plate at the driver's end would be replaced by the stencil POST CAR, and anyone could stop the tram or bus at an official stop and post letters. With buses of the single blind for numbers the blind at the driver's end would be turned to read POST BUS. The post car on the Moston route left Moston Cemetery at 9.09 p.m. and arrived at Stevenson Square at 9.32. The tram was met in Town by Post Office staff, the post box was taken off, and the mail was duly delivered next morning.

CONRAN STREET AND DENTON

This service commenced as a tramcar route between Conran Street and High Street on 23rd November 1903. It was extended to Conran Street and Denton on 1st April 1905. On 4th June 1906 the terminus became Upper Conran Street and Moston Lane. On 14th June 1921 the service was split in two parts: Denton and Piccadilly to be the 19 service; Upper Conran Street Moston Lane and High Street becoming the 55 route. The latter service was converted to motor buses on 10th December 1934, retaining the same number. This in turn was extended to the Ben Brierley, with certain journeys to Chain Bar. The number used for Chain Bar services was 55X.

Trolley buses commenced on part of the route on 4th November 1940 as far as Moston Lane Upper Conran Street. When travelling on the outward journey via Conran Street they would return to town via Moston Lane and Rochdale Road. When travelling on the outward journey via Rochdale Road they would return to Town via Moston Lane and Upper Conran Street. Early in 1941 the service was extended to the Ben Brierley and numbered 32. On 14th July 1941 the service was again extended to Nuthurst Road. A feeder service of buses operated from there to Chain Bar in the rush hours. The service was later extended to the Gardeners Arms and re-numbered as follows: 32 Church Street and Gardeners Arms; 32X Church Street and Nuthurst Road; 33 Church Street and Ben Brierley; 33X Church Street and Moston Lane Upper Conran Street loop. On 23rd August 1943 the service was extended to A.V. Roe for certain rush hour journeys, the same service number 32 being used. Some years later the 33X morning rush hour route Church Street to Moston Lane Upper Conran Street loop, via Rochdale Road and Moston Lane, became the 34 service. On 31st August 1953 these services were re-numbered as follows: 32 service re-numbered 212; 33

The No. 7 Bus at the Ben Brierley c. 1935

service re-numbered 212X; 33X and 34 services re-numbered 214. The last trolley buses on these routes were: 23rd April 1955 on the 214; 24th April 1955 on the 212 and 212X. From 25th April 1955 running through to Sale Moor was commenced by motor buses from the Gardeners Arms. The service numbers given were 112 and 113. Short workings from the Ben Brierley and Moston Lane Upper Conran Street to Church Street were numbered 114 and 114X respectively.

LIGHTBOWNE AND MIDDLETON JUNCTION

This service commenced as a motor bus service, number 25, on 19th May 1926, running between Lightbowne and Middleton Junction. It was extended to Monsall Hospital and Middleton Junction on 19th March 1928, and was re-numbered the 42 service. On 19th June 1932 the service was re-routed via Monsall Street. It was extended to Middleton and Stevenson Square on 1st April 1935, and was re-numbered the 54 service. Later, it was incorporated in the 80 service. This was extended from the Gardeners Arms to Middleton and Chorlton Hardy Lane, via Lightbowne Road, Nuthurst Road, Moston Lane, Kenyon Lane, Lightbowne Road, Monsall, etc. To date the service still runs from Middleton, but is curtailed to Town. The Town terminus was Whitworth Street West; then it became St Peter's Square.

WHITE MOSS AND CHORLTON HARDY LANE

88 became the service number used for the Chorlton Hardy Lane and White Moss bus service, which commenced on 13th August 1956. Rush hours buses ran to Stevenson Square, as indeed did some peak hour buses on the 80 route. Some years later the service was reduced to Chorlton Street Bus Station and White Moss for off peak periods, and Chorlton Hardy Lane and White Moss peak periods only. Some time later the Town terminus became Stevenson Square for the off peak period. After complaints it was decided to send the bus from Stevenson Square to Piccadilly (Littlewoods) and start its journey there in between the 80 service. On Monday 12th June 1978 the 88 service became a full day service between Chorlton Hardy Lane and White Moss, and the 80 service became Middleton and Whitworth St West. On Monday 15th November 1982 there was an extension to Withington Hospital on the 88 service for certain journeys.

BROOKDALE PARK AND WEASTE

On 5th September 1923 the number 7 bus service commenced as Moston Lane (Rochdale Road) and Cheetham Hill, via Central Avenue and Crumpsall. On 1st November 1924 a service commenced from Moston Lane (Rochdale Road) to Moston Ben Brierley. This service was extended to Moston Cemetery on 17th November 1924. It was extended again on 9th May 1925 from Moston Cemetery to Brookdale Park via St Mary's Road. On 14th November 1927 the two routes amalgamated, and the service was extended to Weaste and Brookdale Park via Newton Heath, St Mary's Road, Ben Brierley, Central Avenue, Crumpsall, Cheetham Hill, Broughton, Pendleton, Langworthy Road.

Broadway, New Moston

Manchester Corporation worked a joint service on this route with Salford Corporation during the 1940s. Salford ran the Number 1 service from Mandley Park to Weaste, and Manchester ran the number 7 service from Mandley Park to Brookdale Park. On 28th September 1953 this service was extended beyond Brookdale Park to Newton Road on certain rush hour journeys. On 21st April 1958 it was extended to Lord Lane Wyndale Drive in rush hours, and later to Day Drive. On 27th February 1967 a single deck bus, one man operated, was introduced experimentally on this service. After the local Corporations amalgamated the service was re-numbered 71 and extended first to Weaste and then to Old Trafford.

BROADWAY NEW MOSTON

The dual carriageway along Broadway was designed for Manchester Corporation tramcars to run along the central reservation to Moston Lane (East). The untimely death of Mr Henry Mattinson, the General Manager, in 1928 no doubt played its part in abandoning this idea. Mr Mattinson was pro-trams, and had plans for extending their routes. Mr R. Stuart Pilcher who succeeded him was anti-trams, and in the following year he was already scrapping tram routes in favour of buses. The 53 service was the first conversion. Prior to 1929 the Tognarelli bus company had operated a service from Chadderton to Lower Mosley Street. Manchester Corporation bought out this private company, and on 9th December 1929 began to operate the ex-Tognarelli service as the number 2. On 19th May 1930 the number 2 service was extended to New Hey and Lower Mosley Street. Later, the Manchester terminus became Piccadilly, and eventually Stevenson Square. The number 2 for a number of years now has been the 181 and 182 service. The different service numbers were used to show whether the bus was travelling Heyside or Manchester Road section of the journey. On 19th May 1930 the 2A Firswood and New Moston service commenced. Later, it was extended to Firswood and Boat and Horses and became service number 2X. This service is now part-day and terminates at Stevenson Square as 181X.

The 25 bus service commenced as Philips Park and New Moston on 16th May 1928. On 3rd February 1932 it became New Moston, Bradford Road and Stevenson Square, joining up with the Bradford Road and Stevenson Square service. Certain journeys were extended from New Moston to Rochdale Road from 31st October 1932. Again, from 22nd April 1935 certain journeys were extended to Heaton Park. On 11th August 1948 it became the Newton Heath (Dean Lane) and Wilbraham Road service. Later, it was incorporated in the 76 service Greenheys and Brookdale Park. On 11th August 1948 the 65 bus service was extended from Trafford Park to the Gardeners Arms via Oldham Road, St Mary's Road, Moston Lane East, Hollinwood Avenue, etc. Years later it was re-numbered to 265. It is now a part-day service only. In the 1970s the 77 bus service was running between Fallowfield and Moston Gardeners Arms via Oldham Road, Butler Street, Scotland Hall Road, Old Church Street, St Mary's Road, Nuthurst Road, Moston Lane East. This route is still unchanged.

A private bus company, Holt Brothers, ran a service from Rochdale to Goulden Street, New Cross, commencing on 26th November 1927. This became Yelloway Motor Service in 1932. On 18th June 1944 the service was bought from Yelloway and worked jointly by Rochdale, Oldham and Manchester Corporations. It ran from Rochdale Centre to Stevenson Square as a limited stop service, covering the whole length of Broadway. On 1st May 1949 this service was diverted round Burnley Lane, Victoria Street and Garforth Street in order to give passengers a ten minute service with the number 2 as far as Royton Station. On 2nd May 1949 an express service of buses (part-day) ran from Rochdale to Stevenson Square. This was the 90 service and it was non-stop between Royton Station and Stevenson Square. It is now the 23 service and has one stop along Broadway, Middleton Road.

19

Leisure Activities

Before launching into a discussion of leisure pursuits I wish to say a few things concerning population and boundaries. Even before Moston became a suburb of Manchester in 1890 plans were made to include the township in the Blackley parliamentary constituency. In 1896 Moston ceased to be a township, and became part of the new township of North Manchester. The population of Moston in 1901 was 11,897. There are no further population statistics available for Moston until 1921, because during these twenty years Blackley and Moston figures were totalled as one ward. In 1921 the population of Moston was 19,372; in 1931 it was 23,133. There was no population census in 1941, due to World War Two. In the 1951 census figures we have the first appearance of Lightbowne as a ward. The Lightbowne ward comprised 371 acres from Moston and Newton Heath wards. The whole of New Moston and the parts of Moston north and east of Broadhurst fields lie within Moston ward. Practically all the population of Lightbowne ward is Moston. So, an approximate population total for the whole of Moston (including New Moston) can be reached by adding the 1981 census totals of Moston ward (13,433) and Lightbowne ward (13,481). This gives us a current population of some 26,914. Lightbowne is classified as an inner city ward.

In discussing boundaries we must treat Moston and New Moston as one entity. Otherwise, we shall be sidetracked into questions of minor importance such as why is Moston Station in New Moston? or, why is the postal address of St Matthew's Upper School given as New Moston, when in fact the building is in Moston? Therefore, we shall consider Moston as it was shown on the Ordnance Survey Map of 1848. The surveyors, in drawing up the map, took account of traditional boundaries. In the case of Moston their task was relatively simple. The northernmost boundary of the old parish of Manchester for a considerable distance coincided with the boundary between Moston and the neighbouring townships of Alkrington, Chadderton and Failsworth. There were records of perambulations and precise locations of boundary stakes dating back to the manorial extent of 1322. Adjustments had been made because of the Theyle Moor litigation, notable among these being the incursion of Chadderton into Moston along the line of the present Welbeck Avenue, Hollinwood Avenue, Moston Lane East, Scholes Drive. The eastern boundary was from time immemorial the Moston Brook (sometimes called Morris Brook or Moss Brook). On the western side, from Alkrington to Harpurhey, the boundary was a fencing of stakes enclosing part of the park of Blackley (*palatiu parci de Blakel*, in the 1322 survey of Manchester manor).

No treatment of Moston could ignore nearby Boggart Hole Clough. It was part of an ancient forest, which had only been preserved from assarting or deforestation by being the deer park of the Lords of Manchester. In the 1322 extent of the manor of Manchester we read: "The park of Blakeley is worth in pannage, aeries of eagles, herons and hawks, bees' honey, mineral earths, burned ashes, and other issues, 53s. 4d. The vesture of oaks with the total covert is worth in gross 200 marks for destruction; and it comprises seven miles in circuit, with two deer-leaps, of the grant of kings.' (Harland's translation). To trespass upon such a hunting preserve in Saxon times was to run the risk of forfeiting a limb. In the thirteenth century poaching in the seigniorial deer park was punished by a fine of ten shillings, an enormous sum of money. For generations of children from Blackley, Moston and Harpurhey, Boggart Hole Clough has been a happy hunting ground, a unique and exciting place to explore.

To reach the people behind the statistics will be the object of this chapter on leisure activities. In the early part of the sixteenth century we get our first glimpse of real people. The episodes recounted in the appendix to Crofton's essay, 'Moston and White Moss,' are one aspect of the struggle between peasants and landlords over rights of grazing, turbary and bowking on Theyle Moor. In one incident, which occurred on 20th April 1527, we are told: 'Robert, Thomas, and Henry Shacklocke, Nicholas Jexson, Edward and Anthony Boucker, John Sondeforthe, Thomas Become, senior and junior, James Baresley, Thomas Platte, Richard and George Street, William and Thomas Sydall, Oswalde Mossley, John Schofellde, Ralph Raddley, and Rogger Pendlton, "upon the sound of a horn," arrayed with arms, with sixteen other unknown persons, assembled on Thielmoor, and beat and wounded the servants and tenants of Edmonde Chatherton and James Chetham, and five days later, being the feast of St Mark the Evangelist, with seven score other unknown persons, in the time of divine service, upon the moor assembled, arrayed with bows, arrows, bills, staves, swords, and daggers, having with them a bagpyper of name unknown, at whose pyping the disordered persons "in mooste devilish dancing spent that time which they ought to have spent in being present at divine service, and Edmonde Chatherton, in most neighbourly wyse, aduysed them to geue ouer pyping and dancing and repair to divine service, to which they utterly refused, whereupon Chatherton endeavoured to apprehend the pyper, and called upon the others to aid in conveying him as a rogue to the next constable or justice of the peace, but they not only refused but assaulted Edmonde, and put him in peril of his life, and took the pyper from him, and did continue dancing and pyping all the day long." '

In his essay 'Some Moston Folklore' Charles Roeder describes the way of life of humble folk in Moston that hardly varied for centuries: 'Their habits and mode of life were quite simple, their pleasures and amusements few. They had their wakes, morris dancers, and rushcarts, their pace-egging, and carol singing at Christmas, and led a very quiet existence . . . . . and in the Blue Bell Inn or the few beer houses they discussed, when at leisure, the events of the day. They were fond of a little fowling, hunting and fishing.' Before 1915 pubs were open from morning till night, as indeed they still are in Southern Ireland and on the Continent. The old pubs were meeting places for all and sundry. Every Moston pub (except for the most modern ones, such as the 'Broadway' and the 'Lightbowne') has its own traditions and folklore. The 'Gardeners Arms,' of course, replaced the old pub of the

The old Museum Inn at Streetfold c. 1900

same name, which stood on Broad Lane (present Hollinwood Avenue).

The 'Blue Bell' was the first fully licensed public house in Moston. It was the venue for the old Rushcart procession; and in recent times the Moston Walk began and ended here. The 'Ben Brierley' (named after the Failsworth dialect poet and playwright, who ended his days in Hall Street) stands on the site of two old cottages, later knocked into one and known as the 'Long Vault.' The 'Museum' is named after a taxidermist who managed the old 'Boggart Hole Clough' inn on the same site. The 'Dean Brook' is on or near the site of a beer house of the same name. Likewise, the 'Old Loom', the 'Bricklayers', the 'Blue Bell' and the 'Thatched House', all replaced old cottage inns. The 'Moston' had large stables at the rear, which from time to time housed circus animals performing at the Queens Park Hippodrome. The 'Mowers' is the oldest pub building in Moston, its title commemorating a mowing contest of a hundred and fifty years ago between the owner Jack Sidebottom and one Tom Holland. At the entrance to Moston from Blackley stands the 'Old Loom', that being the nickname of Samuel Taylor the owner of the original cottage inn on the same site.

New Moston has the 'New Moston' and the 'Broadway.' The 'Lightbowne' and the 'Charlestown' were incomplete at the outbreak of World War Two and remained in that condition until peace returned. Of the licensed clubs in Moston and New Moston, the Liberal Club in Kenyon Lane was St Elizabeth's Anglican mission church; the Miners' Club was the Moston Pit baths; New Moston Conservative Club for a time served as a Mass

centre for St Margaret Mary's and the British Legion Club, New Moston, was built as the New Moston Dancing Academy in the late 1920s by Mr Kershaw, whose daughter was an accomplished ballroom dancer.

Until the early years of this century holidays at the seaside were usually in the form of day outings. John Ward (Moston Characters at Play, p. 2) writes of rail trips to Blackpool in the mid-nineteenth century: 'at the time of the introduction of cheap trips, when scholars from our Sunday Schools were huddled together into cattle trucks, and shunted at various stations while luggage trains passed, and kept on the journey five or six hours for a run of forty or fifty miles . . . .' The trucks were open to the sky, and there were no seats other than the floor. Small wonder that people preferred to stay at home. There were lovely country walks from Moston to Middleton and beyond. Families picnicked by Moston Brook. Children played on the slag heaps at Thorp Road and Nuthurst Road; camped out on Broadhurst fields or in the Clough (water and milk being obtained from local farms); swam or fished for tiddlers in the various ponds and reservoirs. In 1911 Boggart Hole Clough was purchased by Manchester Corporation. It was gradually transformed into a magnificent park, with boating lake, playing fields, running track, bandstands, open air theatre, shops, cafe, picturesque walks, and the famous peacocks. Then, in 1920 Moston got its own park. In a letter, dated 2nd June 1919, Sir Edward Tootal Broadhurst made a gift of some eighty acres of land in Moston to Manchester Corporation. The letter was addressed to Alderman Fox, Chairman of the Parks Committee. It reads as follows:

'As a thank-offering for the Victory of the Allies, in the

113

Nanny Fox's Tuck Shop at 'The Ginnel' c. 1915

winning of which Manchester men - and women also - have played such a glorious part; and in gratitude for all that Manchester has done for me, I beg to offer to the Corporation a small piece of property in Moston, for the purposes of playing grounds and fields, and a park for the people.

The property lies between St Mary's Road, Nuthurst Road, Moston Lane and the Cemetery, and a Dingle, and is some 80 acres in extent.

I purposely place playing grounds and fields before park, as I wish these to be the main purpose of the ground, rather than a laid out park, although some of the ground at the lower end being undulating, will probably be more suitable for the latter than the former. However, with this expression, I am quite content to leave the matter to the discretion of the Parks Committee, but I must stipulate that no portion of the land shall ever be used for building purposes, except for such buildings as are necessary for the equipment of the park, etc., or for a public library or council schools.

There are two tenants on the farms, both on yearly tenancies, subject to 12 months notice ending Lady Day. I ask, and I am sure your Committee will grant my request, that the greatest consideration may be shown to them.

I enclose a rough map of the ground, and my Agents, the Earle Estate Office, 88 King Street, will supply you with any further information you may desire.'

This generous gift of land in the central part of Moston served not only to provide excellent playing fields and parks, but also to preserve the rural character of Moston, which otherwise might have been engulfed by housing development. The land was conveyed on 23rd July 1920

with covenants as to use solely as playing fields and park, except for structures in connection with recreation. Soon afterwards Broadhurst Park, as we know it today, came into existence. There was also a bandstand, no longer standing but remembered by many for its concerts; and a little wooden shop, which sold sweets, ices and soft drinks. There had been a tollhouse at the junction of St Mary's Road and Nuthurst Road. This was demolished in 1916. Another tollhouse at Chain Bar was pulled down in 1905. Generally speaking Sir Edward Tootal Broadhurst's wishes have been respected.

During the Second World War prefabs were erected on a small portion, opposite the rear entrance to St Joseph's Cemetery. These were demolished in the 1960s, and the land was returned to recreational use. A transit camp for Polish servicemen and their families was set up on Broadhurst fields after the war. It was only a makeshift affair; but by all accounts the Polish wives made it bright and homely. In 1975 an attempt was made to build houses on the park. Intense opposition, however, from local residents prevented what would have been a breach of the covenant imposed by the donor. A famous haunt of young children in Moston up until the end of the First World War was Nanny Fox's Tuck Shop, which stood at the junction of Moston Lane and Nuthurst Road. When the children of those years grew bored with their legitimate pastimes they could have sport by annoying Mr Carty, who kept shire horses in a field near Lightbowne Road and Sulby Street. In New Moston there was the exclusive Tennis Club, which moved from Eastwood Road to Nuthurst Road in 1910. It occupied a site near the junction of Nuthurst Road and Rishworth Drive.

Nuthurst Park was laid out in the 1930s.

There were four cinemas in Moston. The first one stood on the site of the present 'Adelphi' Bingo Hall. It was an unpretentious structure of wood and iron, built in the early part of the century. It is remembered as 'smaller, much homelier and scruffier' than the later cinema, 'ideal for the penny crush on Saturday afternoons.' The 'Moston Imperial Palace' belongs to the early 1920s. Its first manager was Mr Carl Severs. The M.I.P., now the Moston Market, was a quaint cinema with wooden seats at the front. It was surprisingly capacious; and it was possible to have a good view of the screen from any part of the theatre. The 'Adelphi', built in 1938, was a plush theatre, which made its patrons feel very important. The owner of the 'Adelphi', the 'Victory' in Blackley and the 'King's' in Longsight, was Mr H.D. Moorhouse, after whom the 'H.D.M. Circuit' was named. The 'Fourways', built in 1939, was an extremely modern and comfortable cinema. It opened just before the outbreak of war, closed for a short period, and then remained open for some twenty years. In addition to being a cinema, the 'Fourways' was for a few months in 1940 a Mass centre for the new parish of St John Bosco, Blackley. It was also the venue of North Manchester Grammar School for Boys' Speech Day, until this event was moved to the Free Trade Hall.

The 'Fourways' cinema stood on Charlestown Road, near the junction with Moston Lane. The locality is still called the 'Fourways,' even though there are only three ways (viz. Charlestown Road and the two sections of Moston Lane). The explanation may be found in a Geographia map of Greater Manchester, issued in

October 1950, which shows Tyndall Avenue running from Worsley Avenue to Charlestown Road, where it was to emerge beside the 'Fourways' cinema. This section of Tyndall Avenue, from Croft Hill Road to Charlestown Road, was never built. The decision to build North Manchester High School for Girls on its present site put paid to the projected extension of Tyndall Avenue. The first section of Charlestown Road, from Rochdale Road to the present Grange Park Road, was adopted by Manchester Corporation on 6th December 1905. The second section, from Grange Park Road to Moston Lane, was made in 1938 and adopted by the Corporation on 17th January 1940.

The atmosphere of Moston in the early years of this century is encapsulated in 'A Lightbowne Childhood' by Mrs M. Collins, set down in 1977. Pastimes were simple; recreation was hemmed in by the harsh realities of toil and illness. She writes of a period shortly before World War One: 'The highlights were just before Christmas at a children's dance they had at the Simpson Memorial - we would have our hair in rag curlers, and if our mothers could afford it we would have a very fine silk head shawl. They were sixpence each, and we would go in a cab, four or six of us for a shilling. We thought we were royalty. Perhaps a day or so later we would be going to the coalyard in Egbert Street for half a hundredweight of coal, fourpence halfpenny. We had to pull it in little iron trucks, and our hands would nearly freeze on the iron handles. Perhaps many will remember Nurse Wrigley in Hugo Street. We would go with a cup for one ounce of Jackson's Febrifuge for a bad cold. No wonder lots of babies died in infancy. There was a length of rubber

The Ben Brierley

tubing from the feeding bottles to the teat (they were narrow and about eighteen inches long) - it must have been impossible to clean them.'

In the 1920s Alan Cobham's Flying Circus performed aerobatics on White Moss. For five shillings it was possible to board a plane and enjoy a flight over Manchester. Flying objects would bring chaos, destruction and sometimes (in retrospect) mirth during World War Two. The defensive measures that were taken to protect the primary target of German bombers, A.V. Roe, manufacturers of the famous Lancaster aircraft, constituted a comedy of errors. Barrage balloon cables swept away the chimney pots of a row of houses in Elmwood Grove; the first salvo from the anti-aircraft guns, sited on Broadhurst Fields, caused the glass to fall out of the windows in some cottages near the 'Thatched House' pub. Enemy bombs destroyed two large semi-detached houses on Ashley Lane; five terraced houses in Kingsley Avenue were demolished; the cross and a wall of St John's church, Ashley Lane, suffered slight damage. One lady in Ashley Lane opened her door to let in a frightened neighbour; she was killed, and the neighbour was injured. Moston, and especially the New Moston area, got off very lightly in the blitz on Manchester, considering their proximity to the strategic aircraft factory and the inadequate defensive cover.

The 1944 Education Act and the Ministry of Education's booklet, 'Community Centres,' of the same year, ushered in the era of the Community Association.

This is a neighbourhood organisation that seeks the good of all the residents in a locality, answering a host of needs - social, recreational, cultural and educational, by helping individuals and societies to make the most constructive use of their leisure opportunities. There are three Community Associations in Moston and one in New Moston. The long-established Simpson Memorial C. A. meets in the institute of the same name. New Moston C. A., now in its sixth year, has just moved into its new premises in the former New Moston Board School. Chain Bar C. A., three years in existence, meets in the Sixth Form Unit of North Manchester High School for Boys. The most recently established, Broadhurst C.A., holds its meetings in the Miners' Club.

Planning permission has been given for purpose-built accommodation to be provided for the Chain Bar and Broadhurst Associations. The new building, which will be used jointly, will be erected on the site of the former Lightbowne Road nursery. The estimated cost of the new community centre is £89,000. It is hoped that work on this much needed amenity will soon commence. The New Moston Churches United Action Group, formed in 1969, was instrumental in establishing the Minehead Senior Citizen's Club. With so much good will and neighbourly concern around, and the determination which has been shown by local people in trying to find solutions to the many social problems facing the community, the future of this area looks bright. Perhaps the best part of the Moston Story is still to come.

The Gardeners Arms

The Blue Bell

INDEX

D

DALTON, John 41, College of Technology 103

DANEGELD 13

DANES 14

DANISH WAR 71

DARK AGES 13

DARLINGTON, Arthur 61

DAUGHTERS OF THE CROSS 42, 43, 44, 83, 92

DAVEY, Revd C.H.G. 79

DAVIE, Mary 35

DAWKINS, Professor Boyd 96

DAWSON (alias Halgh), John 39

DAY, Revd H.P.W. 76, 77

DEAN BROOK 16, Dyeworks 47, 81, Inn (old 65, new 113)

DEAN CLOUGH 14, 17

DEAN MOUNT Garage 75

DEANWAY 106

DEANE Church 17

DELAUNAYS 50

DENE HOUSE 27

DENNENY, Fr E.A. 89

DENTON 14, 17, 109

DERBY, Earl 25, 29, 30

DEVIL'S PIT 45

DILLON, Fr Paul 89

DIXON, Elijah 50, 51, 76

DIXON, 'Piggy' 27

DODDITHOKES CLOUGH 17, 23

DOMESDAY BOOK 13

DOUGHTY Family 65

DOYLE, Bill 102

DROYLSDEN 73

DUDLEY, Earl of Leicester 29

DUCHY OF LANCASTER Court 40

DUCIE CENTRAL SCHOOL 98

DUFFILL, Revd J. 75

DUGGAN, Fr Francis 89

DUKINFIELD Colliery 55

DUNGEON, Prison 30

DUNNING, Ray 107

DUNSTAN, St 14

DWYER, Archbishop George Patrick 92

DWYER, Mother Monica 92

E

EAMES, Brother Montfort 72

EARLEY, Monsignor Richard 92

EATOUGH, Sister Gerard 93

ECCLESIASTICAL Commissioners 28, 29, 30

ECCLES, Thomas 24, 28, Sir David 103

EDGAR, King 14

EDWARD THE CONFESSOR, King 13

EDWARD THE ELDER, King 14

EGAN, Monsignor Charles L. 100

ELECTA, Sister Mary 43, 44

ELECTRIC Telegraph 48

ELIZABETH I, Queen 29, 31

ELLIOT, J.K. 97

ELPHEGE, Sister 43, 44

ENGELS, Friedrich 47

ENGLISH Monasticism, Nation 63

EQUAL, The 32, 34, 35

ESPIE, John 61

EVANS, Revd Richard 79, 80

F

FAHY, Sister Pauline 93

FAILSWORTH 12, 32, 34, 76, Industrial Society 55, Cooperative Society 76, Golf Course 76, 77

FALKNER, Fr Thomas 87, 89, 93

FARM YARD Hotel 43, 50

FARRELL, Ged 88

FARRINGTON, Ernest 61

FAY, Alice 96

FEARON, Fr Gerard 91, 94

FERRANTI Radio Works 76, Instrumentation 82, Sebastian Ziani de 81, Products 81, 82

FERRI, Brother Anthony 72

FINCH, John 30

FITZGERALD, Brother Gerald 72

FITZPATRICK, Fr 44

FITZWALTER, Lord 18

FLOOD, Sister de Sales 93

FOLEY, P. 102

FORD, Dr Martin 100

FOURWAYS Cinema 115

FOX, Alderman 113

PRINCE-LEE, Bishop James 52
PRINTERS ARMS 50
PROSPERA, St 67
PRUSSIAN Authorities 67
PUBLIC WASH HOUSE 85

Q

QUEENS PARK 50, Hippodrome 113
QUEENS ROAD Bus Depot 108

R

RADCLIFFES 17, 18, 19, 20, 26, 39
RADULFUS de MOSTON 14, 16
RAILTON, John 79
RAILWAY 48
RATHBONE, Mr 97
RATLEDGE, Revd E.D, 79
RECUSANTS 29
RED CROSS 76
REFORMATORY, Blackley 50
REGINA, Sister Mary 43
REGULARIS CONCORDIA 14
RICHARD de BYRON, Sir 17
RICHARD de CHADDERTON 15
RICHARD de MOSTON 17
RICHARDSON, Fr George 89, 90, 91
RICHFORD, H. 61
RICKETTS, William 51
RITUALISTS 74, 75
ROBERT de BOLTON 17
ROBERT de MOSTON 17
ROBERT, Son of Bernard 14, 15
ROBIN HOOD Locomotive 62
ROBINSON, E. 99
ROBINSON, Revd A.L. 79
ROBINSON, Revd J.J. 76
ROE, A.V. 81, 91, 116
ROEDER, Charles 26, 42 45
ROGER, Bishop Patrick Campbell 91
ROGER Coal Mine 58
ROGER de CHADDERTON 15
ROGER, Son of Orm 14

ROMANS 12, 13
ROSS, Malcolm 42
ROSTERNE, John 35
ROUTLEDGE, Fr James 87
RUSHES GATE FARM 27
RYDER, Fr David 91
RYDER, James 63

S

St ANTHONY'S High School 101
St BEDE'S College 85
St BENEDICT 14
St CHAD'S 13, 19, 73, 76, 77
St CLARE'S 85
St COLUMB'S, Mount 72
St DUNSTAN'S 87, 88, 89
St ELIZABETH'S 75
St GEORGE'S 93, 94, Road 50, 63
St GERARD'S High School 100
St JOHN'S 79, 80
St JOHN BOSCO'S 90, 115
St JOHN VIANNEY'S 93, 94, 95
St JOSEPH'S Cemetery 15, 16, 67, 68, 69
St LUKE'S 13, 52, 73, 74, 75
St MARGARET MARY'S 86, 89, 90, 91
St MARY'S, Manchester 13, Moston 38, 52, 73, 76, 78,
    Mulberry St 69, Road 53, 55, 65, 71, 106
St MATTHEW'S High School 101, 102
St MICHAEL'S 13
St PATRICK'S 86
St THOMAS of CANTERBURY 86
SAFFENREUTER, Fr Gustave 67, 71
SALTERSGATE 13
SANDERS, Brother Edward 72
SANDERSON, Sister Anthony 93
SANDFORD, Samuel 31
SANKEY, Joseph 96
SANKEY'S SOAP WORKS 50
SARGENT, Mother Magdalen 92
SARSNET 48
SAUNDERS, Fr Martin 89
SCHOLES, Luke 58
SCHOLES, William 34, 35
SCHUSTER, Fr 42

126